Smoking Cigarettes, Eating Glass

A psychologist's memoir

Annita Perez Sawyer

sfwp.com

Author's note

Excerpts from the memoir have appeared in *The Healing Muse* (Shocked, 2008; Undercover Agent, 2011), *The MacGuffin* (Pay Attention, 2008), *The Common* (At the Y, 2012), *Literal Latte* (The Other Chair, 2013), and *Southern Humanities Review* (Good Humor, 2014).

The events recounted are authentic and described to the best of my ability. Some names have been changed for purposes of confidentiality and privacy.

First Paperback Edition

Library of Congress Cataloging-in-Publication Data

Sawyer, Annita Perez.
  Smoking cigarettes, eating glass : a psychologist's memoir / Annita Perez Sawyer, PhD. — First paperback edition.
    pages cm
  ISBN 978-1-939650-26-9 (pbk. : alk. paper)
  1. Sawyer, Annita Perez—Mental health. 2. Mentally ill—United States—Biography. 3. Psychologists—United States—Biography. 4. Psychiatric hospital care—United States—History. 5. Psychiatric errors—United States. I. Santa Fe Writers Project. II. Title.
  RC464.S29A3 2015
  616.890092--dc23
  [B]
                          2014026915

Published by SFWP
369 Montezuma Ave. #350
Santa Fe, NM 87501
(505) 428-9045
www.sfwp.com

Cover image: Erica Harney; detail from "Annita in Mind"
www.ericaharney.com

Find the author at www.smokingcigaretteseatingglass.com

Contents

To all children, young or grown, who could not speak and were never known; to all healers with courage to pay attention; to all families and friends who would help if they could understand; and to everyone who has believed in me.

I have woven a parachute out of everything broken

—*William Stafford*

PROLOGUE

Pay Attention

April 2004

Hands on the large round wall clock hesitated, then lurched forward, ticking each minute away. The meeting had started late; it was time for me to speak. I gathered my stack of notes in front of me, patting the edges smooth. I straightened my shoulders and moved a wisp of hair away from my eyes. Two-dozen mental health professionals stared at me where I sat in their midst at a square oak table in the crowded conference room. A small woman across from me, a world-famous psychoanalyst, smiled in a reassuring, grandmotherly way. The director nodded, *Go.*

"My message of transcendence is myself," I began, working to keep my voice full. "Me. Alive. Here. I speak as a seasoned psychologist, and I speak as a woman who was a patient in this institution for several years when I was young."

I glanced up. The analyst smiled again. For a moment, I sparkled.

I'd arrived early, making my way from the parking lot with the help of a map scribbled on the back of an envelope by the psychiatrist who had invited me to attend. Walking in, I'd scrutinized the faded carpets on the old wooden floors, the juxtaposition of windows and walls, the ceiling's odd angles, wondering if I'd ever been in this particular building before, one of many in this well-known mental hospital complex known informally as Bloomingdale's. I was struggling to remember when I'd been a teenager locked in here decades earlier—beyond all the shock treatments that erased most of my memory, beyond the doctors who gave up on me before I was twenty.

I'd worked on my presentation for weeks, writing and rewriting what I wanted to say. I'd practiced in front of mirrors. I'd recorded myself with a video camera and critiqued the tape on my TV. I might never have an opportunity like this again—I had to set them on fire.

I glanced at the men and women seated at the table and lining the edges of the room. Large and small, stylish and frumpy, young clinicians and interns sprinkled among renowned analysts and researchers. I was a thin, ordinary-looking, late-middle-aged woman with trifocal glasses and short hair. Outwardly, I appeared no different from them. *Might there be others like me hidden here?* I wondered.

Beside me sat the white-haired man, a few years older than myself, who had arranged for me to come. We had first met almost forty years earlier in another hospital when he was a young psychiatrist in training. I had been an inpatient on his unit. *Are they expecting a doctor or a patient?* A speck of anger gleamed like dust on a sunbeam. For a moment I was seventeen again, shivering, naked, rough wet sheets wrapped tight against my skin, lying on a gurney in the hall with the smell of sour sweat hovering in a cloud around my head.

My face burned. I ran a hand through my hair, forcing myself back into the present.

I was dressed in a gray Brooks Brothers suit I had found at the outlet, my favorite velvet scarf draped around my neck. A freshly polished leather briefcase my husband had given to me when I'd earned my PhD over twenty years earlier kept my feet company, resting beneath the chair. It held pages and pages of what I wanted to say, probably enough for twenty presentations.

I rubbed my thumb across a tiny silver basket pinned to my lapel, then over the silver ring on my little finger. My children had made them, with their father's help, when they were young. Could I have imagined this scene back then? I raised my head and straightened my spine.

"Forty years ago, I was a patient here," I continued. "I endured years of terrifying treatment for the wrong diagnosis, treatment that made me worse. In the end, I was transferred out for lack of improvement." A surge of energy—*rage? fear? joy?*—swept through me, catching me off guard. Under the table, I clasped my hands together as tightly as I could, so as not to fly apart into pieces. I began to tell them my story.

I described shrinking in high school—my handwriting becoming so tiny it was illegible; my voice increasingly inaudible; my body, like my spirit, withdrawing from the world and closing in on itself. I told them about my diary heaped with guilt and self-loathing. About my suicide plans. I quoted the doctors' assessments directly from hospital notes—patronizing and degrading descriptions of myself.

Then I described my shock treatment and the fear that the electricity inducing the seizures would kill me. I explained that when I'd failed to improve, my doctors had prescribed even more. At this, the elderly hospital director winced. His sad eyes shrank into faraway, dark points as creases in his face deepened around them. I felt myself lift out of my body—for a moment I didn't know who or where I was.

"Should I stop?" I asked him.

"No, no. Please continue," he said, his voice gentle, as if he recognized my distress.

"After three years at the first hospital, I was transferred. My diagnosis: *Dementia Praecox* (schizophrenia); my condition: *Unimproved.* "Another year passed before I was assigned to a psychiatrist who could see me as an individual—as a person, not a syndrome. When I made stupid puns, he laughed. When I told him that evil garbage stank and should be eliminated, he told me he knew someone who found treasures in garbage. "One person's stink is another's perfume," he'd said, astonishing me. No longer utterly alone in the universe, I grew curious about myself and how I worked. My interest in the outside world expanded. I began to heal.

"But, as we all know," I added, "healing can be a long and uneven process, no matter how talented the therapist or how promising the relationship." I went on to describe living without memory of my first twenty years, pretending to belong in a world I no longer recognized, hiding my mental-patient past; often, it had seemed like leading a double life.

I told them about secrets uncovered forty years later when I read the hospital records. An experienced clinician by then, I could easily recognize what had eluded my own doctors so long before. The ensuing memories had somersaulted me deep into the turbulent sea of those childhood times. I'd feared I would drown.

I looked again at the people sitting around me. Tears shone on pale cheeks. A square-set man across the table stared at me from a stern, red face. A few people lowered their eyes or looked away. Icy tendrils spread throughout my chest. *Have I hurt them? Do they feel betrayed?* No one present had worked at this hospital back then.

Yet what could I expect, when I had been describing misguided mental hospital treatment through the eyes of a suicidal adolescent girl? I was telling them what had happened to me so that they would *listen*, because doctors still made the same mistakes. "Oh, yes," I'd heard many times, the speaker ruefully shaking his head, "in the fifties and sixties they diagnosed schizophrenia in almost every patient and gave them shock treatment," as if this were an antique behavior no longer practiced.

But I knew differently. Fads in diagnosis and treatment persist. We mental health professionals are often pressured to label patients quickly, to recommend the newest therapies and drugs, to dismiss disruptions caused by side effects. I wanted these clinicians to acknowledge the significance of their power and its consequences. I was telling them my story so they would pay meticulous attention to every patient they encountered.

The clock urged me to hurry. A tall, slender man not far from me shifted in his seat and began to fidget with his watch, probably worried that he'd have to stop me before I finished. I knew I couldn't possibly deliver all the information I'd worked so hard to prepare. I talked faster. I skipped my last section, even though I knew it was the most direct. I closed by repeating my plea: *pay attention.*

Silence. No one moved. It felt as if a numbing gas had been added to the air. Maybe this had been a mistake.

Then, slowly, people began to ask questions—thoughtful, intelligent questions, carefully phrased.

"What do you think had the most profound influence on your recovery?"

"How do you see the role of the shock treatment in your difficulties?"

They sounded kind and respectful; I hoped it wasn't because they thought I was fragile or sick. I struggled to hold onto their questions and comments, but my vague answers meandered. Promising ideas vanished before I could turn them into whole sentences. Years later I would understand that dissociation had wrapped its foggy curtain about my thoughts, feelings, and everything I could see.

I had to leave. A new set of people were arriving; the next meeting should have already begun.

That's it? I wondered, making my way out of the room. I had expected exultation. I was going to redeem my life. Instead of a flood of sunshine and joyful colors, I felt immersed in gray. Disappointment. Rain.

Still bound in fog, almost out of reach, I waited my turn in line in the hall outside the bathroom, hoping that in time I'd stand with both feet firmly set on solid ground. Two women stopped to thank me for my presentation. "Generous…valuable…inspiring," they might have said. Others approached and used similar words. I stared hard at the speakers, wanting to penetrate each heart and measure the depth of its sincerity. *Should I believe them?*

Maybe I'll be okay, I mused as I wandered out of the building and headed toward my car. No one had criticized me. No one had sneered. I hadn't acted crazy.

By the time I reached the parking lot, I no longer felt suspended in space or entirely incredulous. I was beginning to comprehend that I had just revealed my most personal secrets in public. For the first time, after close to forty years leading a double life, I wasn't hiding half of who I was. Perhaps feeling stunned made sense.

Releasing the scarf tightly clutched in my hand, I unlocked the car door and paused. I stretched out my arms, filling myself head to toe with a deep breath of fresh, spring air. I still couldn't remember having been on this part of the grounds before, but I could picture the desperate adolescent whose fear colored every moment she had spent here. She'd never have dreamed of being in my role that day.

I stretched again and surveyed the scene, taking comfort in the orderly world around me. Clumps of crimson tulips and bright yellow daffodils bloomed along the well-tended walk that bordered the parking area. Beyond the fence, pine trees glistened in the sun. Rows of high white clouds marched across the sky. A cool breeze blew strands of hair into my face. I brushed them away.

"I did it," I said to myself as I slid onto the seat. "I actually did it."

PART ONE
Locked Up

CHAPTER ONE

Swept Away

May 1960

Water on a rising tide splashed and fizzed around rocks on the beach by a tiny cottage where we'd spent the night. The sky was bright, the air brisk and salty. From outside the screen door, Sara urged me to hurry; everyone wanted to go swimming, and I wasn't close to ready. "Go ahead," I said. "I'll catch up with you, don't worry."

She frowned. I hated it when Sara was annoyed with me, but I just couldn't get myself moving. She gave me a long stare, as if she were thinking about what to do. "All right," she said. Then she moved on to join the others. "Just don't dilly-dally," she added over her shoulder.

I'd come to Montauk Point with friends from high school to spend Memorial Day weekend. It was a holiday we had planned for months—or rather, they had. Although we were all juniors, I felt more like a whisper that echoed everyone else's ideas than a true teenager in my own right. When my friends spoke, I heard a funny sound in my head, a sort of ringing or high buzz, and they seemed far away, like toys I could move around.

I intended to kill myself that weekend. When my friends were off together, I was going to take some heavy chunks of rock and wade into the ocean, past where the water came over my head, and hold onto them until I drowned. I hadn't figured out the exact timing.

Maybe because I didn't really like to swim, and because I was mulling over the details of my plan, I took a long time changing into my bathing suit. Sara, Fran, and the others were gone when I opened the screen door and stepped into the sun.

Tightly gripping my towel, I watched my feet press into the warm sand, making deep troughs that filled in once I'd passed. I looked up to see a commotion where we'd parked the cars. A group of people had gathered near a tan Chevy that hadn't been there before. It resembled my parents' car. *Uh-oh,* I thought.

I quickened my pace. The *shlishing* sand and fizzing waves merged with the buzz in my head, which felt light, as if it were a balloon lifting me through the air, as if I were flying. I shook my head to clear it. My feet hurried faster. I soon found myself by the cars, next to Sara. She stood facing my mother and father. *Uh-oh.*

"I really don't see that you have anything to worry about," Sara was saying to them. She was defending me—she truly was my best friend—but she looked more worried than her words implied. What had they told her?

Sara turned to me. "Your parents think you aren't safe here," she said in an apologetic voice. "They want you to leave. Now." Fran looked down at her feet. Emily and Steffi decided to return to the water. Sara stepped back, leaving no one between my parents and me. The wanted criminal, having been tracked down, was about to be taken into custody—I felt as good as handcuffed, right in front of my friends.

And yet, there was a strangeness about the scene that made me think I might be dreaming.

My father drove during the long ride back from the far end of Long Island, my mother glum beside him. Neither spoke. Occasionally cellophane on a cigarette pack crackled as one or the other pulled out a fresh Chesterfield and reached for the lighter. Each exhale that followed filled the car with a terrible, heartfelt sigh.

I sat silent, folded into the back seat. *If only you'd acted more quickly, you'd be gone by now,* I lamented. Concentrating all my energy, I tried to redo reality, to force another chance. I pictured myself heading earlier in the day into the ocean, drowning myself sooner, listening to reports of my death. All to no effect.

Unable to accept that my plan had failed, I moved into a separate plane of existence. The scene inside the car as well as outside of it grew small, as if my life had become a play I watched from seats in the farthest balcony. Colors dissolved into gray. Time lost its moorings.

"Admissions," my father mumbled through his cigarette to a man inside a small gatehouse set at the base of an impressive formal driveway. I cringed at that word, *admissions.* I cringed, too, seeing my usually dapper father's shrunken gray face and dangling Chesterfield, hearing him sound like a gangster heading to jail. What had I done?

I watched as the car traveled in what felt like slow motion uphill to the center of an imposing psychiatric facility—several buildings spread across a sizable estate. I'd often seen them from a distance, since it was located near the center of my town. A tall iron fence surrounded the whole area, keeping ordinary people out. I didn't belong inside.

"I promise I wasn't serious," I said, pleading with my parents beside me. But they focused on the doctor facing us, enthroned behind his vast, polished desk. He was discussing my admission to the hospital. "Please don't leave me here!" I was slipping off the edge of the universe and my parents were my only tether to earth. If they left, I'd be gone.

All three stared at me, unmoved.

"Please, please, please, I beg you, take me home now." I spoke to my mother, palms open, beseeching.

Her face looked hard, her lips pursed tight to keep any contradicting voice from spilling out. Ordinarily my mother's dark, pleading eyes convinced me not to go against my parents'—really my father's—wishes. Her sagging shoulders, sighs, and desperate looks reminded me that if I disobeyed, I'd hurt her worst of all. Ever since I was a little child I'd worried I might damage, even kill her, if I caused too much distress. Now her eyes seemed dull, as if she had already died. Her voice was flat.

"The doctor wants you here," she said, turning her head away from me. "We have to do what's right." I stopped entreating and watched.

My slender, boyish-looking father puffed on his cigarettes nonstop. He spoke softly—not his usual style. Instead of taking over, he was deferring to the doctor determining my fate. His gentle voice and fluttery hands told me that he, too, was afraid.

"Daddy, please, I didn't mean it," I tried one last time. He looked at his hands. No one would protect me. Panic roared through my chest up into my throat.

The doctor, a lanky, imperious man with wavy reddish brown hair and a long oval face, leaned forward to make his point. He warned my parents I might kill myself, that I shouldn't go home, that only the doctors in their hospital knew what to do with me. My parents seemed paralyzed, unable to object.

I saw the evidence against me: I'd written in my diary the plan to drown myself, and my mother had read it. Now the doctor sat there holding my secrets in his large, bony hands. He opened the book and looked at some of its pages, running his fingers across the ink. He stopped to read aloud words here and there—"dangerous...bad...loathsome"—defiling what had been mine but now was his. Then he turned to the last page and read the part about my death. My ears were ringing so loudly I couldn't hear what he said.

"This is a serious misunderstanding," I heard my voice explain. "There's nothing wrong with me. I don't need to be in a mental hospital." No one listened. My parents signed the necessary papers and left.

New York Hospital, Westchester Division
ADMISSION NOTE
May 30, 1960:
Miss Perez was admitted to the hospital today from her home in White Plains accompanied by her parents. In the admitting room, she appeared cooperative but extremely shy and fearful. She expressed doubt that she needed to be hospitalized but was cooperative to her admission and quietly accompanied the supervisor to the admission hall.
—*Dr. Ryan*

In a dormitory style room, I lay in bed, trembling. A terrible mistake was being made. I was not mentally ill. I needed to die, because I was bad, but that was a distinctly separate issue. I couldn't explain how I knew these things, but I was sure that I knew them.

I noticed five other girls asleep sprawled out in beds around me. I didn't intend to sleep. My only hope was that the entire experience might be a dream. I had to stay awake in case it wasn't a dream, because by sleeping I would make the dream come true. As if everything in the world had been switched backwards, and I held the key. I couldn't let down my guard for an instant.

Daddy had seemed near tears when he said good-bye. My mother couldn't speak at all. I was appalled to be causing my parents so much grief. Yet the harder I tried to figure out how to undo the harm, the harder it became to think clearly. Like a ship trapped in Arctic ice, I was beset, my mind frozen. Cold dread swelled in my chest and spilled into my stomach. I had caused some unspeakable damage; only death made sense to me.

A few weeks later, I'd turned into a robot running on low batteries. Medication, plus the sense that nothing was real, left me feeling like a powerless machine in a human form.

At least I'd learned the hospital routine. I knew the names of most of the nurses and patients. I knew what staff meant when they referred to OT (Occupational Therapy) and CO (Constant Observation), PT (time at the gym), meds (drugs handed out at certain times of day—morning, noon, or evening), and EST (Electric Shock Treatment). But I would never agree that I should be in a mental hospital.

Although I kept to myself, I was polite and did what I was told. It was useless to argue with Mrs. Adams, the head nurse, who put the rules first: no talking after lights out, no staying in your room if she thought you needed more social interaction. Miss Thompson, her younger assistant, was more sympathetic and more fun. She liked to play Monopoly and Parcheesi and tell stories about her adventures with her boyfriends and her three cats. I wasn't a game player. If a game was planned, and a nurse or another patient asked me to join, I'd say, "Yes," and pretend to go along, but I'd dawdle while looking for a sweater in my room, or I'd take a long time going to the bathroom and let myself get distracted on the way back. With luck, by the time I returned they'd have started without me.

On this floor most people shared rooms with two or three others. I was still fairly new, so I slept in the larger admissions dorm, which had space for six patients. Patterned bed skirts of pink and red peonies with large leaves fringed the beds, topped by bedspreads that matched. Starchy white curtains decorated large windows that didn't open. We each had a dresser and a small nightstand. Flowered wallpaper gave the rooms a homey feel, until you remembered that you were here against your will.

From the beginning, the shock treatment and accompanying dread dominated my life. Every Monday, Wednesday, and Friday a nurse woke me early for a shot to sedate me. I wasn't allowed to eat breakfast. Afternoons I sat dazed, holding still so as not to worsen the headache and upset stomach that always followed. This meant I rarely participated in activities—occasionally gym on a non-shock day, and sometimes OT, where yes, I made pot holders, the same sort I probably had made in second grade, the same multicolored loops I had interwoven and hooked across square metal frames in Girl Scouts to earn a handcraft badge.

Shock treatment felt like facing death again and again. Not only because the doctor caused a seizure by shooting electricity through my brain, which meant I risked dying if he miscalculated, but because it also interfered with my memory. I'd wake up terrified, not knowing who I was, the world a meaningless blank. It was as if each seizure carved me into a new jigsaw puzzle, and I had to start from the beginning to figure out how the pieces fit together. There was no guarantee they would.

Because I forgot much of what happened day to day, I had trouble getting to know other patients. I lost touch with my friends at school. I told myself that if I didn't see them, I shouldn't miss having friends. I tried not to care, but I was lonely. I felt an ache in my heart that never went away. Soon I'd had so many shock treatments, I barely remembered anything about my life before the hospital.

"Oh, shock therapy does interfere somewhat with short-term memory," my psychiatrist, Dr. Ryan, once explained when I complained, "but your longterm memory shouldn't be affected. To make his point, he showed me a paragraph about it in one of his fat medical textbooks. "See?"

If you're old enough to write a text book or pull the switch, maybe you think five or ten years is short-term, I thought. For a teenager like me, short-term encompassed my whole life.

At night, nursing staff went from room to room, creaking the doors open and shining flashlights on us in our beds, checking to see who was asleep and who was not. I'd slept badly all my life. When I did sleep, I had nightmares. Still, I felt ashamed to be identified as having stayed awake, accused of misbehavior when I was dedicated to being good. Nightmares made me scream. I knew because I woke myself up, or a roommate complained. This, too, might lead to a reprimand by a nurse, although, to be fair, at the time I couldn't tell a straightforward question or a sympathetic observation from a reprimand.

Before long, I'd mastered the slow, even way of breathing that made the nurse think I was asleep when she checked. Dr. Ryan insisted that no one held me responsible for my insomnia or nightmares, but I didn't believe him.

For years I'd worried that as a human being I was despicable. I'd tried to be a good Catholic and go to church every week. Yet, no matter how much I prayed or confessed every bad thought, no matter how hard I worked at being kind and responsible, I couldn't shake the conviction that I was evil at the core and didn't deserve forgiveness. My mission was to rid the world of myself.

The winter before, I'd swallowed part of a bottle of aspirin, but nothing happened. My plan to drown at the beach had been another attempt at fulfilling my goal. I knew I'd been erroneously admitted to the hospital. I wasn't sick; I was *bad*. There was a difference, but Dr. Ryan seemed incapable of comprehending it.

Although I met with him several times a week, I had little to say. Thoughts rarely came, but when they did, I didn't think he'd want to hear them.

"What have you done with other patients your age?" he would ask.

"Nothing," I'd answer. "I don't know what to say to them."

"How do you get along with your parents when you are at home? How do you get along with your brothers? What do your friends like to do for fun?"

"We get along fine. It's all fine," I'd say.

I tried to answer Dr. Ryan honestly, but I couldn't stay interested in the mundane stuff he brought up. I'd find myself looking at something like the plant on his desk and wondering how often he watered it and if he did it himself or had a maid. I often missed what he was talking about. How my friends or my brothers spent their time was trivial compared with eliminating the evil that was *me*. When pressed to name what I considered most important, I tried to justify those feelings, but I couldn't find a way. I kept repeating the same explanation, which clearly annoyed him.

From the center of my being, through all of my organs, to the outer tips of the hairs on my skin, I felt filthy and vile. I couldn't say why. I couldn't provide concrete facts. But I knew it. I felt it. I was absolutely sure of it: I was a walking cauldron of sin.

New York Hospital, Westchester Division
PROGRESS NOTES, CONTINUED
July 31, 1960:
Throughout the month the patient has been receiving shock treatments and will have received a total of 18 by the end of the month...she remains massively self-deprecatory and continues to display the subtly and stubbornly resentful attitudes which are a characteristic of her illness...Thus she constantly reiterates the word "crummy" in describing herself and yet steadfastly refuses to explain why she considers herself so "crummy."

...It seems probable that the patient will require a full 25 EST but it is felt that she will be definitely improved by this.
—Dr. Ryan

In the months leading up to my admission, the chasm between how I looked from the outside and my own frightening, increasingly harsh inner sense of myself had been deepening. In high school, until only a few months before I was hospitalized, I'd earned almost all *As* in Honors classes. My friends were among the brightest, most accomplished students in the school. I'd worked on the yearbook with them and a year earlier had helped start *The Roar*, our literary journal.

As alienated as I felt, I'd been treated as an insider in the clique of smart kids. I cringed at the idea of participating in anything exclusive and took pains to explain that our group was distinct from the popular students, who were especially attractive and well dressed. The popular kids were mainstream and had other priorities: sports, dates, parties, rock 'n roll. My friends and I disdained anything typical or mainstream, (i.e., ordinary), convinced that we were different, (i.e., superior, although I would have emphatically rejected this idea at the time). We eschewed dates. Instead we had *gatherings*. We listened to the Weavers and Pete Seeger and wrote protest songs that we played on our own guitars.

I had also been a successful actress. Although I felt desperately shy in everyday life and questioned my very existence, I excelled at portraying other people, especially if given a script. When I was myself, my shoulders slumped, my handwriting shrank, I spoke almost inaudibly and no longer used the word "I." On stage, however, I could and did project my voice and stand tall. I'd performed in school plays every year since junior high school, the roles advancing with experience. Two months before I was hospitalized, I'd played Betty Parris, a vulnerable ten-year-old caught up in political, sexual hysteria, in Arthur Miller's *The Crucible*. I'd been praised for my authentic dramatic presentation. As the weeks of rehearsals and then performances progressed, I slipped more and more readily into a conviction that I had become a girl dominated by demons. The boundary between Betty's life and mine blurred. Eventually, this disconnected perspective took over.

I knew that even my closest friends, Sara and Sue, didn't understand my growing anxiety and preoccupation with death. I had tested the waters.

"What would you think of someone who felt like an odious criminal and thought she ought to get rid of herself?" I asked Sara one afternoon.

"I'd say she ought to get busy checking out how good she has it and find something better to do," she replied in her matter-of-fact, big-sister way. *Sara's right,* I thought. *I'm just being a baby.*

Decades later Sara told me that my friends had noticed my gradual withdrawal, my darkening mood and diminishing presence, but I had appeared to them as some sort of romantic figure, like a character in a Victorian novel. "You had a mysterious, ethereal quality about you," she said. "We weren't worried. Some of us were even a little envious."

In our therapy sessions, Dr. Ryan often stressed the need for me to become more involved in social activities. I dismissed his advice. Sometimes I read; often I just sat, thinking. Gradually, my conscious awareness deteriorated. The girl who had once worried that the world might not hold enough books for her to read lost interest in everything outside herself. I moved my eyes over Shakespeare's words, but I couldn't take them in. I focused only on death, while I waited for the shock treatments to stop.

After the first three months, Dr. Wilson replaced Dr. Ryan as my psychiatrist. He was younger, cuter, more energetic, and much more sympathetic than Dr. Ryan had been. He even apologized for the shock treatment's unfortunate side effects—the nausea and memory loss. I liked him, and he seemed to like me.

My thinking grew clearer. I found it easier to talk. I didn't always hate myself. Life perked up.

CHAPTER TWO

Hamlet and Me

April 1961

I looked forward to therapy sessions with Dr. Wilson. He helped me to see the relationship between my reactions to situations and what I was feeling. I responded to something as small as a person smiling at me or saying I was wrong and as large as being put on restriction or criticized for not sleeping. Those reactions sprang from emotions, he explained—feelings that I could learn to recognize and eventually control. As my understanding grew, I became increasingly interested in how my psyche worked. I began to grow curious about people around me.

About ten months after I had been admitted to the hospital, I was allowed to commute to my high school, located in the same town, to complete my junior year. In late June, I returned to live at home, on what the hospital called an extended visit, a trial discharge. Every few weeks I met with Dr. Wilson.

Summer slipped by like a barely-rememberd dream. I passed time reading, helping my mother around the house, baby-sitting by playing with my nine-year-old brother, Taylor. I avoided my high school friends, who had graduated and now held summer jobs, even though they made sure to include me when they were home. In my eyes, they had moved on to become adults, while I remained stuck in limbo, nowhere close to being a grown up.

At the end of summer I began my senior year of high school. At first I did well. My classmates elected me president of the National Honor Society—an unexpected affirmation for someone who had spent most of her junior year in a mental hospital—and I played one of the lead female roles in the school play.

My speech at the Honor Society Induction Ceremony was well received. The play, R.U.R. (*Rossum's Universal Robots*), was a success. I worked hard to present myself as the person I thought I was supposed to be: a cheerful, helpful, self-sufficient young woman, certainly not someone crippled with anxiety, burning with shame at being a mental patient, living in dread of shock-induced memory gaps being exposed.

One day in late September I pushed myself through the front door of the sprawling, angular, cement and metal school building like a reluctant soldier forced to advance into enemy territory. I had been doing this for weeks, and each day required more resolve.

Blood rushing in my ears made my head vibrate. Its pounding almost overwhelmed the clang of voices bouncing off the floor and walls and ceiling of the long, hard hallway in my shiny new high school. Rows of green metal lockers heading toward infinity mixed with the cacophonous assault. One face blurred into another. I couldn't identify words in the great streaming body of noise.

My friend Alice appeared in front of me, "Hey, Perez, where are you going? We're supposed to be in English now. Did you read the Shakespeare? Have you written your book report yet? Did you see Becky's new sweater?"

From the midst of the reverberating, incoherent cloud, I mumbled a vague reply that satisfied my friend, "Uh…uh huh," and followed her to class.

Saved again.

Blond wood and metal desks with chairs attached filled most of the large classroom. A chunky teacher's desk, piled high with books, sat at the front. Morning sunlight streamed in through large windows that filled the wall opposite the door.

Mrs. Robacher stood in front of the blackboard, chalk in hand, writing down the words students had suggested to describe Hamlet's mental condition. She was tall and attractive, with shoulder-length, dark brown and white-streaked hair, but she scared me. She had a serious manner, especially with us, her senior Honors class. Mrs. Robacher was Amish, and every day she wore the same plain black dress and black shoes with thick, unstylish heels. She reminded me of an upper-class witch. She expected a great deal from her students and liberally conveyed her disappointment when they failed to meet her expectations. I dreaded disappointing her.

Indeed, I dreaded everything at school, not just my English teacher's criticism. I worried that at any moment, the various strands of my life I was frantically trying to weave together would become so tangled I'd lose my ability to think, and I'd become immobilized. At times I vibrated so much I could barely see.

Many students assumed that I knew them, when in fact, they'd become strangers to me, because the shock treatment had made me forget almost everything. I would never have admitted that, so when kids acted friendly, I just played along, pretending I remembered them when I really didn't. Although no one said this to me directly, they must have known that I was now a grade behind where I should have been. I felt ashamed to be so out of order.

Discussing Hamlet made me especially nervous. I wondered if my classmates recognized the similarities between Hamlet and me. "To be or not to be…" Had they guessed that I, too, was preoccupied with death? They offered Mrs. Robacher words for her blackboard: unhappy, deranged, passionate, depressed, betrayed, miserable, vulnerable, mad. *Are they talking about me?* The air grew hazier, yet the hum of discussion continued unaffected.

The walls began to sway and change form. My head turned cold. The light intensified. I focused as hard as I could on every sentence and on the way each student enunciated it. I concentrated on letters as I shaped the words—s-u-i-c-i-d-a-l, a-n-g-r-y—to anchor myself with my pen to my paper. My sweaty fingers gripped the wet pen even more tightly. I waved my arms in the air to keep my balance. But I kept slipping….

When I came to, I was still seated at my desk in English class. My neck was sore. The skin around my chin felt wet. Objects appeared just a bit out of place, as if there had been a mild earthquake. I lifted my woozy head to discover Mrs. Robacher standing in front of me, her etched face more severe than usual. Unnatural silence had supplanted the room's usual whispers and rustlings. Kids sat hunched over their desks, playing with their fingers or their pens. *Did I miss something important?* The bell rang. Mrs. Robacher swiveled and returned to her desk. The other students moved slowly toward the door, detouring around me.

All the students left, except for Alice, who bustled over to my desk and began to gather my things. With her sleeve she swiped a puddle of saliva off my open notebook, smearing ink across the page. I focused my attention on straightening my wobbly knees and raising myself to stand. As we walked out, I held on tight to Alice's arm. She didn't seem to mind.

New York Hospital, Westchester Division
VISIT NOTE
September 30, 1961:
She is very much on the "side of life" despite the fact that she is suffering from epileptiform seizures of a catatonic nature and etiology. These are of two types

and consist of 1) thirty-second breaks with reality wherein she feels as though she were back in the hospital and sick again and 2) overpowering feelings of the same nature associated with visual hallucinations and probable auditory hallucinations wherein she indulges in agitated posturing in an attempt to ward off the attack. These last from one to two minutes and are less frequent although occurring at the present time, two or three times a week.
—Dr. Wilson   *Dr. perspective foovsal W/J DX*

At home I felt as out of place as I did in school. My parents treated me with odd deference. They stared without speaking. They followed me around. You didn't have to be Sherlock Holmes to detect the fear and worry beneath the masks. However, in our family, we didn't acknowledge unpleasant things or approach concerns directly. We lived in silence, surrounded by inferences and assumptions, wreathed in cigarette smoke and unfinished words.

The family gathered for dinner in the dining room every evening at about six-thirty. When my brothers, Richie and Taylor, and I were young and played outdoors after school, my mother used to ring a bell to call us in. We responded immediately. My job had always been to set the table. When I was in high school, I also helped with last-minute details, such as filling milk glasses and tossing the salad.

A typical scenario unfolded one evening in mid-November. Daylight had ended early. The sounds of rattling windows and radiator clinks intruded into my bedroom, where I was struggling with algebra. The beat increased as the temperature dropped and the wind picked up. I could tell that broccoli was on the menu, because the entire house reeked. My mother used a pressure cooker for all sorts of vegetables, including broccoli, and cooked them too long. Dinner was fraught enough, I thought, without having to breathe foul, ammonia-tinged air or choke down mushy florets and limp, moss-colored stalks. It wasn't her fault. She tried to make the best of what my father was willing to pay for and to eat. Unfortunately, he liked either bland, uninteresting American fare or German food, most of which I found repugnant.

Along with broccoli, dinner that night included boiled hot dogs and boiled potatoes served with a little margarine. The cold house and noisy, wintry weather made any hot food more bearable. Under gobs of mustard, the hot dogs were palatable. Salt and pepper helped the potatoes. I held my breath when I ate the broccoli.

My parents sat at either end of the oval oak dining table they'd bought at Catholic Charities when we moved to White Plains about eight years earlier. Taylor had been a toddler then. They still treated him like a baby, but in some ways he provoked it. He refused to eat much of the food he was offered, especially meat, though he'd learned to manage hot dogs at Cub Scouts. Mom served hot dogs a lot.

A dark oak chest, also from Catholic Charities, sat at one side of our small dining room. Inside a heavy gilded frame, a dark oil portrait of an early nineteenth century man with a beard and black suit hung over the chest and over our meals. This was Uncle Freddie, an obscure St. Louis relative on my mother's side. An educated man from a wealthy family, the story went, Freddie had been a scoundrel who pretended to be a gynecologist, which brought him years of illicit, intimate access to upper class women. I never questioned why she would hang his portrait in our dining room. Or anywhere.

A picture window behind my father's chair looked onto the front porch. Behind my mother's chair, a smaller window offered, in daylight, a view of the bare branches of the cherry tree in our backyard. A framed pastel drawing of a beautiful young woman dressed in a billowy coat and wide-brimmed hat hung beside that window. This youthful portrait of my paternal grandmother, Annita, bore no connection to the small, sickly woman I had feared when she was alive. I liked her on the wall. I almost didn't mind having her name.

Dinner hadn't changed from before I'd been admitted to the hospital. My brothers and father sat first at the table, while my mother and I brought in bowls of food to be served. After we joined them, we all said grace. "Bless-us-oh-Lord-and-these-Thy-gifts-which-we-are-about-to-receive-from-Thy-bounty-through-Christ-our-Lord-amen."

Daddy filled each plate and passed it on. No one could eat until we'd all been served. The bored, hungry boys wiggled their legs and fidgeted with their silverware.

"Sit up straight. Keep your napkin in your lap," Daddy reminded Taylor. "Don't play with your fork," he barked at Richie. "Elbows off the table."

Richie took his fingers off his fork and moved both hands to his lap. He shrugged off Daddy's reprimand—at sixteen, he always looked like nothing bothered him. Taylor wilted like a plucked wildflower.

Although Richie was nineteen months younger than I, he was light-years ahead of me in worldly skills. He spent little time at home. A disinterested, underachieving student and a track star, with a girlfriend and dozens of other teenagers competing for his attention, he'd barely made it through tenth grade. That year our parents had decided to send him to an all male, Catholic high school with the hope of improving his academic performance. He became an even bigger track star, with twice as many friends. Taylor, who was quiet like me, stayed in his room.

"How'd you do at school today, Missy?" my father asked, changing his tone as he turned toward me. He spoke in a pleasant, conversational way, using his special nickname for me.

"Okay," I said.

"What happened to that book report you were working on? What grade did she give you?"

"It was okay. Now we're reading *Hamlet*," I answered softly. *I don't want to talk about this. How can I explain that I don't like school?*

Daddy looked at Richie and resumed his cold tone. "If you applied yourself you might do at least half as well as your sister," he said, "instead of wasting time loafing with your goof-off friends." I stared at my plate. "And the play," returning his attention to me. "How are rehearsals coming? Your role is the female lead, I understand?"

Daddy, stop, I begged in my head. "They're okay," I said.

"Can I please be excused?" Taylor asked in his small, nine-year-old voice.

"After one more bite of potatoes," Mom said quickly.

"Rosanna, can't you see that your son hasn't touched his broccoli? You know coddling only makes him worse."

My parents annoyed me when they argued about making Taylor eat. Neither of them savored their own food. "If I didn't have to eat to live, I'd just as soon skip it altogether," my mother told me a few years later. "My favorite time is before dinner—cocktails and cigarettes when your father gets home." Taylor's food behavior reflected their attitude, but they didn't connect the dots.

He shoved a small forkful of white mush into his mouth, eyes on his plate.

"You're not finished," Daddy said. Taylor quaked. Our mother appeared about to cry.

That's not fair, I thought. She looked so forlorn. I wanted to pull my mother's misery into my own body. I lowered my head.

In the night, a polished mahogany box the size of a coffin sits by itself on a small sandy island about the size of our suburban front yard. A lone palm tree, the only other item on the island, stands nearby, its dark fronds blowing in the wind. The tree's long shadow, illuminated by a silvery half moon in a star-sprinkled sky, reaches across the box on its way to the sea. The moon's reflection on the water magnifies the light. I lay myself in that box, on my back, eyes closed.

"I'll get it!" Richie leapt from his chair to answer the ringing telephone. I blinked.

"No you don't," Daddy snapped. "What do you say?"

"May I puleeeese be excused?" Richie responded, his voice high, almost like a girl's, within a whisker of disrespect. I saw him grin once he was beyond Daddy's view. No one else moved, waiting to see what Daddy would do.

I wish I could be like that, I thought.

"Pat's picking me up at the corner in five minutes," Richie called, as he ran down the stairs and out the front door. "I'll be back after practice, around ten."

"You can go now," Mommy said to Taylor, who grabbed his plate and ran straight to the kitchen. Daddy shook his head and sighed. Before he could say more about Taylor, I pointed to Richie's place. His half-empty milk glass and a dish with part of a hot dog and a few bits of broccoli on it sat where he'd left them when he'd run for the phone.

"See that, Daddy?" I said. "Richie needs to go to practice. He can't clean up home plate."

"*Au contraire,*" Daddy smiled. "I think he will manage to have a ball."

My father loved puns. In earlier years, a comment might have landed in just the right spot to catch fire and grow into an exuberant mood-changer. Daddy, Richie, and I (and Taylor when he was older), stretched sounds and twisted syllables, building together and trying to outdo one another at the same time, contriving the superb last word. It occurred only once in a great while. Daddy's eyes would sparkle. Jamming like an old jazz band, we cooked. Not anymore.

"Let's clear off." My mother stood, picked up two serving bowls from the table, and headed for the kitchen. I followed with my father's and my plates. I removed the last dishes, glasses and napkins from the table.

China and cutlery clattered in the kitchen as we piled them into the sink. The freezer door banged. Metal clanked against the counter. Spilling ice cubes whooshed and clinked against the sides of a bowl before they were dumped back into the tray. They cracked in the warm kitchen air. My father refilled his glass of vodka, added two cubes of ice, and headed toward the living room. Once he'd settled into the window seat that served as his workspace, he lit another cigarette, pulled papers out of the briefcase he'd brought home from his McGraw-Hill office, and began to read.

Psychotherapy with Dr. Wilson helped me see with new eyes aspects of my family I'd never thought to question. My father was the undisputed ruler of the household. On rare occasions when my mother openly disagreed with him, he dismissed her, often with contempt. She withdrew without a fight. He obsessed about spending money—bricks fell from the fireplace, paint peeled off the walls, and water dripped from leaky faucets, but my father refused to pay others to fix things and took ages to do it himself. I grew up convinced that we were poor.

What little my brothers and I knew about our father's history at the time, we'd learned from our mother, confided in rare moments, a hand over her mouth as if she were divulging state secrets. His own father had died when my father was in his teens. His once-prominent family had lost everything in the Depression, she told us. My dad had lived with the bums in the Bowery while he attended Cooper Union, a competitive New York City public college with free tuition. He had been an Ensign in the Navy during WWII. For part of that time, he had taught radar to sailors on a ship off the coast of Florida, work he had truly enjoyed. He seemed to be well respected in his present job as senior editor of a civil engineering magazine.

"How did your grandfather come to die?" Dr. Wilson asked. I had no answer. In our family, personal questions were considered rude, insensitive, even hostile. More to the point, our father would never answer but simply leave the questioner abashed. I'd long ago lost curiosity about my parents' lives. Most questions like Dr. Wilson's had never even occurred to me.

Now, for the first time, I became aware of my father's drinking; the cigarette and short glass of vodka had long since become fixtures, extensions of his hands. On weekends, by afternoon or occasionally earlier, he became maudlin. I appreciated that he wasn't angry, but I cringed when he lavished me with compliments and praise.

"Your dress is beautiful. I wish your mother had your taste," he might say to me in front of her. "You're doing so well in school," he repeated when my brothers were in the room. Sometimes he cried.

"When I die, all I want is for the world to know that I was your father," he told me one Saturday, tears rolling down his cheeks as my mother and I sat with him at the kitchen table eating green pea soup for lunch.

Alcoholic? The word floated through my mind in fuzzy letters, erased before I could remember what I'd seen.

I focused on school. A year and a half earlier, a few months before I'd first entered the hospital, my guidance counselor had allowed me to drop chemistry: at mid-term I'd been dismayed by the first C of my life. Now, the damage to my memory made math particularly difficult, and in English I didn't understand references to classics we'd all read the year before. Perfection required increasing effort. Homework and extra studying took over my days.

As the weeks passed, everyday life, including interacting with my family, increasingly ground me down. My sense of humor disappeared. I struggled not to cry when Richie teased me. I dragged myself though chores and schoolwork. Around other people, I literally shook with anxiety. Most of the time I stayed in my room.

My already significant shyness intensified during the winter holidays. It interfered with my ability to manage socially. At parties given by my friends, now freshmen home from college, I felt like a certified freak.

A few weeks after Christmas, I gave up. I could no longer summon the energy required to function at home or to present a reasonable face to the world. In spite of my initial painful hospital experience, I kept my promise to notify my mother if I became aware I was in danger of hurting myself. Reluctantly, my parents returned me to the hospital.

New York Hospital, Westchester Division
PROGRESS NOTES, CONTINUED
January 18, 1962:
DEEPENING OF SUICIDAL DRIVE, COUPLED WITH DEREALISTIC THINKING, NECESSITATED PATIENT'S RETURN TO THE HOSPITAL TONIGHT

There was momentary remission during the Christmas holidays at least on the surface as she saw old friends, yet an increasing feeling of isolation, ideas of unreality, and continuing feelings of loss of identity, and an increasing preoccupation with thoughts of suicide became evident.

...On the Thursday evening of January 18th, upon return from school, she came to her mother stating she could no longer control herself and that she was in need of help.

...In retrospect, I should like to emphasize that the apparent outgoing readjustment the patient made during the summer had not the solidity of health under it. It is now obvious to the undersigned that it was a schizo-hypomanic state in which she was inclined to be overly optimistic and energetic, lacking judgment about her expenditures, under-critical of other people. Unfortunately the other side of this is the schizo-depressive phase into which she has now entered and in which she first became suicidal in April of 1960. In view of the marked affective component to this patient's illness, I still feel that the prognosis may be good and that surely, as it was before, EST ought to be seriously considered.
—Dr. Wilson

CHAPTER THREE

Shocked

February 1962

It was six a.m. and dark. In the observation dorm, most patients were still asleep. I lay in bed, a thermometer sticking out of my mouth, wishing I could find some way to skip the day. The nurse who had awakened me to take my temperature was back. She removed the thermometer, then jabbed a needle into my shoulder. It stung like crazy. The shot—"to dry up the saliva"—was one of the worst parts of the whole experience, although not the absolute worst.

"Follow me," the nurse whispered. She led me from the dormitory into the treatment room. There, an aide waited with the wet sheet and the gurney, a narrow sort of bed or padded table on wheels. My body anticipated what was coming; I was already trembling.

In the windowless room, I removed my pajamas and stood naked until the nurse told me to climb onto the table. I held my thoughts still, as if nothing were happening, as if I weren't there. "Now," she said, nodding at the gurney. I lay on the damp sheet, which felt like rough canvas against my skin. The nurse and the aide wrapped the sheet around me in the same, particular way as every time before. They lifted me back and forth, and back and forth, and back and forth, until suddenly, they were done. I lay flat, so tightly packed I couldn't move. Enveloped in wet cloth, my body became icy cold. Great shudders ran through me in teeth-chattering waves. For a while, the shaking consumed my attention—eventually I noticed that I was no longer so cold. Gradually the waves subsided. The trembling remained.

I was bound in the wet-pack all the way up to my shoulders, unable to move my arms or my legs. I could wiggle my toes and my fingers, and I did this nonstop. There was a huge energy building within my body and no place for it to go. I wiggled faster.

Soon the nurse rolled my gurney out of the treatment room and into the long, low hallway leading to the room where they shocked patients. They had begun the wet-pack routine with someone else, maybe Allison. As the nurse rolled me down the hall, we passed a woman I recognized from the gym. It was the elderly English lady who said, "Jolly good" whenever her birdie flew over the badminton net. That was all she ever said, "Jolly good."

She played badminton with a younger woman who looked closer to my mother's age. The two badminton ladies lived on the senile ward, which smelled of urine, dirty clothes, and diluted rose cologne. Women wandered around talking to themselves. Early on, when I had lived in one of the medium-level dormitories in the large, old, main house, I'd had to walk through the senile ward on my way to see the medical doctor.

Now I lived in Nichols Cottage, a new concrete building on a different part of the hospital grounds. It felt like a basement, though if you looked out the windows, you could see that it wasn't. Stark, dark wood chairs and couches furnished rooms of pale blue walls, linoleum floors, and florescent lights. The ceilings were low, the angles sharp. Nurses used keys to open the windows. When I'd become too distraught to stay at home and my parents readmitted me to the hospital, the doctors concluded I had to be watched.

Nichols was the disturbed ward, where they put patients who wanted to kill themselves, people like me who were a blot on humanity and needed to be eliminated. I hadn't yet found words to make clear my reasoning on this. That was why the doctors were giving me shock treatment again, I decided—they thought it would make me talk.

My gurney rolled past a few patients who were allowed to wear their own clothes. They sat on benches placed along one side of the hallway. I didn't recognize any of them. Next were a couple of the older women who could walk, and then patients from the unrestricted wards, who were allowed to wear their pajamas and bathrobes. Some of the latter looked familiar: I might have met one or more of them when I was here before. I couldn't say.

Finally we came to the line where the patients on gurneys waited. The nurse parked me at the end—number four. She pushed my bed against the wall and left.

A stray wisp of hair kept tickling my left cheek. I twisted my lips, stretching them around to the side, as I tried to blow it off. My ankles ached from wiggling my toes. I tried to shake out my legs, but they didn't budge. Finally I stopped trying.

Here was where it turned really bad. The waiting.

I hated shock treatment. I hated being naked and wrapped in a cold wet-pack. I hated lying in the hallway on display, like an animal in a zoo. I hated knowing I'd have a headache and feel sick to my stomach afterward. But as I waited and waited, hate gave way to panic. I was smart enough to know that if you were shooting electricity through someone's brain and you measured it wrong, you'd electrocute the person.

Dying won't be so hard, I said to myself. *Isn't that what you want?* But that didn't stop the fear.

Clean up the earth. Get rid of yourself. Go! I couldn't make the pounding blood slow or stop the icy waves from cresting right below my heart.

The line moved slowly, methodically forward. I wondered if this would be the time that I'd die. I was almost ready to choose death, just to get it over with.

The last person in front of me had been wheeled into the room. A nurse emerged and walked toward the gurney. My turn.

In a daze I noted the familiar steps. I was lifted onto the table where they administered the shock. They made sure I was strapped securely across my chest, so I wouldn't fall off. The nurse rubbed a greenish jelly onto both sides of my forehead, near my ears. For a moment I was annoyed that she was messing up my hair. Then came the wires. I looked up to see faces high above me. These were the men who would hold me down while I received the shock. I had to open my mouth for the fat tongue depressor that was supposed to keep me from swallowing my tongue when the seizure occurred. I poured my entire soul into my eyes and pleaded with them to spare me, but they didn't see a thing.

I knew they didn't intend to harm me, but a mistake could kill me. The room gave way to an intense white light. I was filled with burning ice. Then blackness.

I rubbed my hand through the hair near my face; it felt stiff and brittle. Pieces of dried jelly broke off, some in flakes, some in little chunks. My skin itched and my head hurt. I felt both hunger and a deep aversion to food of any sort. I'd let nothing into my mouth, at least I was certain of that. I was bone-tired. It was hard for me to see. How I came to be seated in an old plastic-covered chair in the day room I couldn't recall. I didn't care. My focus was on my fingers in my hair—each flat, thin strand coated stiff with old jelly that needed to be rubbed off. Because it itched. Because it was there. Because there was nothing else to think or to do.

Later, preparing me for bed, the nurse's aide unlocked the bathroom, waiting for me just inside the door. As I looked into the mirror to brush my teeth, I could see pieces of hair sticking out on the sides of my head near the top. I'd learned to know my face in the uneven reflection of the stainless steel sheet mounted on the wall in this bathroom. Yet even with the distortions, I was embarrassed by the odd angles of my hair and the green-turned-yellowish dried patches showing here and there. I thought I'd have removed them all by then.

At night, stiff strands still crinkled between my head and the hard pillow. More itching. More flakes. The telltale dandruff of the girl who needed shock treatment, the girl who was loathsome, the girl who wouldn't talk.

New York Hospital, Westchester Division
PROGRESS NOTES, CONTINUED
February 13, 1962:
REGRESSED AND DETERIORATED. TRANSFERRED TO DISTURBED HALL. EST SERIES STARTED AND CONTINUED.

In the few weeks after the last note was written patient continued deteriorating rapidly. She showed many of her usual regressing, infantile, withdrawing and self-degrading tendencies. In addition, her eating and sleeping patterns became erratic and poor. She persisted in her ideas and attitudes of self-hatred and self-injury....Some weeks ago she was started on another series of EST, which has been continued to the present. Very little thus far in the way of general improvement.
—Dr. Barrett

Despite shock treatment, my behavior grew worse. I began to smash my head against the wall. I stuck straight pins into my thighs and left them there for days at a time. When I refused to eat, food was forced through a nasal-gastric feeding tube. I began to hallucinate. My nightmares increased. I developed a stutter and became increasingly clumsy, falling down and bumping into things. Only pain felt real.

The next year and a half shrank into an elusive, oppressive blur. This murky period included two additional series of shock treatments.

New York Hospital, Westchester Division
PROGRESS NOTES, CONTINUED
April 17, 1963:
EST DISCONTINUED. STELAZINE DISCONTINUED. GENERALLY UNIMPROVED. RECENTLY SELF-INJURED.

After completion of a regular series of 20 EST treatments almost 2 months ago, patient was placed on weekly maintenance EST treatments, which were discontinued 2 weeks ago, after a total of 6. She showed no significant change or improvement in her pathologic patterns of thinking or behaving during this time. She persisted in thinking of herself as a "stupid jerk," spending much of her time idly and unproductively and withdrawing from others by curling up and sleeping on a couch or chair...She has remained essentially unresponsive to therapeutic efforts and advice.
—Dr. Barrett

In the end, they gave up.

The hospital recommended to my parents that I be transferred to the New York State Psychiatric Institute in New York City. Because my prognosis was so poor, and I was a significant suicidal risk, that hospital—referred to as PI—was reluctant to take me. Many years later I learned that the director had agreed to accept me as a patient only after my mother asked the lieutenant governor, the husband of her best friend from childhood, to intervene. Their acceptance included the understanding that no improvement in my condition was to be expected.

New York Hospital, Westchester Division

April 24, 1963:

A copy of the abstract of Miss Perez was sent along with a letter to Dr. Lawrence C. Kolb, Director, Psychiatric Institute, New York City. Miss Perez is being considered for admission to Psychiatric Institute.

—Dr. Barrett

How long could a body hold together once the person inside of it had gone? Except for some veins and maybe a few wasting muscles, when I thought of myself, I saw hollow corridors with cobwebs hanging in the dark, empty spaces. I recognized a smell that lurked in basements, damp and mildewy, from dust and dirt and dead animals. From old newspapers, rags, oil, and sweat that had become too cold and hung in the air too long undisturbed. All of these fell apart if you touched them. I wondered if I were destined to fall apart like that, or if the move to a different hospital might save me. I wondered how long I would last.

Seated on a pale, lumpy love seat in the alcove of a room in the Admissions Building, I pressed my body into the small sofa's cushioned arm. Mrs. Callahan, a big nurse from my ward, crowded beside me. We were waiting for my parents to drive me to the psychiatric hospital in New York City.

I heard nurses and doctors talking and laughing as they walked through a hall past the room. Some startled when they saw me. They stopped short, then moved slowly, as if I were asleep and shouldn't be disturbed. Patients weren't usually there.

I'd left my ward early, before the others were up. "Could I say goodbye to Jill and Megan?" I'd asked Mrs. Callahan, while I tied my shoes. "I promise I won't make noise."

"No," Mrs. Callahan had said. "We'll have no scenes on my watch. Move along."

My doctor said it was good news for me to be going to another hospital, and I believed him. It was good news for me to be getting a fresh start. And it was good news for him to be getting rid of me.

New York Hospital, Westchester Division

July 18, 1963:

DISCHARGED TODAY UNIMPROVED FROM COTTAGE FOR DISTURBED PATIENTS. ADMITTED TO PSYCHIATRIC INSTITUTE IN NEW YORK CITY.

For the past three months the patient has remained essentially unchanged. She has been off medication and has not received any additional EST. She has made no suicidal gestures but has remained markedly catatonic, has slept poorly, having terrific nightmares, and on the whole has continued with her childish, withdrawn, apathetic behavior.

She was accompanied to New York City by her mother, father, and a staff nurse.

DIAGNOSIS: DEMENTIA PRAECOX, OTHER TYPES (depressed).

CONDITION: UNIMPROVED.

—Dr. Barrett

CHAPTER FOUR

Let's Try Again

July 1963

It felt like a recurring dream. Remembering the forced smiles on my parents' stricken faces, their wistful "Byes" still echoing in my head, I followed a tall nurse out of the social worker's office into an elevator nearby. We got off at six. Some of the nurse's keys spilled from the fat clump in her fist, clanking against the wood as she stooped to unlock a large door across from the elevator. With the door opened, she pointed me onto the ward.

Another yellowish hall with linoleum floor. My shoes landing loud, her words drained of sound. *I've been here before*, my old dream observed. *The new girl. Alone.* While everyone stared.

Deja vu may have ruled, but the transfer was real. I had just arrived at PI; my new ward was 6-South. Yet how many times had I made the same walk? *Welcome to first grade; welcome to second grade, to fourth, to tenth? Welcome to the Disturbed Ward. And now, Welcome to 6-South.*

Only a few weeks later, I'd settled in. 6-South was PI's female serious-but-not-hopeless ward. If you were hopeless, you might have been locked up on the eighth floor where they did drug experiments and lobotomies, or they might have you shipped to one of the large state hospitals, probably Rockland. According to Marcia, whose cousin had been a patient there more than once, Rockland was huge, packed full of scary, truly crazy people, managed by mean, overworked nurses, and staffed by doctors who spoke only Romanian. Being shipped to Rockland was every patient's worst dread.

On 6-South, we had all kinds of patients, but no one scared me. We had a lady who was a concert pianist, someone who worked in publishing, and a stockbroker. We had a prostitute and an anesthesiologist. We had a nurse who got into trouble from handling too many pills and a teenager whose parents were psychoanalysts. We even had identical twins who traded off which one was so sick she had to be hospitalized. They never came in at the same time.

Some of us were students from high school or college, without jobs or careers. My new friend, Emily, had been in the honors program at her college and made perfect scores on her SATs. Cheryl, one of the teenagers, came from a special boarding school for gifted students. I was twenty and hadn't finished high school. I tried not to think about that.

The doctors hoped to unravel my pathology by using another feature of the new girl routine. *Welcome to psychological testing.*

"Let's try again," said the small, quiet man beside me, trying to sound kind. "How many weeks are there in a year?"

The consultation room was empty except for a wooden table, our two chairs, and a dented, gray metal bookcase with old magazines stacked on its shelves. The table stretched almost the entire length of one bare, cream-colored wall. A worn black briefcase, stuffed with papers, lay open on its side near the table's far edge. On the next wall, an old-fashioned window with lead-lined panes let in dim light. Outside the glass, a thick safety-screen smudged the view of a hazy, late-summer sky.

"Could I please have a minute to think about it?"

I moved my chair, straightened my hair, checked the pencil, looked out the window and around the room. I coughed. "Sorry," I mumbled, trying to smile.

The ceiling slipped lower, the walls began to shrink. I couldn't take a deep breath. The buzzing in my ears grew louder. My tongue stuck to the roof of my dry mouth.

The man's round head and bird-like face—dark, shiny, wide-set eyes behind an elegant patrician nose—leaned over the collar of his white shirt, just above the knot of his thin, striped tie. My eyes followed the tie's pattern. Against a sky-blue background, delicate royal-blue lines ran beside broader burgundy ones as they emerged from under his collar and reappeared in a different direction on the front of the knot. I could imagine the path of those stripes, where they looped inside the knot before reappearing, repeating diagonally down the long ends that hung at the center edge of his shirt. The tie moved in and out with his breath.

The psychologist cleared his throat. I jerked upright in my chair and stared him square in the face, pretending to be poised. I was trying to figure out where I was.

"Would you mind saying that once more?" I said, praying he hadn't noticed my lapse.

"The question was, 'How many weeks are there in a year?'"

Weeks in a year...Weeks in a year? ...Come on, I pleaded with my brain. *You have to know this.*

My muscles tightened. Everything turned white.

Then, like a miracle, the fog lifted. A solution appeared clear before me. There were seven days in a week and three hundred and sixty-five days in a year. All I had to do was divide them and I'd know the weeks. *Okay, so...seven into thirty-six goes five and uh...*

Now he looked bored. I was taking too long.

"I just need another second," I said as calmly as possible, excitement wrestling with panic.

So then the seven goes into sixty-five...is it four? Okay, I had it. I slid my chair around to face him. "There are fifty-four weeks in a year," I said quietly, although part of me wanted to shout it so loud my lungs would turn inside out.

The psychologist stared at me, eyes wide open over his beak, but there was no expression. He wrote down my answer as if nothing were wrong.

Good. That was close.

Psychiatric Institute
REPORT OF PSYCHOLOGICAL EVALUATION
WAIS, SCT, DAP, BENDER-GESTALT, RORSCHACH
August 12-Augsut 13, 1963
A tendency toward specific repression is notable in her conspicuous failures on the Information subtest. Among items she could not answer were, "How many weeks are there in a year?" and "Where does rubber come from?"
—G. Fried, PhD

I blamed shock treatment for the dramatic holes in my memory, although as far as I knew, no psychiatrist from either hospital had identified it as a serious problem—or referred to it at all. I, too, chose not to consider the impact of shock treatment on my experience; it might have made me angry. I'd have obsessed about the condition of my brain. What was done was done, I decided. There was nothing I could do about it.

On the ward, I passed time reading books and occasionally playing cards with my friends. However, of all life's activities, thinking held the most appeal, even more than reading, at least when I was upset and couldn't remember what I'd read right after I'd read it. I pondered things like the meaning of reality and whether one could tell if something actually existed. For instance, I wondered if there were other people outside of myself, or if I had created everything out of my own imagination. What if I were the only person in existence? Or, what if I weren't real? What if *I* were just a manifestation of someone *else's* imagination?

Sometimes I felt very smart and wondered if I were exploring ideas no one else had considered. At other times I thought only about how odious I was and that I had to die, as if I were a scientist who had discovered that she herself was the source of a deadly pollution, and her responsibility was to eliminate it.

Either way, I had trouble turning my thoughts into words. Despite my best efforts—pictures, poems, stories about animals trapped by wildfires in the woods—I couldn't convey what was important to me in a way that made sense to my doctor.

Of course, I was in a psychiatric hospital, where doctors were interested in people who often didn't make sense—genuinely insane people, like schizophrenics. Some patients on our ward, such as Ellen, were definitely not in touch with reality, but most of us knew quite well what was going on, or so it seemed to me. Yet even I had been diagnosed schizophrenic.

I knew my diagnosis, because I'd seen it when I was interviewed during rounds. Soon after I'd arrived at PI, I'd learned how to read the nursing notes, which were upside down from where I would stand at the half-door of the nurses' station, passing time, or discussing medication, or waiting to clarify a pass. At rounds, I could see the sheet of paper the nurse showed the doctors when they stopped at each bed to ask questions. Printed clearly at the top was the patient's name and diagnosis. Mine read: CHRONIC SCHIZOPHRENIA: AFFECTIVE PSYCHOSIS.

Clearly a mistake had been made. I knew I wasn't schizophrenic. I didn't talk to myself out loud, or walk in circles nonstop, or giggle or scream for no apparent reason, or refuse to take my medication, or spit at nurses who tried to tell me it was time for gym or for bed. Ellen did those things, not I. Being schizophrenic might have made me a more interesting patient than my old, blah self, but I needed to make sure there was no confusion about the matter. Hence, my first rule: never say anything that might sound crazy.

Even when I really wanted to talk and ignored my rule, I had little to say. My thoughts glued up and I felt stuck. After a few months, I gave up trying to communicate. Instead, I decided I would learn to smoke.

All mental hospitals had rules about smoking, although details varied, not only from one hospital to another, but sometimes by ward. On the disturbed ward at Bloomingdale's, what we called my old hospital in White Plains, a person was allowed to smoke one cigarette while a nurse or an aide stood close by. On 6-South you could smoke in the day room any time. You just had to ask the nurse for your pack of cigarettes and your matches and return them when you were done. I figured that if I were sitting in a chair staring into space with a cigarette, when staff noticed me by myself they wouldn't worry that I was depressed or hallucinating. They would see that I was smoking and leave me alone; I wouldn't have to explain anything to anybody.

Cellophane crinkled as I pulled a thin strip from around the top of the pretty red and white pack. I tore off a corner of silver paper with a modest rip and tipped the pack downward. Out slid my first Chesterfield.

The cigarette felt a little softer than I'd expected. Bits of dark brown tobacco spilled onto my tongue when I tried to see what it would feel like in my mouth. It tasted like rich dirt, a sort of nutty raw taste I'd never encountered before. The tiny bits felt like foreign bodies I wanted to pick off and throw away.

The pungent cigarette smell seemed bigger than I'd imagined. I sniffed each end and then the middle to see how much the white paper covered up. The paper itself was fragile, and I wondered how it could hold all that tobacco together and not tear. I'd been surrounded by cigarettes all my life, but I'd never examined one before.

I set the matchbook on the edge of my chair. The chair had wide flat arms and a low seat. I'd turned it so that my back was to everyone else in the ward's large day room. I wanted this moment to be private.

The row of flat cardboard sticks inside the matchbook seemed insubstantial. "Post Road Liquor" it said on the outside. "Close cover before striking." Slowly and deliberately I closed the cover to make sure I knew how to do it.

With grand ceremony I raised the cigarette to my lips. Then I worried that my lips would wet the dry paper, so I held the cigarette in place using my teeth and lifted my lips away. The inelegance of my pose registered briefly, but not enough to break my concentration. I focused on the higher goal.

I bit the cigarette to keep it in my mouth, while I bowed my head over the single match I carefully separated from the others. A few tobacco bits spilled onto my lap. More pieces ended up on my tongue. This annoyed me, but I let it go. I had a plan.

Holding the tiny match in my right hand, I closed the matchbook cover. I rubbed the match over the rough strip on the back. It bent without lighting. I tried again. Once more the little matchstick bent without a spark. On the third try, it worked. I lifted the flame to my cigarette, brought down my lips to seal my hold on it, and inhaled.

I gasped and gagged and coughed. I flailed my hands and extinguished the flame that was about to burn my fingertips. Choking, folded almost in two, I flapped like a magazine in the wind, grabbing my throat and gasping for air. I had wanted not to be noticed, but my hacking, wracking figure must have been obvious to anyone in the room.

Miraculously, just prior to suffocation, I found some space and inhaled again. I'd barely caught my breath when the barnyard taste of the tobacco cut into my consciousness. In response my stomach seized, but I continued battling to keep my balance, to avoid disappearing completely into a cloud of smoke.

Awhile later, the fight was done. I'd submerged my impulse to throw up. I'd accepted my seared throat as a necessary step in the process, a nuisance I could ignore. I'd mastered the breathing, taking in warm smoke with a slow, steady rhythm—lungs moving like waves deep under the sea.

My poise regained, my mission complete, I rubbed the cigarette butt in the ashtray until the fire went out. Then I stood and rotated my chair back to its position facing the center of the room. Shoulders back, head high, I pocketed my pack of cigarettes and matches and strode toward the nurses' station for my evening medication.

One afternoon, late in November, I was passing time as I often did, sitting on the long bench opposite the nurses' station. I was preoccupied with my personal dilemma: did I or did I not want a pass to leave the hospital? My high school best friend Sara had invited me to a party the following weekend. Did that mean I had to go? I'd lost touch with almost everyone from school; how would I know what to say? Deep in my thoughts, head down, arms wrapped around my neck, I was startled by a key rattling in the large door at the end of the hall. Dr. Martin, my stout, stodgy psychiatrist, walked onto the ward. I straightened up.

Dr. Martin moved in a deliberate, tense way, shoulders raised, eyes jerking from side to side, as if he were in a jungle anticipating attacks from natives lurking in the bushes. He rarely smiled. Like most of the ward psychiatrists, he looked young, but his attitude was old. If you asked him a question he wasn't sure how to answer—"Are you married?" for instance—he'd flip it around and criticize you for putting him on the spot. "How does that concern you?" He never stayed around patients if he didn't have to.

There was a reason for his fear. As soon as they saw Dr. Martin in the hall, Lori and May, two of his teenaged patients who'd been hanging out near the day room, hurried to the corner just out of his sight and called in stage whispers, "Chubs! Oh, Chubs. We love you, Chubs."

Almost at the nurses' station when he heard them, Dr. Martin stopped and looked around, glaring, his face deep red. Then, as if he suddenly remembered that his mom had told him to ignore bullies, he acted as if nothing had happened. He gave me a giant, fake smile before he bolted into the office and closed the door.

I struggled not to smirk. It wasn't the first time Lori and May had done something like that. I was too much of a coward to tease him myself, but I had to admit I enjoyed the show.

I knew it was wrong to make fun of Dr. Martin. At times I felt sorry for him, when I considered how brazen some patients were and how insecure he must have been. He wasn't really so bad. I wished I were brave enough to tell them to stop.

"I'm not sure I can handle Sara's party," I told Dr. Martin the next day.

We were in a tiny office without windows on a floor near the basement. As far as I knew, this was a floor of nothing but therapy offices tucked behind rows of closed doors. The doors lined a maze of low-ceilinged halls that branched at right angles. Outside the office, metal fixtures spaced evenly along yellow walls gave off white light, minimizing shadows. A musty basement smell suffused the warm air. Footsteps on linoleum reverberated in the narrow space.

A small desk, two chairs, a low, wooden table, and a green plaid rug filled the office. Dr. Martin sat behind the desk. I occupied the chair across from him. Occasionally, the muffled sound of a slammed door or a raised voice in the hall made its way into the room.

"Why not?" Dr. Martin stared at me. "You could benefit from activity with your friends."

I have nothing to say to them. I'd stand out like an ugly statue covered with lichen. "They wouldn't like me," I said. "I'm disgusting."

"Where does that come from?"

My pores exude noxious fumes. If I opened my mouth wide enough, sewage would run out like a river. "I smell bad," I said.

"You aren't making sense."

I knew I couldn't explain.

Silence.

Dr. Martin's raised shoulders slipped lower. He looked at me and then at the wall. I was supposed to say whatever came into my mind, but any clear thoughts that formed quickly flew beyond reach or popped on contact, like soap bubbles we'd chased as children.

Dr. Martin's spine curved forward into a C. The bottom of his tie drooped onto the desk. He glanced at me again and sighed. His head bobbed. He leaned his elbow on the desk, resting his chin in his hand. He slumped lower. His eyelids fluttered.

For the next twenty minutes, silence settled onto every surface in the room, adding to layers of tacky dust, accumulated from years of empty talk. It reminded me of home.

Because PI was a teaching hospital, we were accustomed to psychiatry educators and researchers from around the world passing through the ward. Famous psychiatrists came to speak in the hospital's auditorium, their names posted on a sign in the hall like stars on a theatre marquee. Patients were sometimes "borrowed" for their clinical presentations.

One such celebrity visitor was Dr. Herbert Spiegel, the hypnotherapist. We'd all heard dramatic stories from patients whom he'd regressed back to early childhood. In front of his assembled colleagues, hypnotized patients talked like babies or young children and disclosed events no one had imagined. Dr. Kennedy, one of Dr. Heller's friends who presented patients to the great doctor, asked me if I'd like to be interviewed. Here was a chance for me to discover a whole life I couldn't remember; I was thrilled.

Alas, although we tried and tried, I couldn't be hypnotized.

"Are you worried you'll say something you don't want to say?" Dr. Heller asked when I told him.

"Well, maybe I'm afraid I'd say 'penis.'"

"Your assignment," he responded, "is to repeat 'penis' out loud one hundred times."

After my session I went straight to an alcove at the end of the hall and stuck my head inside an empty locker. Keeping track with my fingers, I whispered "penis" until I made the count.

When I tried again with Dr. Kennedy, nothing had changed. I never met Dr. Spiegel.

I did end up being borrowed successfully, however. Three or four times a tall, friendly doctor in a white coat approached me on the ward and asked if I were willing to be interviewed by her medical students. It was part of their clerkship in psychiatry, she explained. I'd be helping with their education.

Bright red hair distinguished this psychiatrist, a woman maybe in her forties. She wore it bobbed, with short bangs across her pale forehead. Lustrous lipstick colored her lips the same vivid shade. I must have been too nervous to pay attention when she introduced herself—I never knew her name. Calm confidence, coupled with an easygoing friendliness, made me eager to agree to anything she suggested.

"Here goes Exhibit A," I called to Emily and Lori and whoever else was hanging around in the hall each time I followed the red-haired doctor out the door to another interview, a big smile on my face. I hoped they would focus on my joke and not see how much I relished her attention.

At night I lay in bed and imagined her talking to me. I wished she could be my doctor.

Years later, when I tried to recall details of those interviews, their content eluded me. I remembered only the smile on the doctor's face, the earnest way her students addressed me, and how easy it had been to talk. I remembered the way they'd listened with care, as if what I had to say was important.

CHAPTER FIVE

Ode to Joy

January 1964

I'd arrived at PI with a mixture of optimism and despair. I'd failed at the first hospital; PI was to be another chance.

But when Dr. Martin and I couldn't find ways to communicate effectively with each other, I lost heart. I resumed the behaviors that must have caused the first hospital to transfer me: I scratched my face and bit my arms and fingers; I smashed my head against the wall; I burned myself with cigarettes and held my hands against radiators to burn them. Constant Observation, Suicide Observation, denial of privileges, and withholding passes were effective short-term deterrents, but nothing made me stop altogether.

Dr. Martin didn't pursue the underlying motives for my actions and symptoms. We didn't discuss what had happened in the first hospital or the reasons I was re-admitted after living at home for eight months. It wasn't entirely his fault; I gave him little help. I didn't tell him that dread and a deep sense of shame increasingly preoccupied me. I was convinced he wouldn't understand.

From my bed upstairs in my family's house, I scanned the room I'd occupied since I was ten, half-heartedly looking for a box of Kleenex I knew wouldn't be there. Daddy said tissues cost too much to have in our bedrooms. I needed to blot blood from a hangnail on my thumb. When I was nervous, I picked at the skin on my fingers, and I couldn't seem to stop. I'd been home for a day on a weekend pass. My anxiety kept growing.

For as long as I could remember, I'd felt that my essence was evil. I'd tried to undo it by going to confession and being good, but woven through sermons and psalms and prayers and Mass were references to sin I couldn't escape. At some point I would have to cleanse the world of my presence.

Recently my condition had become unbearable; self-loathing darkened every day. As I lay stretched out the length of my bed, sucking my hurt thumb, I pondered questions of life and death. What would be the most honorable choice for a vile creature like me?

Sometimes when I felt close to despair, powerful music would bring relief. If I turned the volume on my record player to its highest decibel, huge thundering chords might absorb the malevolent energy festering inside me. So I decided to listen to Beethoven's Ninth Symphony, part of a complete set of all of Beethoven's symphonies Genny, my favorite aunt, had given to me that year for my twentieth birthday.

I placed the record on the turntable and clicked the switch. Its arm hovered over the slowly spinning record, then lowered the needle and began to play. At first the music soothed me, but its intensity built quickly. As the symphony progressed, I became overwhelmed with grief, swelling with sorrow for my sinful existence. Like a ship beaten by waves against rocks, I began taking on water in a cold, dark sea.

The symphony reached its final movement, the *Ode to Joy*. Tympani reverberated through the walls and floor; above, voices soared so beautifully that all I could see were showers of sunshine cascading into the room. "*Freude, schöner Götterfunken, Tochter aus Elysium,*" they called across ages.

I was transfixed. I couldn't translate the words, but I knew that God was speaking to me. *GOD*. Through this music He was giving me the solution to my dilemma: I could kill myself, and, because I would then face Judgment, I would see Him. I could end my unbearable anxiety, purify the world, and meet God—all with one act. I would be bathed in the glorious light I heard in the music, and, for a few brief moments, I would feel happy and free. The prospect was irresistible.

Yes, Hell awaited me at the end, where I would suffer forever. I didn't care. Right now, all of my problems were going to be solved.

I gathered the pills I had brought home for the weekend—five large, orange 300 mg. thorazine pills for my anxiety; four red chloral hydrate gel capsules to help me sleep; two pink colace tablets for the constipation caused by thorazine—and headed for the bathroom down the hall, where I began to down the pills with a large glass of water.

I hadn't anticipated how long it would take to swallow that many pills. Water splashed all over the small sink, onto the dingy white-tiled floor, drenching the front of my sweater and blouse. I coughed and choked on some of the pills as I attempted to shove them too fast into my mouth and down my throat, drinking in great gulps to move them along. I did remember to turn off the faucet.

Back in my bedroom, I unscrewed a light bulb from the lamp on my dresser and returned with it to the bathroom. With my foot I crushed the light bulb against the hard floor and begin to eat bits of ground glass I scooped up with my fingers, along with a few smallish pieces. I had trouble swallowing those, too.

Next I removed a bottle of Clorox from a tiny closet that held towels and supplies, unscrewed the cap, and started to drink. My stomach lurched. I gagged and stopped after only the first or second try. Inside my mouth, skin peeled off in lacy sheets.

My hands shook; my eyes wouldn't focus. A huge roaring filled my head. It took enormous effort to concentrate on the task at hand, as if I were working outdoors in the middle of a hurricane. I felt the pressure of time—I must fulfill my mission quickly if I wanted to succeed. I moved on to the next step.

I lifted a razor blade from a box on the top shelf of the medicine cabinet. The world slipped into slow motion as I watched the razor's edge slice each of my wrists. I thought if I opened the large dark veins on the inside of my arms, I would bleed to death. I figured this bleeding would happen while I was in a deep sleep caused by the concoction of pills. The Clorox and glass were added insurance to safeguard my plan.

The blood didn't rush out in a flood, so I made a few more slices to the inside of my left arm, up near the elbow. I pulled the sleeves of my sweater over my hands and in slow, unsteady steps returned to my room. There, I placed myself on the bed, flat on my back, arms crossed over my chest, to await my death. By now the hurricane had passed. Everything around me—the hall, my room, even myself—appeared distant and indistinct.

I began to feel anxious about my encounter with God. Our meeting didn't seem like such a sure thing anymore. I shut my eyes and lay still. I hoped. I waited.

And I waited.

I was still not asleep. I wasn't even drowsy. And I had nowhere near bled to death. My hands had a cold, tingly feeling, but that was all. Nothing hurt.

When I couldn't stand waiting any longer, I sat up and moved to the edge of the bed. I lifted a sleeve of my sweater, intending to check the damage on my arm, but I couldn't look. Blood dripped onto the floor.

For a few minutes I sat without thinking. Then reality began to register.

Have I truly failed?

No, it takes longer than you thought. Death's coming.

That's not true. I've blown it. What'll I do?

It has to work. Wait a bit. Think yourself dead.

With all the focus I could muster, I tried to move the world with my thoughts. Nothing happened.

Nope. You're a complete dud. There's no way out.

Gradually I accepted that my mission had failed. I realized that I had to do something to mitigate the damage. With my arms gathered close around me, I stood and shuffled to the top of the stairs outside my bedroom. "Mommy," I called to my mother, who was in the kitchen preparing dinner, "I think I need to go back to the hospital."

My mother stuck her head around the corner separating the pantry from the stairs and looked up. "Why would you want to do that?"

"I think I hurt myself," I said.

Without a word she walked into the living room where my father was reading the paper and drinking vodka on the rocks. They put on their coats. She looked unhappy as she helped me gather the few things I'd brought home for the weekend. She didn't speak about what I had done.

The large red sweater I was wearing gave me comfort as well as cover, since its oversized sleeves had soaked up who knows how much blood. It was a wool cardigan, patterned with cables and elaborate vines. A friend at Bloomingdale's had knitted it for me, and I always felt her message of caring and patience speaking to me in the beautiful design. I shuddered and held myself taut inside the sweater.

Our car ride into the city was cold and silent. My parents sat in the front seats; I was in the back. The scene had become a dream that I watched unfold from somewhere else. Within me, nothing moved.

We arrived at the hospital at probably seven or eight o'clock in the evening. In winter, telling late afternoon from night was difficult, but I knew it had been dark for a long time. The building's harsh, florescent lights sliced into me. As if through thick glass, I watched people running around talking loudly and asking questions. I was able to keep them from appearing real, as if they were cartoons I didn't have to watch if I chose not to. But the lights hurt, and I couldn't escape them.

Out of all the noise and confusion, the doctor on call appeared. She was a pleasant-looking woman wearing a nicely tailored, dark-pink suit. Her smooth brown hair was pulled away from her face into a tidy bun in the back. Everything about her was in the right place.

My heart began pounding. The glass barrier vanished. All my energy shimmered with an immediate, desperate hope that I had found the right doctor at last—the person who could lift me off the rocks and repair the holes in my battered hull. Every cell in my body reached out for her attention.

"What happened?" she asked, her tone focused and business-like.

"I, I can't say," I replied, my mind frozen, unable to think.

"Why did you do it? What did you take?"

"I don't know," I said. Indifferent to questions, I stared at her face. I needed to absorb her miraculous presence.

"You must have had some idea about what you were doing." The doctor looked increasingly skeptical. Her voice rose.

"I don't know." Now I wasn't sure why I had done it. I knew better than to tell her about my message from God—she might think I was crazy.

The doctor sighed. She studied the report in her hand.

"What did you swallow?" she asked after a minute or two. "If you go to surgery, we'll need to know what you put into your stomach."

"I'm not sure."

The doctor's expression hardened. I truly couldn't remember what I'd eaten, or how much of anything I had actually swallowed. My existence had turned into a singular longing to be rescued by the psychiatrist in pink. I couldn't explain how this worked. I just knew I was almost drowning in Darkness, and she was Light.

The doctor glared. "You're not helping," she said.

As quickly as she had come, the doctor on call disappeared. The glass that separated me from the rest of the world descended. I watched an aide thread me through a warren of tunnels to the emergency room of Presbyterian Hospital across the street. There we waited in silence, squeezed into a white-curtained cubicle that barely fit two people. The lights still hurt. Beyond that, nothing registered. A surgeon stitched up the cuts on my arms. The razor's blade had gone deeply enough to nick a tendon in my left wrist, but it wasn't severed. Only a local anesthetic was needed. When I finally reached my bed in the ward's dormitory at one or two o'clock in the morning, I didn't sleep. I lay awake, very still in the darkness.

The psychiatrist who had been on call Saturday returned Sunday afternoon.

"Let's see those cuts," she said, lifting my left arm and raising the bandage. She gently pressed a finger against some nearby skin. "Looks okay," she said, more to herself than to me.

Fluttery excitement convulsed through me when I smelled the bloody gauze. For a moment I felt alive. Immediately my stomach turned. *You should be ashamed,* I thought.

"Let's have the other one." The doctor lifted the bandage from my right wrist and inspected the cut. Then she was gone.

She had not looked at me, and I had not spoken. I never saw her again.

ON CALL NOTE

January 25, 1964

Pt returned to the hospital this evening saying she had scratched her wrists. Examination revealed 4 deep slashes & on further questioning pt said she had swallowed Clorox, glass from a light bulb, and her weekend meds (@1500 thorazine). She did this at 4 o'clock according to pt & her mother. Pt's story about what she swallowed, if she vomited, how she felt varied with each telling.

—Dr. Gordon

CHAPTER SIX

Gargoyles, Saints, and Harold Searles

April 1964

The day room air hung heavy, dense with the body odor that comes from waiting for bad news. As all twenty of us settled in, the atmosphere was hushed. Even Ellen, who ordinarily spoke loudly to anyone who would listen and usually ended up talking to herself, was silent. Lori and May weren't poking each other or rolling their eyes. They huddled on the small rust-colored sofa, legs folded under them. Their sallow faces echoed the pale walls. At the edge of the circle of patients waiting for Miss Riley, our head nurse, to speak, I sat cross-legged with my arms locked around my chest, rocking.

"Some of you may be aware that Bella has not returned to 6-South following her medical stay at Presbyterian across the street," Miss Riley began. "Because I knew you might be wondering where Bella is, I called this community meeting to let you know that she has been transferred to Rockland." Several gasps and at least one person's sobs, along with subdued murmurings of "Oh God" and "I told you" and

"Shit" broke our silence, but those outbursts didn't convey the level of fear reverberating throughout the room. I felt as if I were watching a large gasoline can slide toward an open flame. Something terrible was about to happen.

Last month Bella had swallowed poison at her lab job up on the 8th floor. She didn't tell anyone, which gave the poison hours to work before she collapsed at the end of an early evening bridge game. As her partner, I'd noticed that she was unusually quiet and that her skin had an odd greenish sheen, but I never guessed what she had done.

Her plan almost succeeded. Bella spent a week in ICU before it was certain that she'd live. After that, the doctors didn't want her at PI anymore. I'd sensed that her transfer was coming, but I still couldn't believe it.

Bella had been one of my two closest friends on 6-South, the kind of friend who saw things the way I did; I didn't have to explain myself to feel understood. Marie had been the other.

Marie was a student nurse at Bloomingdale's during my stay there, someone I'd appreciated as an individual. She'd blended in with the other students, but she'd been kind to us patients. Respectful, too. She didn't treat us like dumb animals to be herded around, or poisonous snakes that might bite.

One day after I'd been at PI a few months, Miss Riley told us to expect a new patient. I was stunned when Marie walked in. It took me a few seconds to figure out where I knew her from, and by then she had recognized me, too. We ran and grabbed each other with happy hugs and squeals, the way girls do. I was so delighted to see her, that for a moment I didn't register that this was, in fact, bad news: Marie was being admitted to a mental hospital.

Most of the time she looked darkly troubled and kept to herself. Patients on 6-South abided by an unofficial rule not to ask each other about problems. Marie never volunteered personal information, so I didn't know what made her so despondent. When we talked, it was about our cats or our favorite books. Or what kind of birds we'd be, if we could choose.

In February Marie killed herself by jumping off the George Washington Bridge. She had run away—"eloped" was the hospital term for it—and never returned. The police found her body downstream. Even though I'd known other patients who had done that before her, it was hard for me to accept that Marie was gone. The loss weighed me down, as if a heavy shadow had settled over my heart. Eventually I became numb when I thought of her.

Thinking about Marie's death after news of Bella's transfer set my heart hammering in my chest. What if I never saw *Bella* again?

I followed the last stragglers out of the day room and into the hall. Grotesque images of gargoyles and monsters flashed before me nonstop. I moved closer to the nurses' station, as if proximity to the staff would help hold me together. I began to hop from one foot to the other, unable to stand still. I was trying to stay ahead of the enormous energy racing inside of me. Faster and faster I hopped. Then gasoline hit the flame. I blew.

Exploding bits of mountains and trees, dogs and cats, rivers and buffaloes, dead faces with arms and legs came raining down on me. I dug my fingernails into my cheeks. Stinging scratches, speckled scarlet where the nails cut through, streaked down my face. Blood glistened on my fingertips. I clenched my teeth deep into my skin, leaving marks.

The explosions wouldn't stop. I threw my head against the wall with all my force to counter the flaming assault. Through the fire, two male aides and a nurse appeared. They grabbed my hands and shoved me into a large canvas jacket that opened in back. The men wrapped my arms tightly across my chest so I couldn't move them and tied the sleeves behind me—I was forced to hug myself and hug myself with no end. The nurse pushed me down the hall. I resisted, but not for long. I couldn't breathe. Deflated lungs made me collapse in on myself, and I ended up curled into a ball on the floor.

I was inside the quiet room. Shabby white quilted pads covered the walls. A rubber mat lined the floor space. It smelled like sneakers rotted from stinking feet. A mattress lay on the floor on the side of the room farthest from the door.

A crowd of staff stood outside the door looking in at me, talking among themselves in words I couldn't make sense of. Then they moved aside for the doctor on call. It was Dr. Roberts. He spoke to me, but I ignored him. I stayed in my ball.

He spoke again.

After a long wait, I looked up. I felt desperately unreal, untethered in space, reeking with shame.

"You know, Annita," he said, "I think you must be enjoying this." His words ricocheted inside of me and would have set off another explosion, except I had nothing left. I was empty.

I have to make this not be happening, I thought. *I will stop time. I can do that.* I held absolutely still—if I didn't move, perhaps I would be absorbed into another dimension.

Nothing changed.

Summoning my very last molecule of breath, I made my voice calm. "Please, go away."

Dr. Roberts stood, thinking, then turned to leave. The staff stepped aside as he walked out. The lock on the heavy metal door, with its little wire-embedded window in the center, clicked shut behind him.

My life will never be right. I headed down the hall toward the ward's back dormitory, hoping to find privacy in my cubicle, where I could cry. I'd had a miserable week leading up to my birthday. Nightmares plagued my sleep, including one with my mother raging at me, and another in which my brother tried to kill me with a baseball bat. I wasn't looking forward to the pass on Saturday to celebrate with my family—at home I felt lonely and out of place. I hadn't the heart to celebrate turning twenty-one.

As I approached the dorm, lost in a forest of demon trees with pointing fingers and scowling faces, lacking energy or will to tell myself it wasn't real, I failed to notice what was going on. All of a sudden someone grabbed my waist and hoisted me from behind.

"Yikes!" I screamed midair. Judy, my cubicle-mate, twisted me around and flung me over her back. Her shoulder socked the wind out of my stomach as I landed on it.

"You're coming with me, young lady," she said, while I gasped. She carted me down the hall fireman style, as if she were a professional who did this every day of the week.

"I've got her," Judy shouted as she bounced toward the day room, showing me off like a trophy to the others who appeared, as if by pre-arrangement, and joined our ragtag parade. I laughed and flapped my arms and legs.

"Save me!" I yelled, once I could breathe. "Come on. Please?" I jutted my chin toward Carol and some teenagers who had stopped to watch. I nodded toward my captor, "Can't you see she's crazy?"

Judy flopped me down in the day room next to the Ping-Pong table, where evening snack was about to be served. I was so dizzy I nearly lost my balance, but I grabbed the edge of the table and managed not to fall.

I noticed a pile of small items near the net, one or two with ribbons tied around them. A moment later, Billy, a tall, handsome black man who was one of our favorite nurse's aides, produced a large aluminum steamer tray of cinnamon toast and placed it on the end of the table with a grand flourish. To judge by his beaming face, it was cake for a queen.

A tiny flame flickered on a small candle stuck in a piece of toast at the center of a sea of thin, sandy-colored, barely toasted bread. Streaks of warm brown spice, white sugar, and yellow margarine spread across it in uneven lines.

"Happy Birthday!" everyone shouted.

I took a moment to grasp what was happening. It seemed as if I were watching a movie without words playing across a screen in disconnected pieces—nothing fit together to make sense. I saw my friends with smiles on their faces. In the distance, I heard sounds of their singing, "...Happy Birthday, dear Annita..."

Oh, I realized, *this is for me.*

Gratitude swelled through me. Tears welled into my eyes but stopped before they could fall.

They love me.

You're an unworthy bitch, how could they love you?

They're being kind; they didn't have to do this.

They had to do this; you're arrogant and selfish; they should hate you.

But, they're acting like they love me.

They'll despise you when they see who you really are.

Clouds covered the sun. I knew I had felt joy, but it was gone. I was struggling not to cry again, this time from frustration, when a space opened in the midst of all the back and forth.

Maybe you don't have to be worthy to be loved...

"Wake up, for Chrissake," Rita pulled on my elbow and gave me a shake. "You're not done."

"The candle," others yelled. "Blow out the candle!"

I blinked and shook myself. Inhaling deeply, I leaned way over the table to reach the middle of the tray of toast and blew with all my might. The flame hesitated, then gave up. Everyone applauded.

"Don't forget these," Leah said, as she helped Judy move the gifts closer to me.

Lori and May gave me a coconut with two round, dark spots on its pointy end that made it look like an enormous cute mouse with big eyes. Leah gave me a handmade mug in an artsy shape with a beautiful, blue-green glaze. Carol gave me a set of colored pencils.

Judy gave me a tiny spiral-bound notebook. "It's to help you keep track of your new year," she said. Tina gave me a large cookie she'd probably bought for herself. Other patients didn't have presents, but even Ellen said, "Happy Birthday."

"Thanks for not saving me, guys." I smiled at a clump of younger patients. "And I highly recommend Judy for rescue if this place ever catches on fire."

"Or if you need someone to sneak you out in a sack," added May.

I laughed. "The perfect elopement for two with their hearts on fire."

"Who's crazy now?" Judy laughed, too.

We turned our attention to the cinnamon toast. I handed a napkin to any individual who looked vaguely in need of one and offered sugar and powdered cream to each person holding a cup of the warm coffee Billy had filled from the large metal pitchers that appeared every evening.

"It's your birthday. You don't have to wait on us," Leah said.

"It's the least I can do," I replied. I meant it. They had been so good to me, and I wanted to make sure I gave back.

The happy aroma of coffee and cinnamon lingered, while the party faded away. Most of the patients moved on to watch television. I gathered my presents and carried them to my cubicle, where I arranged them on the bureau next to my bed.

As I prepared for the night, the quarreling resumed.

Don't forget you're hopeless.

I have friends. They care.

Hopeless and unworthy. Don't think you're so great.

Maybe I don't have to be worthy to be loved. I think maybe they love me.

No, not you, not love.

Blah, blah, blah....

I lay in bed, but I couldn't sleep. Opposing thoughts still crashed and clattered inside my head. After a long while, seeking distraction from the fight, I decided to focus on my gifts. I pictured each one in order, as I had received it. I imagined every detail—every texture, every color, every curve and corner. Somewhere along the third or fourth time through, I drifted off.

Our psychiatry residents moved on from the ward at the end of June. Before he left, Dr. Martin shook my hand and wished me well. He sounded sincere. "Thank you, I wish you well, too," I said.

I wasn't sorry to see him go. Long before June, my early dream of a dramatic recovery had shrunk into reluctant consent to survive each day.

Then, on July 1, 1964, I met my new doctor.

Stanley Heller scored high on essential, universal criteria: he was handsome, funny, and smart. His broad shoulders were perfectly proportioned for his tall, strong frame. His wavy chestnut hair was just long enough to look stylish without appearing unprofessional, and his large brown eyes were kind.

Dr. Heller's sense of humor matched mine. When I made stupid puns, he laughed. "What a pain in the neck!" he said once, after I'd crashed my head against the wall yet again. I had to laugh at myself. In the spark of a good joke, we were peers; we connected.

For a while, I worried that Dr. Heller might be a sex maniac. I'd seen him on the ward one day carrying *The Complete Works of Freud, Volume 1*. Later, he'd added volume two, then three. Everyone agreed that Freud was the man who wrote about sex. I also knew that only very intelligent people understood Freud.

Dr. Heller was definitely intelligent. He could explain things to me. He wasn't offended when I told him I thought everyone hated me. Instead, he expressed sympathy for my distress. Rather than trying to talk me out of my painful assumptions, he gently showed me where my thinking might not make sense.

Unfortunately, good feelings about Dr. Heller didn't solve everything. Rage still erupted without warning and drove me into the wall. My sincere promises after each episode—"That was absolutely the last time....I'll never, ever do it again."—had no effect. The staff ruled that I would have to wear a football helmet if I acted out again.

"This is getting old, Annita."

Miss Riley sounded sad. I didn't care.

"We warned you. You brought this on yourself, Annita."

The helmet was heavy. It buffered me from the full force of the blow as I crashed my head against the wall outside the nurses' station. Again. And again. I had to purge the black energy that had invaded every molecule of my being and turned me into a shuddering mountain ready to explode. I had to derail the brain that housed my thoughts or risk demolishing the universe. I had to defuse my volcanic force or go insane. Some might have said I was already insane. They were the fools who didn't understand, who didn't deserve the gift I offered by eliminating myself.

The effort left me spent. My body turned from molten lava into leaden ash. I dragged it away, wondering how I would get it into the trash. A table adjacent to the plastic-cushioned couch, where the hallway turned into the day room, offered the first opportunity. I crawled underneath it, folding myself up like a collapsible umbrella—a collapsed umbrella with a black, plastic football helmet on top. I had imploded, my rage reversed into a vacuum, sucking me into nothingness. My shame roared so loudly it completely filled the space where I'd been.

After a while, I noticed a large white figure sitting on the floor beside me. I had no idea how long she'd been there.

"Annita?" she said.

Why is she here? I wondered. *What does she want?*

It was Miss Vilna, a nurse I hadn't liked, because she was aloof and sarcastic. *She hates me. She's always cold. She doesn't understand patients.* I dug in deeper, head bowed, arms crossed over knees I'd folded against my chest. She reached out and placed her arm around my back and shoulders as she rested beside me.

Time stopped.

As if there were a locomotive approaching, somewhere between its early faint rumbling and the eventual preemptive screech of its brakes,

I noticed sounds of shoes clumping on linoleum, doors opening and closing, and excited voices down the hall.

"The doctor is here," someone shouted. "Where is she?"

"Annita, your doctor is here. Annita, come over here."

I dreaded leaving what had become the sanctuary of Miss Vilna's sheltering arm. My body ached. Humiliation stirred up the smoldering remains of lava. But I complied. I unfolded myself to stand upright in the hallway, the already-heavy helmet now grown gigantic on my head.

Fitting punishment, I thought. *I am shamed forever.*

"Take that silly thing off," Dr. Heller said in his matter-of-fact way. "You look ridiculous."

"Thanks," I said.

HOSPITAL NOTE

December 5, 1964

Banged head in context of my seeing two of my other pts & not her while on call. In view of past behavior & previous ultimatums of staff, was given helmet and placed on observation.

—Dr. Heller

The hall was empty. In the afternoon most patients not on Observation were at their therapy sessions or some regular activity such as occupational therapy, or art therapy, or maybe an accompanied walk. I sat rocking on the long bench across from the nurses' station while I waited for Dr. Heller. A few minutes earlier, Judy had passed me going to her session. Before that, a group had left for the gym.

"So long, Granny," Rita had called to me on her way out the door. Patients teased me about rocking wherever I sat. I would have gone to gym with them, if I hadn't been scheduled for a meeting with Dr. Searles.

I didn't mind missing gym. Nothing mattered to me as far as what I did or didn't do. Yet it felt strange to be there with the ward relatively empty. "Harold Searles is an internationally acclaimed authority on psychotherapy and schizophrenia," Dr. Heller had explained to me before our first meeting. "He offers consultation to hospitals all over the world. He's my supervisor. He wants to meet you."

I didn't know Dr. Heller had a supervisor, I thought. *Is it because I'm not getting better fast enough?*

I moved my fingers across my forehead and along each side of my head to check my hair. I'd put it into a ponytail to look neat, but wisps always slipped out and tickled my face if I didn't keep them tucked behind my ears. I was wearing my favorite blue blouse, and I hoped the sweat wouldn't show; although, like all of my clothes, this blouse was already discolored at the underarms. I cared more about how I might smell.

Before I could take a discreet sniff, I noticed a white coat approaching.

"Let's go," Dr. Heller said. "We'll be in a conference room upstairs."

I liked Dr. Heller. Sometimes I thought he liked me. More often, I decided that I'd ruined my chances and he would never again want to deal with me, because, no matter how hard I tried, I still misbehaved and attacked myself.

I approached each therapy appointment almost giddy with excitement, as if something wonderful were about to happen, something that would leave me happy and unafraid. I was usually disappointed. As Dr. Heller walked me back to the ward, my mind would race ahead trying to think of something to make him reassure me that I hadn't spoiled his opinion of me and that he still cared. I felt deflated after he left. Sometimes, if I thought he was upset with me or when he'd ended the session a few minutes early, I became desperate and burned myself with cigarettes. To get relief. That never worked for long; it was how I'd caused trouble in the first place. Everyone—doctors, nurses, even my friends—

would end up angry, and I'd feel worse. I figured that was the reason for the consultation with Dr. Searles: they didn't know what to do with me.

I ended up in a dimly lit room with no windows. I wasn't sure of which floor it was on or how I'd arrived there. Three men, each wearing a white coat over his shirt and tie, occupied chairs near mine. One was Dr. Heller; one was Dr. Mesnikoff, the chief psychiatrist of my section; and one was Dr. Searles. Dr. Mesnikoff's presence jolted me awake—I hadn't expected him. All three doctors shot into hyper focus. *They could ship me to Rockland, like Bella,* I thought. *They're here to determine whether I'm hopeless.*

Dr. Searles moved his chair closer to mine. With doughy pale skin, near-white hair, and a deliberate way of moving, he seemed old and puffy around the edges. I stared at his round face, struggling to pay attention. The world had slipped back to unreal; the vivid clarity from just moments earlier was gone. My body moved without volition, as if I were a marionette.

"Well, hello, I know you," Dr. Searles began. He must have been referring to the first meeting, a few weeks earlier that I'd dismissed as completely useless. "Aren't you the girl who wants to be a saint?"

Oh yeah, that crazy idea, I recalled. *How could an irredeemable sinner be a saint?* His ignorance made me feel frantic.

"When you're a foul, shameful person you don't actually believe you could ever be a saint," I said after a long pause, not looking at him. The room smelled of stale, dirty bodies. I shuddered.

Dr. Searles didn't move. He stared at me with an expression I couldn't translate. I pressed harder into the back of my chair.

"You look like a frightened young fawn sitting there in front of me," he said.

He sees I'm afraid. Is that wrong? Hammers began to bang inside my forehead.

"The way you look at me makes me feel like a dirty old man," Dr. Searles continued, leaning forward as he spoke. "If talking to me frightens an innocent girl like you, I must be a terrible person. I feel awful. The way you look at me makes me feel so guilty I want to kill myself." The room's air vanished; my ears popped. *I make him feel suicidal? Me?* I couldn't fathom having that kind of power. My stomach churned as I replayed his words:...*dirty old man...innocent girl...You make me feel...so bad I might kill myself.* He didn't make sense. *Yet he knows I'm afraid. He feels guilty.* I felt guilty, too. I began to feel sorry for him.

Dr. Searles brought his hands together and nodded. He stood, signaling the interview's end. Although there'd been more discussion, I hadn't heard anything further that he and the other doctors might have said.

Oblivious to my surroundings, focused only on my noisy brain, I followed Dr. Heller like an imprinted duckling out of the conference room and back to the ward. I walked straight to my cubicle and lay flat on my bed. Gradually the hammers softened. Day turned into night, and I hardly noticed. I thought of nothing but the phenomenal idea that I'd had an effect on Dr. Searles. *He understands my fear...He wants to kill himself...because of me.* I'd become obsessed with the power of that connection.

The next evening in the informal group of patients that gathered every night for coffee at the end of the hall, I described my conference with Dr. Searles.

"I'm still amazed," I told them. "The first time I talked to him he said I acted like a saint. Now he says I look so frightened I make him feel like he's bad. Can you imagine?"

"Hell, yes," Rita said. She was a pale overweight teenager whose major pathology, as far as I could tell, was extreme defiance and swearing all the time. "You're always doing shit for other people."

"Yeah," Cheryl, who was more sophisticated, chimed in. "When someone sneezes, who's the first to run for a tissue? It's sickening."

"Don't you know how it makes us feel?" Judy's round face was flushed; she waved her hands for emphasis. "Like you have to be better?"

Leah, whom I'd thought of as my closest remaining friend, practically jumped out of her chair, shouting at me from across the room. "Do you think you're the only person around here who can help anyone?"

Even Carol, who didn't eat and rarely spoke, added her two cents. "Yeah, like I feel useless, totally, because you're always first."

You, too? I thought, as I forced myself to listen to Carol's version of my oppressive helpfulness. *How could I have had it so wrong?*

My head ached with the painful news. Yet I wasn't devastated, which I would have predicted. I could see their point. I could see how annoying I might be, running around gung-ho trying to fix everything, crowding out their chances to feel useful and worthwhile.

Shouldn't I feel ashamed? Doesn't this prove I should disappear forever? Still, I wavered. *Maybe I could change how I go about these things…*

While I felt brought up short by my zealous, goody-goody behavior, another part of me felt as if I'd been handed a prize. From their reactions—first Dr. Searles' and then my friends'—I grasped the idea that my behavior affected every person I met. I influenced how other people saw themselves, not just what they thought about me.

Suddenly I understood the *inter* in interaction. I had a place in a process, in a relationship. For someone who'd felt invisible and unreal—perpetually on the brink of disappearing, with absolutely no power or influence—this was an amazing discovery.

I wanted to dance.

HOSPITAL NOTES

December 3, 1964

Seen by Dr. Searles, consultant from Chestnut Lodge, who will supervise treatment. He felt she was saint-like in appearance and action. Spoke of the envy her innocence must cause and attacked her use of the second person in referring to herself. He felt prognosis was not favorable.

December 16, 1964
Presented to Dr. Searles, who informed A she had progressed from saintliness to being an adorable child and that her purity so bothered him he fantasized suicide. Feeling was to encourage open expression of hostility.
—Dr. Heller

No one, not even Dr. Heller, seemed to understand the motivation underlying my so-called saintliness. I was annoyingly good, because I felt loathsome. I was trying to make reparations for my existence, not seeking sainthood. Yet Dr. Searles had touched me in a way no one before him had. As inappropriate as his words may have sounded, and as misguided as his assumptions appeared at first glance, he had cut through my isolation. He might have saved my life.

CHAPTER SEVEN

More Life Inside

August 1965

Summer was not a good time to be a patient in a mental hospital. Humidity seeped into every corner of the ward. In the sweltering day room, bare thighs snapped like masking tape ripped from dispensers as we shifted position on the vinyl-covered chairs and couches. Many patients just moped around, assorted stinky damp rags. If we'd earned certain privileges, we could take walks with a group, but only a fool would have chosen to go. Outdoors was often hotter than inside 6-South.

It was August, when any doctor or nurse who could do so took vacation. Those who stayed were mostly inexperienced psychiatry residents, schedules were in flux, and no one knew what to expect. That, plus the heat, put everyone on edge.

Occasionally, those of us with building privileges were allowed onto the roof to lie in the sun. The roof could be blisteringly hot, and there were only a few small wooden benches to rest on. Car exhaust and smokestack fumes from roofs along the whole complex of hospital buildings stifled our lungs, while traffic swarming down the West Side Highway thrummed in our ears.

But hospital girls were like girls anywhere—we'd suffer whatever we had to if it meant getting a tan. A heavy wire screen covered the entire space; the effect was like being in a huge birdcage. Once, I fell asleep up there. I returned to the ward with a serious tan, but what impressed my friends even more was the pattern of square white lines on my skin where the screen's wire had blocked the sun. They celebrated me as an exotic freak.

Dr. Heller, who was now Senior Resident, had already returned from his vacation. Every day I thanked God that I was still his patient, since very few people continued with the same doctor once the psychiatric residents switched to their new assignments in July. To guarantee that the doctors in charge knew I appreciated Dr. Heller's investment of another year, I needed to show improvement and make sure I didn't lose ground. This meant I had to control all the self-destructive stuff: no more bashing my head against walls, or scratching my face, or burning holes in my arms and legs with cigarettes.

I'd worked hard at not burning myself. Still, there were times when I felt as if I'd stepped off a cliff into a chasm I hadn't seen coming, and I needed to cause pain just to keep from falling too far down. This could be triggered by a nightmare or a criticism, by saying something I wished I hadn't, or by intense feelings I simply didn't understand. Regardless of the cause, I had to make the darkness stop. A certain kind of blackness, like molten lead, would grow and spread inside me, so dense and unremitting that I feared once it filled me up, I'd sink through the center of the earth into a void that would never end. The fire of a hot cigarette pulled me back to the outside edge of myself, where my skin was. From there I could figure out what to do, and I'd feel better. I'd no longer be in danger of disappearing.

I had made progress. I could still be very depressed. I still became jealous of other patients. I often felt loathsome and vile. Sometimes I still wanted to die. But I recovered my perspective faster than I used to.

Going to the ninth floor by myself to meet with Dr. Heller in the new office that came with his advanced residency helped me feel more grown up. In our sessions he sat behind a modest desk and swiveled his chair closer to face me. On sunny days the Hudson River and the George Washington Bridge gleamed through a window on the far side. This room was smaller than his old one, but with the view and our chairs closer together, I liked it better.

When Dr. Heller first became my doctor, I had felt so shy that often words wouldn't come out. Yet as I became used to his accepting, un-hurried style, room for thoughts opened in my brain. After I'd bashed my head or burned myself, he and I would talk about what it was that had pushed me into feeling so desperate that I lost control. As I became more comfortable discussing my ideas, we often ran out of time. "Let's follow up on this next session," Dr. Heller would say. "Unfortunately, we need to stop now."

On one occasion, I took his "We need to stop now" as proof that I was worthless and he hated me. The thought festered; it wouldn't let go. A few hours later I burned myself. "Slow down; don't take those ideas so seriously," he said when we talked about it later. "I think you have enough pain already." He wasn't angry.

Sometimes Dr. Heller pretended he was my mother. "Oh, Annita," he said one time in a high, whiny voice, "you haven't paid enough attention to me and I feel neglected." At first, I enjoyed the absurdity of this tall, confident man's impersonation of a small, timid woman. I grinned.

"It's not meant as a joke," he said. Then I worried I'd offended him by taking it wrong. I was trying to figure out what he wanted to get across, playing his words back in my head, when I was hit by what felt like a sudden rockslide. Boulders tumbled through my chest and landed in my stomach—cold, hard, and heavy.

"My tummy's a little queasy," I said, half apologizing.

"How come?" he asked.

I went over Dr. Heller's imitation again. This time I pictured my mother's hunched shoulders and apprehensive face. I heard her put-upon sigh. The scary feeling intensified.

"Yeah," I said. My voice came out high, as if I were a little girl. "Lots of times I feel my mother is unhappy with me, and I try and try, but I can't cheer her up." My eyes filled with tears. A second later all my feelings vanished; I'd become like the rocks, numb. I took a deep breath and stared at my doctor. His sincere eyes looked terribly sad. *He really thinks I was hurt,* I thought.

I sensed that Dr. Heller was angry with my mother, because he thought she had made me suffer somehow. "Don't you see," I'd tried to explain more than once. "Mothers love their children; it's what they do. So my mother wouldn't do anything that hurt me. Don't you see?" If I'd felt something missing, it would have come from a flaw in me.

"Aren't you a bit old for fairy tales?" he asked.

"Oh, Annita, stop feeling sorry for yourself," Dr. Heller said a few months later, impersonating my mother again. "You are so smart and your brothers aren't. How could you possibly be unhappy?"

"Yes!" I said, delighted that he understood some of the things that bothered me most. "I worry that if I'm not happy, I must be feeling sorry for myself. I *do* try to be happy. On the other hand, I feel like disgusting dirt most of the time." By then I'd figured out that he wanted me to see that how my mother treated me might have caused certain problems. At times I could see his point. *But you're too harsh,* I thought. *She tries hard.*

I worried I was being disloyal to my mom, yet I liked when Dr. Heller stuck up for me. My confusion and fear, my tremendous anxiety, seemed reasonable to him, as if bad things really did happen, and they really were beyond my control. Whatever had gone wrong wasn't solely my fault. Sometimes I basked in his positive view. Often, though, I panicked, as if thinking I deserved more than hatred or contempt could put me in serious danger, and only punishing myself first kept me safe.

At least I had become better about asking for help before doing something dangerous.

One day a week earlier, we could barely touch the air without getting burned. It was too hot for the roof or a walk. The yellow walls of the central day room vibrated in the sunlight, making some patients dizzy. We were miserable. And bored. From where I was reading on the smaller rust-colored sofa I heard Jake taunting Ivy. I knew it wouldn't be long before someone blew.

From my place on the couch, I watched Jake move toward Ivy in the center of the sizzling day room, his lips twisted into a wicked smirk. My heart began to race. *Please no, Jake. Don't.*

"Your boobs are dying to jump out of that shirt," Jake said in a serious tone, pointing at Ivy's chest, as if he were the weatherman noting in which counties it would rain the following night. He stepped back and surveyed her body, eyes wide with mock concern. "Maybe I could help them."

I held my breath.

"Go back to nursery school, asshole." Ivy's eyes narrowed. "Obviously, you flunked kindergarten."

"You calling me stupid?" Jake's voice grew louder. His face turned red.

Marcia, who'd been lying near me, set aside her book. As Jake's volume increased she pulled herself upright, staring at them. My head was about to explode, but my body couldn't move.

"Who are you calling stupid, whore?" Veins bulged in Jake's neck. He pushed his face into Ivy's. With viper speed she reacted.

Smack!

Jake held his cheek, crouching in pain.

"Stop it, you fuckers!" Marcia screamed. She threw herself at Jake and Ivy, who turned from each other to confront her.

"Shit!" "Dumb ass!" "Cool it, jerk." "Go Ivy!" Practically everyone was yelling something. Nurses' aides came flying.

As Marcia moved in, Jake or Ivy shoved her. She flew backward and landed with a thud on the edge of her butt, her wrist underneath her. The sounds of her fall and her outraged shrieks intensified my guilt. *If you weren't such a wimp you wouldn't have let this happen.* My head throbbed. Adrenaline surged with no place to go.

The last time I hurt myself had been a month before that. It was a deep burn on the inside of my ankle, behind the bone. I covered it with my socks, and it became infected. It felt like a knife slicing into my leg when I put my weight on it, but I didn't tell anyone.

Around then I had a special pass to go with Genny, my favorite aunt, to see *The Mikado* at a theater on the Upper East Side. We walked from the hospital to a subway station at the end of the block, past the row of massive gray hospital buildings on one side and The Silver Palm Restaurant on the other. Although my foot was killing me, I smiled and chatted as usual.

An evening breeze kept blowing my hair into my face, but I didn't mind—at least it was cool. I told myself what mattered was that for those hours I was out of the hospital, and I was free. But by the time we emerged from the subway tunnels and began the short walk to the theater, every step felt like someone was shoving red-hot coals into my leg. It took all my concentration to pretend nothing was wrong.

The next morning I couldn't stand the pain. I showed the oozing pink hole to Miss Lang, one of my favorite nurses. She put ointment on it and gave me a lecture about why burning myself was a bad way to manage uncontrollable feelings. But she wasn't angry. Perhaps because so much time had passed since I'd done it, they didn't take away my privileges.

I liked the way this hospital managed rules. If we improved and controlled ourselves, we earned more privileges and higher status. If we misbehaved, we were demoted. After I tried to kill myself they put me on suicide observation, and for months every move I made was watched. I couldn't even use the toilet without a nurse or an aide standing right outside the stall.

Since then I'd worked all the way up to accompanied walks and eventually building privileges, which meant I could move freely through the whole hospital by myself. If they had punished me for burning my ankle, I'd have lost that freedom. I realized what I risked if I hurt myself again. Without building privileges, not only would I never get a tan or go on passes with my aunt, there'd be no watching the river from the 12th floor, or eating toasted English muffins in the coffee shop, or taking orders and bringing Linzer tart cookies back to patients who couldn't leave. And I was looking forward to a job shelving books in the medical library. I wasn't giving that up.

Once it was clear that Marcia's wrist had been injured, Jake and Ivy calmed down. They hadn't meant to hurt her. However, by then I'd become a leaking cesspool of dread. At first I thought that by failing to stop the fight sooner, I'd caused Marcia's fall and could be cited for negligence. Later I realized that idea was nuts, but at the time shame swamped any rationality. My stomach writhed. I couldn't breathe. I needed to attack myself or drown.

Yet I realized this was the same feeling that had made me burn myself before. If I gave in to it, I'd surely be punished when the staff found out. I decided to tell Miss Riley that I needed to talk to my doctor. She was busy with the crisis from the fight, but she said if I could wait, she'd call him.

So I walked. Up and down the long yellow hall, I paced, my eyes locked on the floor. Back and forth, around and around. Toward one end I passed a clump of teenage patients discussing Marcia's intervention. Others had dumped themselves on the long bench across from the nurses' station.

"Will you slow down?" Leah, my best friend, said, after maybe the fourth pass. "You're making me dizzy."

"Leave her alone, at least she's creating a breeze," Cheryl countered.

"Hell, no," shouted Rita. "She's making me sick." Rita placed her large body in front of mine, blocking me in the middle of the hall.

"Look, you," she said, scowling into my face, "Do you want me barfing all over this fuckin' floor?" I turned and resumed my rapid pace in the opposite direction. I knew she wasn't kidding, but I ignored her, just like I ignored the streams of sweat flowing down my body. I didn't even feel hot; nothing registered on that level. I had to last until Dr. Heller arrived. I was wondering how much longer I could hold off bursting out of my skin when I saw his white coat come through the door at the end of the hall.

Dr. Heller didn't seem to be angry at me for bothering him, and he showed no interest in the fight. "Come on," he said. "Let's get out of here." I figured we were heading for his office, but we stayed in the elevator all the way to the ninth floor.

I followed him past a few faded music festival posters into an alcove lined with vending machines. Under the ubiquitous florescent lights, the crass machines and old artwork just intensified the area's lonely, institutional feel.

"I'm dying of this heat," Dr. Heller said. "I could really use some ice cream." He took a quarter from his pocket and slid it into the slot in a large Good Humor machine. A vanilla bar covered with chocolate dropped into the basin at the bottom.

"How about you?" He turned to me. "Want one?"

I was stunned. I didn't know doctors were allowed to do that sort of thing. My face flushed—now I felt the heat for sure. I couldn't form words, so I nodded my head vigorously, not wanting him to think I lacked enthusiasm.

It can't be wrong if he offered, right? I'm not making him do this.

Dr. Heller dug into his pocket and produced another quarter, which he inserted into the slot for ice cream bars. Maybe he realized that I was too surprised to speak, because he pushed the button for one like his without asking me to choose. He handed the ice cream to me, and we settled side by side on a plain wooden bench set against a wall of the alcove. I ate slowly, luxuriating in the smooth, creamy texture of ice cream on my lips, savoring the sweet chocolate I held on my tongue for as long as I could. The need to burn myself faded like a midday moon.

Dr. Heller didn't seem to mind that I no longer had an urgent problem requiring his attention. He never mentioned it. We talked about the weather, about when it might cool off, what I used to do if I was at home when the temperature climbed this high.

"Sometimes the Good Humor man came to my neighborhood, but my father only let me buy a five-cent popsicle, and not every time," I explained.

Dr. Heller stroked his chin, mimicking deep reflection. "I see," he said. A big smile spread over his face. "So that would give you two cheap pops."

"You got it!" I laughed. "A two-for-one special."

He knew I loved puns. In that moment it seemed as if we were two old friends who had stopped for a snack together. The world around me changed texture: walls, windows, he and I—everything appeared crisp and vivid, where before I'd only known anxious fog.

A while later we returned to a quiet ward. All were back where they'd been before the fight. Dr. Heller left.

For the next several hours, I sat by myself in the little meeting room at the end of the hall and thought about what had happened. I felt as if I'd been dancing at a magnificent ball, my partner and I moving with a grace I had never imagined—my mind was still twirling. I vowed to remember that feeling.

HOSPITAL NOTE
August 16, 1965

Able to handle my vacation and return without self-injury. Using privileges well and continuing to socialize.
—Dr. Heller

A week later, the old hatred was back, catching me off-guard. I'd spent days thinking I was disgusting—hideous, despicable—but when Dr. Heller asked why I was so upset at this particular time, I had no answer. By Wednesday morning my level of abomination required action. I considered jumping off the bridge to kill myself. But that also frightened me. Part of me didn't want to die. So I told Miss Riley.

She didn't scoff at me or seem angry. "What's up?" she asked. "I'll need to tell the doctor on call."

I didn't know the man who came to speak with me about half an hour later. "It's like I'm a village that's been invaded by Nazis, and they turned it into a place just like themselves," I told him. "My mind has turned into a tangle of terrible, hateful thoughts. I have no say."

"Your mind doesn't feel like your own?" the doctor asked, looking worried.

"Nothing good is left. I've become one of them. I'm as evil as a Nazi inside my own skin." I began to cry.

The doctor on call said I was restricted until I met with Dr. Heller. Before then, I wouldn't be allowed to leave the ward for any reason.

The Nazi feeling kept growing inside of me. By afternoon I felt like I was possessed. I needed to hide. I knew of a space off the hall, an alcove behind the lockers. I crawled as far toward the back as possible, underneath the stored winter clothes—jackets of all sorts and smelly woolen coats. I squeezed myself into a ball, as low on the floor as I could go. I was trying to disappear.

Dr. Heller found me there—I had no idea how. He crawled into the alcove and sat on the floor, too, so we could talk.

"What brings you here?" he asked, as if we'd crossed paths by chance in a general store.

"If you've turned into a Nazi, there's no hope for escape."

He looked puzzled. I searched for words that might convey the horror I felt at who I had become. "Repulsive, reprehensible, putrid. You can't live with yourself like that. You must die."

But Dr. Heller wasn't afraid of my evil the way I was. "I know you didn't see yourself this way last week. Something had to make your feelings change," he said. "Anything new on the ward?"

"Believe me, I've thought about that. Nothing happened. Evil is evil. You're forever exposed; it shows." I was trying my best, but the words didn't make sense, even to me. I ached for him to understand what I was trying to say.

"What about your visit home on the weekend?" Dr. Heller asked. "How'd that go?"

Then I remembered.

On Saturday my parents and I had visited one of Daddy's work friends who lived with his wife in a glamorous white Colonial house in Greenwich, Connecticut. Their perfect green yard included a lovely blue swimming pool. White wrought-iron tables with matching filagree chairs sat on a patio around the pool's edge. An umbrella shaded each table. Yellow rose bushes along the perimeter perfumed the scene.

After our swim, the adults settled into lounge chairs on the lawn, smoking cigarettes, drinking cocktails, and chatting for quite a while. I had been reading at one of the tables by myself, when Daddy wandered over and took a seat beside me.

"What are you reading there, Missy?" he asked. He leaned in to check my book. *Jane Eyre*? Of course, something worthy of your superior intelligence. How do you like it?" He didn't wait for me to answer but moved his chair closer to mine.

"Your hair looks particularly lovely against your skin," Daddy said. "Your skin glows in this light."

A rancid cloud of cigarette smoke laden with alcohol wafted into my face. My bathing suit began to shrink. I froze.

Daddy stared at me. "You are the daughter all fathers dream of," he said. Then he paused. "I can't...help, I...can't...help...myself," Daddy faltered, starting and stopping his words as if he weren't sure of what he was saying. "I'm in love with you," he blurted out.

I must have looked startled, because he added quickly, "Of course all fathers feel this way about their daughters."

He reached toward me as if he were going to touch my arm with his hand. Suddenly he pulled back. "No, much too tempting," he muttered. "I don't trust myself." He rose abruptly and left to rejoin the group across the lawn.

My head vibrated with the buzzing of a thousand bees. *He's been drinking,* I thought. *He doesn't know what he's saying. People say all sorts of things they don't mean when they've had too much to drink.* The bees continued. I decided nothing was wrong. I forgot about it.

Dr. Heller's jaw had dropped. His mouth hung open. *He thinks something serious happened.* He asked me to repeat the part with my father, as if he couldn't believe he'd heard it right the first time. *He probably doesn't understand that Daddy was drunk, so it doesn't count.*

Dr. Heller didn't seem to blame me for my suicidal thoughts or feeling possessed or having to hide. He wasn't angry that he'd been requested to see me after I'd been restricted. I was grateful, as well as surprised. Instead of burning me at the stake—which I felt I deserved—Dr. Heller just sat with me under the coats. *He's disturbed by this himself, I can tell.* Yet I didn't feel guilty for upsetting him. I felt as if he were protecting me from my own hatred.

The mixed-up, filthy, Nazi version of myself receded. Killing myself no longer felt urgent or even relevant.

Bleak sadness was all I had left.

HOSPITAL NOTE:

August 25, 1965

Extraordinary sequence of events…When I saw her re restriction, she reported her father had seated himself next to her on Saturday and told her he was in love with her, that she was luscious, and that he'd have to get up since he couldn't trust himself with her. Annita was horrified, and there has been some suicidal ideation since the dynamic significance is, of course, spectacular….

—Dr. Heller

Later, when I thought about Dr. Heller's reaction, none of my standard explanations—*he has to act thoughtfully because he's my doctor…he's just a handsome robot who would treat anyone like this*—addressed the way Dr. Heller had looked, gaping in astonishment. At last, someone I cared about was aware of me and upset for me. I mattered.

I'd found the essential human connection at the center of psychological healing.

Once a year the National Psychiatry Boards took over PI. Psychiatric patients were needed as subjects for the assessment interview part of the exam, and we fit the bill. All our usual activities were suspended for the day. We were roused, fed, and dressed early, so we would be settled on the ninth floor by 8:00 a.m. when the doors opened and dozens of brave-faced, tired-looking, business-suited men and a few women flooded onto the floor. For once, we patients were the gawkers. Anxious doctors were the gawked.

Although my job in the medical library was small, I resented that I'd been required to miss work, as if my responsibilities didn't matter, compared with the doctors'. At the same time, I was surprised to see psychiatrists, individuals in the same category as the powerful men who ran the institution, reduced to the status of lowly students lined up for a test. The idea that they needed my help moved me. I was excited by the prospect of having something to offer, energized to think that I could give back.

Seated on benches and folding chairs set up in roughly the same space used for visiting hours, we watched the ragged array of nervous postulants advance slowly down the middle of the hall. They talked among themselves and ignored us, even though we sat but a few feet away. Overhearing conversations, I learned that they'd traveled from as far away as Maryland and Oklahoma. I didn't recognize anyone. I wondered if Dr. Heller would have to do this, and, if so, how far he would have to travel.

Occasionally one of the more obnoxious teenagers would sass a doctor stuck in line. "Hey, asshole," Rita yelled in the direction of a very tall, overweight man with dark, curly hair, conspicuously focused on a textbook he held close to his face. "You didn't have to come here to see a genuine nut-case, you know. You could've looked in the fuckin' mirror!"

"Ha ha," a few of her friends laughed. I cringed. Some of the doctors who heard her turned away, one or two with a nervous smirk. Tanzy, a woman who had been a nurse's aide on our ward for years, hurried over to Rita and chewed her out. I wondered how much of her concern was serious and how much was for show. My guess was that we all secretly rooted for Rita.

When it was my turn, an examiner beckoned to me from a room a few steps down the hall. I could see the bridge through a back window as I walked in.

A pale, gray-haired woman sat behind a bare desk next to the window, while the examiner, a rotund, ruddy-cheeked man with wispy white hair smoothed across his head, filled a chair to her right. He wore wire-rimmed glasses and a psychiatrist goatee. I took the remaining seat, facing them both, in the middle of the small, plain room. This wasn't the first time I'd been required to serve as an examination object for the Psychiatry Boards. I'd come prepared.

"Tell me about yourself," the examinee said to me in a quivery, airless voice. I felt sorry for her, so vulnerable in her anxiety. After the last time, I'd figured out that the point of these interviews was for the psychiatry-board candidate to talk with us and come up with a diagnosis. I decided to help.

Eager to show off results of the multidirectional, long-distance reading skills I'd honed through years of deciphering the days' notes while hanging around the nursing station, I looked her straight in the eye. "I'm a chronic schizophrenic with an affective psychosis."

"No!" she cried, raising her hands over her head. "Stop!" The examiner jumped out of his chair and stood waving his arms in front of me, as if he could disperse my words like flies and prevent them from reaching their target.

I didn't move.

The next several minutes passed with intense, agitated whispering between examiner and candidate as they huddled at the desk. When they finished, the examiner turned and told me I was free to leave. I offered to try again, but he made it clear that the interview was over.

On my way back to the ward, I felt abashed, yet my face insisted on smiling. I'd intended to help the frightened candidate. I'd also been at least half-aware of what I was doing. However briefly, I had triumphed over the cringing goody-goody in me, whom I hated, and dared to be mean.

I felt almost proud.

Except during psych boards, every Tuesday, Wednesday, and Friday morning I reported to work in the medical library upstairs. For two hours, I filed index cards and sorted books. Performing well in my job led to promotion from Building Privileges to Unaccompanied Walks, the highest level available short of discharge. Now in the afternoon, if I didn't have OT or a therapy appointment, I was free to leave the hospital and go where I pleased. To maintain this advanced status, I had to resist giving in to impulses to cut or burn myself or hit my head against the wall. And I had to return to the hospital by 8:00 p.m.

For my first solo excursion I chose a tiny park a few blocks from the hospital. I'd been there on walks with a group, but never alone. I selected an oak tree at the edge of the grass, away from the swings and the people. I dropped my book on the ground, slipped off my sweater, and settled in, resting my back against the tree. Its trunk felt scratchy through my cotton shirt, so I stuffed the sweater between it and me. From my jeans pocket I extracted an apple I'd saved from lunch, opened the book, and began to read. Before I'd finished the first bite, a lovely cloud of sweet apple mingled with the fresh scent of onion grass enveloped me. For the duration of my tiny picnic, their mingled fragrances prevailed over the city smells of car exhaust, factory smoke, diner grease, and hospital-kitchen blends. I could have been in an orchard in the country.

I Never Promised You a Rose Garden was a true story. "Dr. Searles knows the psychiatrist who helped Debbie, the main character, get well," Dr. Heller had told me. I was nearing the end, and I anticipated exhilaration as I followed the triumphant trajectory of a fellow patient's recovery. Instead, I watched Debbie grow despondent and return to the hospital after her first venture out on her own. I read on, but my heart began to sink.

All of a sudden I realized the sun had set; the day was growing dark. I scrambled to my feet. In the twilight I paused to look around the park. Figures in the distance had flattened into silhouettes. Streetlights glowed in the dusk. I gathered my things and headed back to PI. I ached for Debbie, and I worried for myself if her story didn't end well. But as I walked, I was taken by the rhythm of the cars, cabs, and box trucks rushing by. The screeching, honking road noises filled the neighborhood, pulling me under their urban-symphony spell. At exactly eight o'clock, I stepped off the elevator onto the sixth floor, thankful to be alive.

I still gave in to dangerous impulses occasionally. A few weeks later, distraught, I dashed out of the hospital toward the street thinking I'd kill myself by running into traffic. I stopped short, just past the curb. While I worked up enough courage to try again, I stormed up the twenty-six blocks from 168th up to 181st Street and back—I didn't pause once. By the time I returned to the ward, my anger was spent. I was hungry for dinner.

The weekend after that I brought my portable AM/FM radio to the park, where I listened to a Metropolitan Opera broadcast of *Aida* on WQXR. And I ate another apple under my tree.

CHAPTER EIGHT

Finishing Touches

October 1965

Ever since July, when Dr. Heller had become Senior Resident and decided to keep me as his patient, my goal had been to improve enough to live on my own outside of the hospital. I needed to be discharged if I wanted to continue with him in his private practice after he left PI. Few patients remained at PI for more than three years. Rockland lurking in the background intensified my motivation.

Since PI was a state hospital, if a patient was serious about leaving, one of the first steps in the process was to meet with a counselor from DVR: the New York State Department of Vocational Rehabilitation. I surprised my parents when I told them I was expecting an appointment.

"How will you prepare for your interview?" my father asked.

"I think she'll need a suit," my mother said.

My mother and I planned a shopping trip with the explicit goal of finding an interview outfit. When my father said I could buy a suit, my reaction was mixed. A year earlier, home on a pass, I'd bought three new $4 summer dresses at a super sale at Genung's Department Store, the most I'd ever purchased at one time. I'd gained enough weight from the high doses of thorazine prescribed in the hospital that my dress size had changed and my clothes were too tight. "Unless you think you're very fancy, you don't need more than one dress," Daddy said to me when I showed him my catch. Then he sneered at my mother, "What on earth were you thinking, Rosanna?"

For Daddy spending money was akin to having his blood squeezed out by a giant vise, drop by drop. If I failed to find a suit worthy of his suffering, I'd have that blood on my hands. If he blamed my mother, I'd hurt her as well. No wonder we rarely shopped and owned few clothes.

Yet by giving me permission to buy this suit, my father must have believed that I could find a job worthy of his investment. I'd thought about that myself.

I'm striding down Fifth Avenue, dressed like a model in the New York Times Sunday Magazine. *My high-heeled shoes are the latest style, as is my hair, pulled away from my face and pinned up. I'm made up with lipstick, powder, eyeliner, rouge, mascara—the works. I enter a tall office building. Completely at ease, I climb the stairs and proceed down a hall, where I pause at a polished oak door, third on the left, with a large gold-leaf sign and a solid brass handle. I twist the handle, open the door and walk right in—I work there.*

Daddy would be so pleased.

On the morning of our shopping expedition, I awoke early. With "Unaccompanied Walks" still my privilege status, I need only sign out if I had a pass. When Miss Riley saw my name and destination in the book, she smiled and wished me luck.

I practically danced to the end of the street. The M10 bus took me to Grand Central where I caught the 9:15 a.m. train to White Plains. I found a seat by myself with a good view out the window. I was too stirred up to read. Initially the ride was disappointing. After about five minutes in the dark, the train emerged from a tunnel under the station and traveled past ugly, burned-out, broken-down buildings in the Bronx. At the end of my car, a scruffy old drunk in a ragged coat sat by himself, holding a bottle in a brown paper bag. I felt sorry for him. A few seats away from him, a little girl, eight or nine years old, with long straight hair cringed while her mother shouted and waved her hands in her face. I worked not to cry.

As the trip progressed, and the scenery improved, my mood improved with it. By the time the train arrived at White Plains, my exuberance had returned. The air felt cool in that fresh, fall way. Autumn leaves in reds and golds vibrated against an intense blue sky. I strode out of the station and right away spotted my parents' car.

"Hi!" my mother said, as I waltzed up and opened the door, slipping into the front passenger seat. "So glad to see you." But her forehead wrinkled, and her cigarette trembled in her hand.

Faster than I could think, anxiety supplanted the confidence I had gathered on my trip. Ever since I was a little girl, I'd tried to comfort my mother by absorbing her distress, as if her fear had been water and I'd been a sponge.

My words jumbled on top of each other. "Mow, hom good you be seeing, too," I said.

I'd had enough therapy by then to know I needed to slow down. I took several deep breaths, and began again.

"How are you doing?" I asked. "Isn't this the most perfect day?"

"Yes, yes. Couldn't be better."

"How's everyone? When's Richie's next leave? How's Taylor?"

Maybe this reassured her that I wasn't going to be a problem, because soon she seemed okay. I relaxed, too.

We headed first to Genung's Department Store. I didn't know if Genung's was my mother's favorite store because she liked the merchandise or because the prices were low. I couldn't tell what my mother truly liked; she made herself fit what she thought other people needed. She gave the impression of being friendly and easy to please, but to me she often seemed out of reach.

When I was in high school, before the psych hospitals, my friends thought I had the best mother of all of us. She enjoyed their company. She took them seriously in creative ways. Once when we had a half-day at school, Sara, Sue, and Fran came over for lunch. My mother suggested a picnic in the back yard. She made little sandwiches, wrapped each of them in wax paper, put them into a basket, and gave us a blanket to spread out the way we would if we were in a meadow far away.

My mother was a great resource for pleasant things, but she struggled with difficult ones. A few years before, when I told her that Sara had said I was emotionally immature, she sounded upset and reminded me that kids always said those things, that Sara's remarks shouldn't bother me. I tried to explain to her how very shy I was and how that left me afraid to go on dates, but it was clear from the look on her face that my insecurity caused her pain. In my therapy, when Dr. Heller pretended to speak as my mother, he made her sound weak and guilt provoking, like the mother in the book *How to Be a Jewish Mother*, which I'd given him as a joke. (He told me it wasn't a joke, and after we'd analyzed it, I'd agreed.) I knew he was enacting a caricature, but it got me thinking about how my mother actually did come across.

One evening, a few weeks before our shopping trip, I'd experienced a painful, stabbing feeling in the center of my chest, near my heart. It went on for quite a while, and I had trouble catching my breath. I was home for the weekend, so I told my mother about it.

"It's anxiety," she'd whispered close to my ear, her hand covering her mouth, as if she needed to hide the words. Apparently, being anxious was a shameful secret. What did that say about me?

As we traveled along streets I could no longer recognize reliably, since the shock treatments had taken so much of my memory, I stared at my mother and tried to figure out how I should be for her on this trip. Emptiness was all I could feel—nothing connected us emotionally. Next, as if I were watching an actor in a movie, I heard myself burst out with enthusiasm.

"The train was a bit late but not very and I noticed the sky as soon as we came out from the tunnel and there was a drunk in my car but he wasn't scary and a girl with long hair and a woman with a Chihuahua in her pocketbook I'm so excited about this shopping trip and about getting a suit and I think about getting a job maybe where Emily works she said and last night at coffee group when I told Leah and Cheryl I was going they said be sure to check out Macy's and Lord and Taylor both Women's and Designer departments and they have good sales if you hit it right and even Miss Lang said I shouldn't settle for something unless I really liked it I can't believe we're doing this thank you so much for bringing me to the store thank you thank you." Like a wind-up doll with her springs freshly twisted and set loose, I jabbered away, filling in all the space around us.

We were fortunate that downtown wasn't crowded. My mother found a parking space on the street, not far from the store. She put a nickel into the meter, and I followed her into the tall, drab building.

Genung's was like many department stores I'd visited. Racks of dresses and skirts filled the floors, which were broken up into sections by standing counters offering cosmetics and accessories like hats, gloves, belts, and scarves. I was dazzled by all of the items calling me to consider their various shapes, and colors, to experience their textures in my hands.

I stopped before a collection of scarves from India, examining each one, imagining what I would wear it with. I slid some through my hands, delighting in the smoothness of the soft, shiny fabric. Some of the more delicate ones caught on the ragged edges of my fingertips; I still picked skin around my nails when I was nervous.

Next to the scarves were wool felt hats, some little boxy ones, and a few with lovely, wide brims. I tried on a mustard-colored hat with a soft brim and a woven ribbon for a hatband. It was huge. When I looked in the mirror on the counter, I could barely see my face. I looked like a child playing dress-up. I tried on a red one to see what happened with a smaller size. I liked it. Then I saw more scarves, but they weren't where I'd remembered them. My mother was nowhere in sight. I was lost.

Stay calm, I told myself. *Act normal.*

I was determined not to do anything that might identify me as a mental patient. However, my body had disconnected from my brain. I couldn't make it work.

Don't worry, Stupid. Pretend nothing is going on.

I stuck out my right foot and put my weight on it. I repeated this with the left one. *See, you can do this, even if you are a nincompoop. Now walk slowly toward the escalator. She'll find you. She'll come back.*

I was embarrassed to think that I was twenty-two and could be this frightened in a department store in my home town, just because I didn't know where my mother was at that moment. Perhaps my shyness made me insecure. Maybe I'd been in psych hospitals so long that I hadn't had a chance to practice ordinary things like shopping by myself. But what if I really were hopeless?

My mother showed up as I arrived at the escalator. "Where have you been?" she asked, looking severe.

"I got distracted. I'm sorry."

"Suits should be on the floor with Ladies' Dresses," she said.

As we stepped onto the escalator for a ride to the third floor, the wind-up doll went into action. "I'm so excited!"

"Yes? Good." My mother's relief was clear.

The Ladies' Dresses department offered an assortment of suits, but they all looked stodgy, appropriate for middle-aged executives, or psychiatrists, or high school principals trying to impress rich parents, not someone young. The colors were dark, mostly black and some brown, one navy blue. The fabrics were heavy. Most of the suits were not in my size. On top of that, they cost more than I had expected. I didn't want to hurt my mother's feelings, but I feared my suit was not there.

Luckily, my mother knew this without my having to say a word. "Let's see what Macy's has," she suggested before I offered to try on one of the stodgy suits. She didn't even sound upset. Because Macy's was just down the street, we could leave the car where it was. She added another nickel to the parking meter.

Macy's was a much larger and more expensive store than Genung's, and the selection of suits was certainly better. I found three I wanted to try on. This raised the issue of whether my mother would accompany me into the dressing room and how much her opinion would determine my choice. I was twenty-two years old, but I felt as if I were twelve. Or five. I couldn't tell whether I wanted her with me or not.

I felt so uncertain about the nature of my connection with my mother that I didn't even know what to call her. Before I went to the hospital, I'd always called her "Mommy", but that didn't feel right anymore. Mommy was what little children called their mothers. It was whom you cried out for when you were in danger, the one with the power to protect you. When Dr. Heller made fun of my mother, I didn't completely agree with his assessment of her. She tried hard and did her best to help, and it wasn't her fault if I was too emotional. But she never seemed comfortable with me. "Mommy" was not the right word.

Some of my friends called their mothers "Mom", but in my family, that perfectly acceptable moniker had become an insult. Since admitting me to PI, my parents had been required to have counseling. Apparently, their social worker, Mrs. Eichner, noted that my mother was overprotective, worrying more than she needed to about my brothers and me and being too indulgent. My father grabbed onto that idea like a boy who'd discovered his sister had started her period. He called it "being a Mom" and drew it out—"Maahhhm"—like it was something disgusting. I personally believed he was jealous when our mother paid attention to us instead of to him, so he made her suffer for it. He sneered, dripping with sarcasm. She would actually cringe. For me, that name for my mother was ruined.

To avoid using a name, I never addressed her directly. I made sure she heard me by speaking close to her face, or I touched her arm to get her attention. At times I must have been obvious, but I couldn't tell if she'd figured out what I was doing.

I didn't take a stand on my mother being in the dressing room with me, either. I didn't know if she wanted to be with me or not, and I didn't want to hurt her feelings by saying the wrong thing. She was probably embarrassed to have a daughter who needed her help. Or maybe she wanted to keep an eye on me. Neither of us said anything about it. She huddled on a bench close to the wall, while we both looked miserable and tried to act as if nothing were wrong.

I hated taking off my clothes with my mother there, but somehow I endured it by pretending I wasn't. The first suit was dark blue wool, and the skirt didn't fit. That was easy. The second one was tan and so bulky that I looked like a stuffed squash. But the price was reduced, so I considered it. The third one, a brownish plaid, fit well. I felt a little uncomfortable, because it looked quite stylish, and I wondered if I'd be too self-conscious to wear it. I didn't want to come across as someone who thought she was overly important. My mother really liked that one, but it was expensive. I worried about what my father would say. To buy time, I decided to look around again.

I found a clearance rack toward the back. Squeezed in among the odd discards nobody else wanted was a beautiful suit for half price. It was size 5 and made of fine wool in a lovely light green shade, a color softer than emerald but just as intense. The suit fit perfectly. Its skirt fell straight over my hips and had a fancy pleat above each knee. The jacket was unusual, featuring a deep, curved scoop in the front with a trimmed collar all around the edge.

I loved that suit. It was inexpensive, it fit well, and it was the sort of beautiful color and fabric that was just right for a girl like me. And it looked fashionable without making false claims of professional superiority. I was thrilled.

My happy reaction to the suit made my mother happy, too. She quickly paid for it.

"Of course you'll need a blouse to wear with it," she said to me as she pocketed the receipt. "Let's go find one."

Our search for a blouse went smoothly. We had already agreed it should be white. I wanted it to have a high neck, and we found one, also on sale, with a big collar that more or less met my specifications.

"Do you have an appropriate slip?" my mother asked.

"I, I, uh, no, perhaps not."

In fact, I did have an assortment of old slips—discolored, torn, frayed at the seams like the skin on my fingers. I jumped at the chance to buy a new one, even though it meant stretching the truth.

We left the store secure in our accomplishment and headed for home. Neither of us was afraid that my father would be angry. This was probably my best visit ever. No blood spilled. No sarcasm. I even had a new slip. Daddy was pleased that such a well-made suit had been on a half-price sale. When they dropped me off at the hospital on Sunday afternoon, he wished me luck with DVR and a future job.

Now I just have to live up to his expectations, I thought, as I walked into the building and pressed the elevator button for the sixth floor.

My first attempt at job hunting failed. I'd interviewed for work as a nurse's aide at a hospital where Jerry-Ann's uncle was the doctor in charge. He said lifting people for bed pans and changing sheets would be too hard for someone as skinny and inexperienced as I. He'd known his niece was a patient at PI, which meant he'd known I was one, too.

By mid-November, following want-ads in the *New York Times* and *Daily News*, I'd secured a real job—a holiday sales position at Gimbels Department Store. Sales clerk selling goods in the glassware department of a major department store sounded much better than patient shelving books in the library of a mental hospital.

I loved the subway ride from PI to downtown. At Gimbels I learned how to work a cash register, how to identify glass sizes and functions, and how to locate each pattern's display. I tried to be cheerful; I smiled a great deal. I listened to the other salesgirls, most of whom had been there longer than I, but I rarely joined their conversations. I felt unreal and my head vibrated. Sometimes when my hands shook, I'd down an emergency thorazine pill at the water fountain in the stock room when no one was looking.

"We'd like you to stay for a permanent position," the department manager announced shortly after Christmas. "You'd work the same hours, but your pay would increase."

They don't think I'm nuts? I was flabbergasted. "Thank you," I said.

My new position required more paperwork and a physical. "I'll just check you over," the company nurse told me. "It won't take long."

What'll I say when she sees the scars? Already I couldn't breathe. I'd rehearsed my story. *"I slipped and fell on a tin can lid by mistake."* Who would ever believe that?

The nurse listened to my heart and lungs and checked my eyes and ears. Lifting my left arm for a TB test, she noticed the two prominent scars across the vein at the inside of my elbow. From there she couldn't help but see my wrist scar, too.

You'll never get the job now. I turned my head away and focused on the far side of the room, avoiding her face—no thoughts, no feelings, full consciousness suspended.

"What's this?" The nurse sounded alarmed. While I struggled to find enough air to answer, my eyes filled with tears. "Oh," she said, speaking gently. "It's a cut down. I see that. An IV. From surgery?" *A cut down? Surgery?* I looked at her kind, yet urgent expression. She waited.

Slowly I grasped that the nurse was offering me a viable response. I nodded. She signed the report. Done.

A month later the well-dressed, attractive department manager asked me into her office. "I need to talk to you," she said. "This is private. It stays entirely between you and me, period."

Stunned, I responded by becoming an automaton. *What did I do wrong?*

"I was in a hospital once. I wanted to die. Sometimes I feel so depressed I don't think I can go on. I need to share this with someone. I believe you would understand."

I wandered out of the meeting in a self-contained, disoriented fog. *Does she know about me? Was it the nurse?* True to my family's rules and her request, I never spoke of this to anyone. A half-century passed before the scene reappeared in my memory with a jolt. *Oh, my God! She was* suicidal. *She was asking for help.* And I, unable at that time to conceive of having any authority in the eyes of a superior, had failed to recognize and heed her plea.

I'd been in love with Peter Marks ever since he threw a snowball at me on my return from a walk in early January. I'd been optimistic about my life at the time. For three months I'd held a part-time job, and I'd just been promoted to 5-South.

Peter seemed intelligent. He was tall with gentle brown eyes and thick brown hair—the kind of square-jawed good looks that reminded me of Dr. Heller. For a month we'd sat side by side in the central day room on matching plastic-cushioned armchairs, holding hands. Everyone knew that patient inter-gender physical contact was forbidden, but in our case staff overlooked the rules. I caught more than a few fond smiles in our direction.

At the end of February, Peter was discharged. He moved to an apartment near Columbia where he was planning to attend graduate school. By then I was working as a regular sales clerk at Gimbels, and I was used to traveling away from the hospital. When he invited me to dinner at his apartment, I accepted. We had a date.

Peter picked me up at PI on his Vespa motorbike. Then we flew down Broadway, white with packed snow, Peter steering his tiny vehicle while I hung on behind him, my butt squeezed onto the seat, my arms clutching his back for dear life. Yet I felt no fear as Washington Heights, Amsterdam, and Harlem streaked by. My very own golden eagle was carrying me away to a beckoning world. Wind buffeted my ears and joy my heart.

For dinner Peter broiled a luscious steak just right. His baked potatoes were delightfully fluffy. His salad, made from non-iceberg lettuce and dressing he put together himself, particularly impressed me. He served wine with dinner, and we ate peppermint ice cream for dessert.

After dinner Peter lit a fire he'd laid earlier in a tiny brick fireplace in the center of his small apartment. We sat on his couch holding hands and watching the flames' flickering dance. With Pete Seeger on his record player, life was complete.

After about ten or fifteen minutes, Peter put his arm around my shoulders and pulled me closer beside him.

Uh oh, I thought.

His hands reached behind me and stroked my back, then moved around to my hold my breast. Suddenly I was in a scene from the summer before. I had joined an accompanied walk and we'd stopped at a playground in the park. Some patients wanted to use the swings. I found a seat on a bench set among a clump of trees where I enjoyed looking at the sky. A shabby old man appeared on the bench. He squeezed himself close beside me. I held my breath. He reached under my blouse and unhooked my bra. "I love you," he said in a raspy, smoker's voice while he fondled my breasts. I didn't move; I didn't want to hurt his feelings.

When our nurse called for us to reassemble I stood and walked away, pulling my sweater around me to hide the loose bra. I never mentioned what had occurred.

As I sat on Peter's couch, again I didn't move. He slowly withdrew his arms. With his right hand he stroked my thigh, watching my face. My head began to sound hollow. I felt dizzy. I smiled at Peter—I knew I should show appreciation for his efforts.

He turned toward me and pulled my head toward his. His lips on mine, we merged in a giant kiss. He touched my leg and my breasts again. *You have to like this; you have to,* I told myself. But my thoughts scattered incoherently; my body had disappeared.

We'd been stuck in the kiss for what seemed ages when he finally let go. "Did you like that?" Peter stared at my face for signs. His voice sounded tentative, possibly tinged with anger.

"It was nice," I said, not wanting to hurt his feelings.

"Didn't you feel *anything*?" he asked. This time his frustration was clear. I was completely numb. He was on to me.

"I'm really sorry," I said. "But no."

Earlier we had planned that I'd take the subway back to PI. A grim but responsible Peter walked with me to the station: two bereft souls on our way to a funeral. Later as I jolted and rocked on the clattering train, I revisited the promise of our magic Vespa ride and delectable dinner. A fresh crater caused sharp pains in my chest.

Living outside might be more complicated than I had anticipated.

PART TWO
Moving Out

CHAPTER NINE

By the Front Door

May 1966

The room itself was tiny; its air felt warm and full. The walls of pale green tile seemed to bend with the heavy film of water exhaled from my hot bath. Wet hair stuck to my face, which dripped with sweat. My cheeks burned. My eyelashes spilled water droplets so large I couldn't see. I was sunk up to my neck in hot, sudsy bath water, soaking in my elixir of independence. I was taking my first bath on the first evening of my first day in my new home—the Y. My first day on my own. Ever. I let the water from the faucet keep running just a little bit, so it stayed hot.

This just might be the most delicious event in my life so far.

I hadn't had to ask anyone for permission to take this bath. I had only to see if a room with a tub was available. I slipped off my skirt and my blouse and put on my bathrobe. I gathered my towel and my soap and some clean underwear from my room. I carried them into the bathroom and locked the door. I locked the door! No one could open it unless I let them. No one knew I was there. I hadn't had to tell anyone.

My flushed face had swelled into a balloon. The skin on my fingers had wrinkled and was turning white. Time to go. With a great whoosh, the water fell away from my body and rocked around the tub as I staggered to stand. Unsteady in the slippery heat, I held tightly onto the bathtub's edge and stepped over its high side to reach the floor. I was set. Quickly drying myself, I rushed to leave the now oppressive humidity and returned to my room.

If I'd spread my arms wide, then doubled myself, I'd have reached from one side of my room to the other. The distance was a bit longer in the other direction. A window over the radiator let me see way down onto 8th Avenue. There was enough space for a straight chair, a small bed and a bureau, where I put the hand-me-down record player from my devoted aunt, Genny. My parents had brought it and my records with them when they'd moved me there from PI that morning.

Although my father had written the check, the lady at the Y had made a point of handing me the key, along with my room number and a book of rules. One elevator trip was all it took to transport my things. Years of living in an institution had taught me that I didn't need very much.

After my parents left, I'd eaten my first dinner in the dining room. With serving stations set out of the way, attractive food, and lots of tables, this arrangement far outclassed the hospital's for comfort and congeniality. I'd selected breaded chicken cutlet with peas and mashed potatoes. I could have chosen meat loaf or green beans if I preferred. Nobody noticed me. I could have eaten whatever I wanted.

And now, fresh from my bath, I planned to listen to my records until it was time to take my medication and go to sleep. As I settled into bed, arias from the first act of *La Boheme* filled my room.

I can't imagine a better way to celebrate my first day of freedom, I thought, before I fell asleep.

I had moved out of the hospital into the 8th Avenue YWCA on May 6, 1966, the anniversary of Freud's birth and the day before my twenty-third birthday. A few days later, I returned to PI for my discharge conference.

"Tell us what you've been doing to prepare for your next stage outside the hospital?" queried the psychiatric resident seated across from me on the auditorium stage. She didn't look at me directly. Dr. Heller and Dr. Mesnikoff also sat on the stage, off to one side. What looked like miscellaneous students and staff were scattered through the front rows of seats in the large auditorium. I could see my parents a few rows back, on the aisle. For some reason I wasn't nervous at all. *It's like being in a play,* I thought. *I know my part.*

The doctor fidgeted with her note cards.

"Well, last November I began selling glassware at Gimbel's," "but that was only part time. As for serious full-time work, in March I got a clerical job at David Kaye Shoe Distribution Company. Now I work as a clerk in the bookkeeping department of Parklane Hosiery." I paused, judging the fall of the shot. "I'm working my way up."

Everyone but the nervous interviewer laughed. I felt ten feet tall. At least for a moment, I'd taken control of my life.

HOSPITAL NOTE:

May 14, 1966

Patient handled discharge conference quite well, joking with interviewer and showing her sense of humor. When asked why she'd stopped hurting herself she recalled my telling her after banging her head that I thought she wanted to leave the hospital by the front door and how ludicrous this made the self-injury.
—S. Heller

Several months before discharge, I'd met with my DVR counselor, Mrs. Lipka. Following that meeting, she had sent me to an Upper East Side psychologist for an evaluation, which included a series of psychological tests. Reading the top paragraph of his report on Mrs. Lipka's side of the desk, I saw: "The patient rocked back and forth in a manner typically schizophrenic…" True, I often rocked where I sat. How that related to schizophrenia I couldn't fathom. Fortunately, he decided that I should go to college, despite my pathology.

Mrs. Lipka served as an anchor in the bewildering sea of adult commerce. She helped me apply to New York University's speech therapy program, a three-year degree. I was already far behind my high school classmates. I couldn't wait four years to begin a career. Shy and easily unsettled, I struggled to communicate, even without evident physical impediments. If I were a speech therapist, my thinking went, maybe I could help bring to the starting line some who might otherwise not have a chance to run the race at all.

When NYU rejected my application I was outraged. The process had required an interview with one of the most depressed psychiatrists I'd ever met. He was sicker than I was, yet he had the nerve to judge me unfit.

Mrs. Lipka assured me that the School of General Studies, Columbia's adult community education program, would suit me better than NYU anyway. I met with a soft-spoken Asian man for the admission interview. "Welcome!" he said at the end of our meeting, as he reached to shake my hand. "I'm sure you'll become one of our shining stars." I was stunned—and inspired—by his belief in me. When hope seemed lost, when discouragement threatened, I remembered his words.

Dr. Heller's steady presence also sustained me. We were meeting twice a week, and this continued throughout my college years. His office remained the one place where I could always be myself without secrets, although, ironically, the fact of my being in therapy was something else I felt obliged to hide.

At the end of January 1967, with Mrs. Lipka's guidance, Dr. Heller's blessing, and my parents' transportation, I moved into a small, single room in

Johnson Hall, Columbia's graduate women's dorm. I was a freshman, not a graduate student, but there was no other university housing for females attending the School of General Studies.

My skill in absorbing others' messages, which had been a problem in a mental hospital, proved an asset in college. It was easy to for me to immerse myself in all sorts of philosophical and literary worlds. With subjects that interested me—especially ones that involved human relationships, the nature and construction of reality, and the influence of language on culture—I felt like a long-caged bird set free: inexperienced and ignorant, yet eager to test my wings in exotic new habitats. I reveled in fascinating and unanticipated ecologies. Only the practical choice of where to alight first limited me.

April 1967

One morning, a few months into college, I was on my way to the library, when I stopped for a moment on the sidewalk at Broadway and 116th Street, just outside the large iron gates that marked the entrance to Columbia. Blossoming fruit trees perfumed the air, their scattered white petals forming lacy patterns on the ground. The area bustled with chattering students and rattling cars, all rushing past each other up and down the street. Despite the morning's chill, my blouse felt warm and damp from nervous sweat. I shifted my stack of books and freed a hand to tuck a loose wisp of hair behind my ear. I wanted to compose myself, to make sure that I looked normal.

An attractive, curly-haired girl hurried toward me.

"Hey, Annita, what are you doing here?" She was smiling. She sounded enthusiastic.

"Hi!" I replied, grinning warmly. I scanned her face and searched my brain for any indication that I'd seen her before, while I prayed for divine intervention and hoped that my pause wasn't lasting too long. *Dear God, who is she?*

"What have you been up to?" I ventured. By now I was feeling disembodied, like a robot reciting a script. But I'd won acclaim for my acting in high school, so I pulled myself together and focused on my part. I took a deep breath—*no sweat stink yet*—and grinned again.

She launched into a report on her recent activities. She shared an apartment in the Village and dated musicians and MBAs, but there was no one special yet. After college she had taken a year off and lived in France. Now she worked in a bank downtown at a job she didn't like. She was here to check out the law school. She paused for a moment. "You?"

"It's been a while, hasn't it?" I responded, as if I were answering her question, as if we were old friends. She returned to talking about herself, and whenever she looked for something from me I produced sympathetic phrases that encouraged her to continue. "Yeah?...No kidding... He didn't!" What looked like a conversation might have qualified, in essence, as a monologue.

I was pretty sure she hadn't guessed that I had no idea who she was.

Like an experienced undercover agent, I was buying time while I gathered strategic information. My concealed identity: former mental patient, now returned to the world close to six years out of step, with almost no memory of life outside an institution. My public persona was congenial local college student. I matched my responses to my friend's emotional tone as I noted her age, her dress, and her choice of words. She looked as if she were about my age. I was almost twenty-four, but people often assumed I was younger, which meant age alone wasn't enough. She was dressed in an ironed green corduroy skirt with a clean white cotton blouse and a cardigan sweater. Her speech wasn't pressured and had a nice rhythm. She was lively. No tics, dishevelment, or ghostlike transparency, which would have suggested someone from the hospital. She was probably from my high school.

Confessing my ignorance was not an option. If I told her I'd lost most of my memory, I would have to explain why. If I said it was due to loads of shock treatments in a mental hospital, she would likely run as fast as possible in the other direction. No sane person would choose to destroy their social acceptability with psychiatric revelations if they could avoid it. And someone who had known me before my hospitalization wouldn't believe I could have forgotten so much—especially who she was.

I'd seen the dismay on faces of people I told before I knew better. I assumed that classmates had been aware of the psych hospital, since I'd left school suddenly and never returned. Certainly Sara and Sue knew. And kids talked; nothing in high school stayed secret for long. Thinking I should be honest, I became tongue-tied and awkward when I tried to explain that I couldn't remember experiences they knew we had shared.

Some of my friends had seemed deeply hurt, angry even. Their skin paled and their eyes flattened. My guess was that they imagined I didn't consider them important enough to remember. Others might have worried I was truly insane. They stammered and fidgeted and beat around the bush, although no one ever said anything directly. And how could I blame them? I stammered as badly as they did, if not more so.

I first realized how delicate a situation my forgetting could be one evening when my brother's best friend, Bobby, came by when I was home on a pass. He rang the bell, and I let him in. I asked him to wait while I went to find Richie, who was home on a pass from the Army. They soon left to go drinking, and my brother didn't return until after I was asleep. But the next day, before I returned to the hospital, a scowling Richie stopped me in the hall. He shoved his face close to mine and glared into my eyes.

"I'm very disappointed in you," he snarled, pointing his finger at me. "I expect you to treat my friends with respect, do you understand?"

"Wha—what do you mean?" I mumbled in response. I had no idea what I'd done wrong.

"Bobby said you were cold," Richie growled. "You ignored him. You acted like you didn't know him."

"I was polite. He's your friend. I wasn't rude."

Then I learned that Bobby and I had been friends, too. He had been looking forward to visiting with me as well as with Richie. I could see why he had felt rejected when I assumed he was interested only in my brother.

"I'm sorry," I said. But I was also disappointed. I had thought my brother knew about my memory problem. I slunk off without defending myself, glad I'd be returning soon to the hospital.

About a year later, just after Thanksgiving, I was visiting home again. Richie was home, too. I had been out of the hospital for a few months, working at the hosiery company, living at the Y. During the years I had been away, my friends had graduated from high school and gone to college. They were moving on with their lives. My brother, who was very sociable, had become good friends with Lynnie, my childhood best friend. She had married and moved to California, but this week she was visiting her old hometown.

On that chilly November day, when Lynnie stopped over to see my brother, I didn't recognize her. When she saw me she looked flustered. So many years had passed since our best-friend days of elementary and junior high school, and she may have been worried about how to address a possible nut case.

"Annita, wow, uh, how's it going?"

By then I knew enough to act like we were friends. "You look great. Uh, have a seat." I said, gesturing toward the couch. "Can I get you some juice?"

"What a treat," Lynnie said, smiling. I could see her relief. "When was the last time? Remember those sleepovers we used to have? And the games! Do you still play?"

"Richie told me you might be over…Yeah, I'm good, uh, how's it with you? I can't believe how cold it is—last week wasn't so bad…."

Lynnie looked beautiful in an up-to-date, stylish way. I stared at her fashionable hat, her clothes, and especially her face as she brought up stories of old times together: "…and the time we went to the beach with your mother and decided to go to that party without asking, remember?…when your brother took your books…Remember how we hated dancing school…Don't you remember?"

I had nothing to say. Still seated on the couch, Lynnie fiddled with her hat.

My face burned, and I began to sweat. I stared at her as intently as I could. My ears examined every word. Inside my brain I urgently reviewed my life, and still I came up empty. I couldn't remember anything about us. It was as if I had gone into my garden and found only asphalt and rocks where bright flowers and ripe vegetables were supposed to be growing.

I had no choice but to explain. "You know I was in the psych hospital here for a few years, right?" I paused. Lynnie didn't move. I couldn't look her in the eye. "Well, they gave me lots of shock treatments, and it makes you forget everything. I can't remember anything about school— elementary school or high school. I hate that. I'm really sorry."

At first she looked crushed. Inhaling slowly, Lynnie considered further what I had said. Her finely penciled eyebrows lifted, questioning. She tilted her head and tightened her lips into a thin, straight line. Then she sighed. "That's good to know," she said, while her tone implied that it wasn't. "Please tell your brother I was here." She grabbed her purse, picked up the jacket beside her, and left the house. I heard her say, "Bye" a second before the door closed.

I knew Lynnie didn't believe me. I might even have scared her. After that, I neither saw nor heard from her again.

"Have you been in touch with anyone else—Mac? Sara?"

The question brought me back. I was right: the girl in front of me was a friend from high school. The people she named had been in my class. I answered her without lying, "Not recently. What about you?"

She took off again with stories about her friends and her adventures. Eventually I could even deduce who she was—Irene. A group of us had shared most of the honors classes. That time I was lucky. I'd gathered enough clues to identify her by name. I didn't remember any specific incidents involving Irene and me, but at least I knew her name.

"Well, this has been fun. Tell the others 'Hi' for me when you see them."

"I sure will."

She smiled, picked up her book bag, and walked away toward the street.

"See you...Irene," I added, when she'd moved on too far to hear me.

Over time, I concluded that no one could understand my condition of missing memory. It was incomprehensible, as though I were a visitor from another planet with customs known only to myself. So I developed a system to avoid alienating or frightening people I met. If I listened, sooner or later I'd hear enough details to figure out the context in which they had known me. Then I'd make some reference to what I thought we must have in common, and the person would leave satisfied, grateful even.

I learned from this how hungry people were for someone to pay attention to what they had to say, and how little they noticed what actually transpired. I began to feel like an expert in listening. And, more importantly, in the process of seeking information to prove I was the person they thought I was, I learned a bit more about myself—who the Annita was they had known as their friend.

CHAPTER TEN

Courtship

B ecause I hadn't scored high enough on the General Studies test to pass out of English, I was assigned to an elementary class. I needed remedial math as well. I'd won a national poetry contest in high school, yet I could no longer define an adverb or diagram a sentence. I didn't dare explain that I once knew those things, that my ignorance was a result of shock treatment.

Long before this, I'd decided I wanted to be a child psychologist. That first semester, the prerequisite introductory psychology course met at an awkward time, so I signed up for Sociology 101 instead. My professor, Alan Blum, was a brilliant, peripatetic man who talked about how people constructed reality, how societies gave meaning to actions, and how humans communicated with one another.

Along with the classic sociological philosophies, he presented a radical 1960s sociology called Ethnomethodology. We looked at the essential pieces of human behavior that took on shared meaning and made communication possible. "How would a Martian make sense of all those signals we give to one another that let us know what is going on? What are the minimum necessary pieces?" His specialty was the sociology of mental illness. What behaviors identified someone as crazy?

"If we come across a disheveled woman in a telephone booth screaming, sobbing, and pounding her fists on the glass, does that tell us she's psychotic?" he asked as he paced from one side of the room to the other, chain smoking cigarettes, his arms' urgent gestures emphasizing his point. "What if we knew that during the phone call, she'd learned that her child had been killed by a bus?" My mind whirled with possibilities. I inhaled his ideas. I applied them to everything around me. As if I had just discovered colors, I noticed them everywhere and couldn't wait to name and to analyze every shade.

Psychology 101 was a requirement for psychology majors and for any advanced psychology courses. I learned from the course catalogue that this class was about rats and pigeons—the scientific principles, history, and classic experimental concepts of general psychology. But rats and pigeons did not engage me emotionally. I fulfilled the requirement by taking the class in an intensive summer program. I was done with it in five weeks.

Although I continued to think I should study psychology, I found myself entranced in sociology courses, delighted to learn about the arbitrariness of categories like psychiatric diagnosis, how certain behaviors came to be identified as symptoms of mental illness, and how these varied from one culture to another. Required courses in English, French, history, music, and art appreciation kept my schedule full. When I could choose, it was more sociology. By following my heart—people over pigeons, at the time—I was becoming a sociology major.

Meanwhile, I conducted my own sociological research on 'normal.' I observed other students, checking my actions against theirs. I copied the dress and manners of the students and teachers I admired.

One day, a former classmate who had been part of our high school group recognized me on the street and invited me to a party at her apartment nearby. A group of my closest friends had graduated from college and moved to the city. Sara had a job as an editorial assistant at a publishing house. Sue was writing her dissertation for Harvard with a boyfriend who lived there. Jeffrey was studying journalism. They were strangers. At the party I stayed in one chair, unable to speak. Ashamed to be so far behind them in school, I felt I lacked any life details I could comfortably share. No one mentioned the hospital. A powerful sense that the scene was a dream about to vanish dominated my experience. While my friends discussed office politics and avoiding the draft, I spent the evening in a state of panic, pondering the paradox of perpetual annihilation. A trill of terror played at the top of my stomach, as if I were falling off a cliff and death was but a flicker away. Outwardly, I survived the evening without incident.

Kindly ignoring my miserable showing the first time, my old friends invited me to a second party a few weeks later, this time in the Village. While they mingled, laughing and sharing stories, I decided that getting drunk might alter my status as an alien. Alone in the kitchen, I downed a large glass of vodka mixed with enough orange juice to endure swallowing.

Before long, I couldn't stand; I spent the rest of the evening in a small room on a mattress piled high with coats, while the walls spun. Disabling whirlies were ghastly, but temporary. Shame and regret for my appalling behavior persisted. Decades passed before I saw any of them again.

I met Bill the day of our first class in Professor Blum's Sociology 101. He was on his own search for normalcy following four years in the Navy.

I thought of Sociology 101 as my first real college course. It wasn't English, math, or history—subjects I'd studied in high school—which made my enthusiasm feel all the more legitimate and mature. Bill was as excited as I. He was taking some sociology courses in order to figure out his choice of major before returning to Yale to resume his education there as a college junior.

When I read James Joyce's *Portrait of the Artist as a Young Man*, I absorbed a sense of words as actual physical items akin to ants or crackers or skyscrapers. I loved watching my own thoughts—now visible to me thanks to Joyce's stream-of-consciousness style—as they circled upward through the air. Similarly, my early conversations with Bill unfolded as sparkling duets of words and ideas soaring together in fascinating patterns, in this instance close to the high ceiling of the lounge in Dodge Hall, where General Studies students were offered tea and cookies at four o'clock on Wednesday afternoons, immediately following our class. I marveled at the ease with which Bill and I understood each other.

Bill developed a crush on me and began to appear everywhere I went on campus. Although I loved conversing with Bill about sociology, I wasn't prepared to date him. When I realized that he had figured out my schedule and was waiting for me after my classes, I became frightened. I began to delay my departure. I'd check to see if he was in the area, then run to the ladies' room, where I remained until I was sure he had left. I didn't want to hurt his feelings by asking him straightforwardly to stop. We laughed about it later, but it didn't feel funny at the time.

Bill left Columbia after the semester ended that June of 1967. Later that summer, in August, as I left the administration building where they'd posted grades for summer classes, I met him on the sidewalk outside the front door. He'd come to take care of paperwork for transferring his course credits to Yale. At the sight of him, a great surge of happiness surprised me. My annoyance at learning he'd been in the city for two weeks without contacting me was even more startling. I accepted his offer for dinner.

For the next few months, Bill traveled often between New Haven and the City, ostensibly to get his Yale papers typed by a Bronx couple he considered first-rate. He usually visited me, too.

If I was to be part of a serious relationship, I had to do the honorable thing and let Bill know about my psychiatric history. I knew I might lose him once he found out. *Before each date I promised myself that I'd tell him, but before we parted, I'd managed to forget or to invent a reason to put it off. Next time.* One Saturday afternoon, as we sat in a coffee shop close to campus sharing forkfuls of Viennese pastry, I suddenly felt ready.

"I'm older than most freshman, because I spent several years in two different psych hospitals," I blurted out. "I don't remember most of my life before that, because I was given so many shock treatments at the first one." I lifted my plate of raspberry layer cake and, with a nod, offered him a second bite. "Want some?"

Bill stared at his fork. My cake trembled on the plate.

He began slowly, taking care with his words as he accepted the cake. "My family is really messed up," he said quietly. "My half-sister was in a hospital when she was a teenager. She had shock treatments, too." He nudged his plate of chocolate mousse cake closer to mine. We both looked at the food. "My mother made me see a psychiatrist when I was a boy," he continued. "When I return to Yale, I plan to start therapy as soon as I can find someone good." He poured coffee from a silver carafe into a cup, which he handed to me. "May I?"

I laughed a laugh close to tears.

After that, Bill regularly returned to New York, dazzling me with dinners, taking me to concerts and plays. He brought champagne, fresh strawberries, and whipped cream for picnics on the Palisades, across the Hudson River from New York City. We visited museums, art exhibits, a flower show. But no matter what activity captured our attention, we never stopped talking.

From the moment he strode into that first sociology class after the bell rang, then sat in the front row and asked questions, I'd known that Bill was an exceptionally intelligent man. More than a year later, I still reveled in our vigorous discussions—analyzing and building on all sorts of ideas and theories that we'd discovered in our classes, in books, in the news, anywhere. Bill grasped what I meant right away, better than anyone I'd known before. I thought I might have found my soul mate. By spring of 1968 I was traveling by train to New Haven to be with him on weekends, although we spent most of our time together in the City.

One balmy evening we headed out to *La Crêpe*, a restaurant near Lincoln Center. It was one of our favorite places.

With the bearing of an aristocrat entering his ancestral home, Bill swept open the door, nodded for me to pass, then followed me inside. An elegant, black-haired waitress in a starched white apron and elaborate, lace-trimmed cap, bobbed a friendly curtsey.

"*Bonsoir, Madame, Monsieur,*" she greeted us, smiling. We followed her through the golden, herb-scented air to a little table at the far side of the restaurant.

"*Bonsoir, Madame,*" Bill smiled, returning her bow, as French phrases in colorful ribbons spun from his mouth. The glow on the waitress's pink cheeks intensified, and her dark eyes shone. My heart beat faster. How I delighted in the company of a man so sophisticated, so knowledgeable in the ways of the world!

There were times when I could tell that Bill was trying to impress me. Once he'd taken me to dinner at The Four Seasons and arranged for us to be seated next to the fountain. He'd brought his own bottle of wine, which a *sommelier* opened at our table. I liked that he thought I was important enough to impress. But I especially liked when he was being ordinary and revealed without trying that he knew so much. We'd eaten at *La Crêpe* many times. We even called it "our restaurant." I didn't think Bill was trying to make me admire him when he spoke French to the waitress. He just enjoyed talking with her in her language.

The warm evening air caressed us. Oil lamps glowed on each table. Perfume from purple lilacs in cut-glass vases mingled with the fragrance from herbs and buttery *crêpes*. We'd finished the main course.

Bill ordered champagne. I was about to light a cigarette to pass the time while we waited for dessert when Bill raised his hand to say *don't*. "It interferes with tasting the champagne," he explained. I knew he didn't like my smoking, so I stopped.

During the quiet pause, I took in the candlelit scene. How could I reconcile myself the college student in an attractive French restaurant being courted by a charming and well-bred man, with the girl who'd spent more than five years locked in a mental hospital, the girl who couldn't remember what she'd learned in high school because she'd been given so many shock treatments? The disparate images confounded each other, like two photographs trapped in a double-exposure. I smiled at Bill to reassure myself that I was there with him. I returned my cigarette to the pack and slipped it into my purse. I smoothed the napkin in my lap.

Bill lifted his arm and placed his hand on mine in the center of the table. My heart sped up again. He leaned forward, staring intently into my eyes. "I love you," he said, carefully enunciating each word. Without warning, my head turned cold. Little sparkly lights like shooting stars darted around me. My skin prickled. I started to fall....

Some time later, I noticed that I was lying sideways on the banquette where I'd been sitting. My head felt too heavy to move. I was groggy, as if I had been forced from deep sleep in the middle of the night. Sharp, icy points scattered throughout my body, tingling the way that hands and feet react when you first try to use them after they've gone numb. I fought to wake myself and to see through the tingly fog.

Worried-looking people had gathered around the table. I watched them for what seemed like several minutes. *What's wrong?* I wondered. "No problem," I heard Bill say to our special waitress, "This happens all the time."

Uh oh, it's me, I realized. *Shoot! I must have fainted.* I forced myself upright, grabbing onto the table edge with one hand while brushing hair away from my face with the other. I smiled and tried to reassure everyone that nothing was wrong. Some of the patrons continued to stare at me. Others glanced, then turned away.

Bill went to find our waitress and pay for dinner. When he returned to the table, I staggered to stand. As we made our way slowly out the door, I leaned heavily on his arm, apologizing along the way, "I'm so sorry...I'm fine...really...so sorry."

"I'm sorry," I said again, as we stood on the street corner, breathing in the now-cool night air. "I'm just glad you're okay," he said. "I was wondering if I should call an ambulance." I was feeling better by then, and we both laughed. I decided that I'd fainted because Bill was the first person to say, "I love you" to me, whom I wholeheartedly believed.

At the end of the month, Bill and I became engaged. We planned to marry a year later, on the first weekend following his graduation from Yale.

Being engaged meant no more dancing around the topic of intimacy.

"Give me three months and I'll have her in bed," Bill had crowed to his roommate at the end of the snowy day on which we'd met. For my part, after my experience with Peter, I was wary of any sexual relationship. Nevertheless, the sexual revolution was happening in full swing all around us. As a college student, I felt enormous pressure to participate. Besides, I'd never felt right about another man the way I felt right about Bill.

Bill hadn't anticipated my visceral fear of sex, which was so automatic and profound that even I was surprised. I justified my resistance by citing Catholic rules against intercourse before marriage. He complained, but since I didn't budge, he adapted.

Eventually I made progress sexually, although I pretended more than I would admit. Between Bill's skill at encouraging me, and my wish to please, I became pretty good at heavy petting; I learned what orgasm was.

Summer passed before I agreed to consummate our relationship. I needed a ring to prove that I was almost married.

CHAPTER ELEVEN

Champagne, Cake, and Uncooked Rice

Summer 1969

From its first moment, the day stood apart, as distinct from ordinary life as if I were in a dream or a fairy-tale.

I'd awakened early to a bedroom filled with sunlight filtering in through thin white shades, slipping around the edges in pale stripes. The pastel walls had been pink when I'd lived there long ago, but my mother had painted over that childish color and replaced it with a fresh, spring yellow. She'd made curtains out of an unusual quilted fabric she must have bought on sale. They were gathered across the top, with panels that hung down on either side. A rod halfway between the top and bottom of each window held an additional filmy white curtain. This added privacy; the neighbor's house was just across the driveway. The half-curtain allowed a view of the sky when the shades were pulled up.

I hadn't spent much time at home since my return to the hospital eight years earlier. I hadn't slept in that room for more than a brief weekend since I'd tried to kill myself there when I was twenty. The yellow walls reassured me that things were different now. *You'll be married today. You'll never be alone here again.*

Instead of the hammering anxiety I was used to, a splendid calm spread through me. I imagined my heart a pitcher of warm milk, sweetened with honey. Peace poured into my veins all the way down to my toes and out to my fingertips. I lay still under my old covers, basking in the wonder of it all.

A need to pee interrupted my reverie. I moved the blankets aside and set my feet on the floor—a princess emerging from her royal bath. When I returned from the bathroom, I raised the shades on both windows and slid back into the sheets—this princess craved more time to soak. From where I lay in my old Catholic Charities twin bed set against the wall, I could see bits of blue sky through the leaves of the cherry tree outside the window. This was the tree that flowered on my birthday in early May. *My tree.*

By now the sun was bright. Outdoors, a perfect day. I gazed out the other window, facing the neighbor's house, and around my room.

On the far wall, shared with my parents' bedroom, a set of worn, white wooden shelves held books and mementos. My yearbooks, beginning with junior high school, were there. A few Nancy Drew mysteries stood next to a faded green, bound version of *The Complete Works of Shakespeare, Vol. III* with "New York Hospital, Westchester Division - Library" written on tape on the spine. Boxes full of trinkets from trips, movie tickets, notes from friends, old letters, programs from high school plays, and dried flowers from a prom corsage filled space on either side. I hated that I couldn't remember where most of them came from. *Let it go. You're starting over.*

Bill and I had agreed on a wedding as small and simple as possible. Because he'd lived away from home for years, and because I'd lost most of my memory in the hospital, we had few longtime friends. For this reason, and also to avoid upsetting my father by spending a lot of money, we had invited only our closest relatives: twenty-seven people altogether. We decided to marry in the garden at the side of the house. Our reception would take place on the porch.

Bill's best man, Bob, had been his closest friend since their time in the Navy together in the early sixties. They were sharing an apartment when I first met Bill at General Studies. My brother Richie's wife, Bobbi, had agreed to be my matron of honor. I'd been one of her bridesmaids, and we were all friends. A few months before my wedding, Bobbi had told me she was pregnant. I loved the idea that her child would somehow be present when Bill and I exchanged our vows; it felt like a blessing, a sign of the rightness of our marriage.

I'd made my wedding gown myself. I spent $ 0.49 for a pattern and $20 for the white linen fabric—the easy style didn't require much cloth. I'd sewn real Belgian lace onto a strip around the hem and onto the top of the sleeveless bodice. I'd used the rest of the money my father had given me for a gown to buy a portable Singer sewing machine. It came with sewing classes, where I made the dress. That provided the help I needed with the tricky bits, like getting the facing to lie flat around the armholes and adding the lace.

Bobbi also had sewn her own dress, a soft green cotton with adjustable ties on the sides. Instead of a veil, I'd be wearing a crown of woven daisies from a flower shop downtown. We decided on daisies and white lilies for each of our bouquets.

Bill lived in a tiny house in a friendly, half-rundown neighborhood between projects and a woodsy mountain on the far edge of New Haven, about an hour and a half drive from my parents' home. I planned to move in with him after our honeymoon on Nantucket. A friend of Aunt Marjorie, my father's sister, was lending us her summerhouse for a week, before the high season began on the Fourth of July. Perhaps part of my generous calm came from our June 21 wedding date: the Summer Solstice. The Solstice connected us to weddings and ceremonies in civilizations past and to something beyond this world, a kind of goodness or unique power. What many people called God.

I didn't know how to think about God anymore. I'd been Catholic until about a year earlier. I'd confessed my sins every week and diligently considered my shortcomings—I was glad I took my religion seriously. Sundays at Mass I'd recited the Latin words by heart. Then, one evening, I realized that what I'd been saying in church hurt me.

I'd been kneeling in a basement room of a church in New York City, preparing for Confession. *Domine non sum Dignus* I repeated three times as my right fist hit my chest over my heart, "Lord, I am not worthy." I was trying to feel sorry for my sins, although at the time I hadn't been able to identify them specifically, such as robbery or murder or even deliberate meanness. Yet I worried that if I didn't feel remorse for being a squalid, reprehensible person, I might be guilty of lacking humility.

All of a sudden, I saw the impossibility of my remaining a devout Catholic. I thought about the hours and hours of therapy I'd spent trying to understand and accept the fact that many difficult and painful incidents and struggles in my life had not been my fault. Focusing on guilt and feeling bad couldn't be right. *A true and loving God wouldn't want people to turn against themselves.* I bowed my head and searched my heart for what to do. A few minutes later, I walked out of the church and into the arms of a noisy, smelly, welcoming city evening.

On my wedding day, as I looked at the sky through the leaves on my tree, I could feel a sense of sacredness without exactly believing in God.

A cheerful aroma of coffee and bacon drifted into the bedroom. The rest of my family was up, bustling about downstairs, preparing for breakfast. I heard Taylor call out something to my mother. At the sound of Genny's voice, my heart did a little dance. Genny was my godmother, the person who'd always loved me and believed in me; she made me feel complete. I longed to stay in bed savoring my thoughts, but I knew it was time for the princess to appear and do her part.

Reluctantly, I pulled myself upright. I moved aside the covers, letting their fur-like softness—that condition just short of threadbare that old sheets and blankets achieve with age—linger on my skin. Every movement I made seemed to reverberate and expand within and around me, as if it were reflected on a vast movie screen in full hi-fi and brilliant color; every word of every thought, every sound, every smell, the hairs on my skin, the light, the air—all magnified and clear. I slipped into the pink-checked bathrobe I'd had since I was twelve and slid my feet into ballet slippers at least as old. *I wish I remembered all that these clothes have seen,* I thought as I buttoned my robe. I brushed my hand across my forehead and hurried down the stairs into the kitchen.

Dressed in my white gown, a crown of flowers in my hair, I was ready. The sweet scent of lilies arose from my bouquet. Only the faintest hint of makeup graced my face; my lipstick was more pink than red. I felt beautiful, and I'd been calm all day. As if I were in a lovely dream.

I stood at the back door, listening for my cue. Bill's sister-in-law would play Bach's hymn "My Spirit Be Joyful" on the harpsichord he had carefully delivered to my parents' front porch from his house in Connecticut. His two nieces would be playing flutes. When I heard the tune, I would walk to the side of the house where the porch over-looked a pachysandra-covered slope that led to a tiny garden; a flat area of scraggly rose bushes, azaleas and impatiens planted around a circle of aging slate tiles, it looked like an underachieving version of an old formal garden. The same cue would prompt my father to come from the front door. We would meet below the porch, and he would escort me down four stone steps to my place on the circle, in front of Bobbi, who would be there already. Then he'd walk to a chair at the front edge of the garden and sit. Next from the front door, Bill was supposed to meet up with Bob and arrive at the spot where Bobbi and I would be waiting, along with the minister.

Dr. Parker, the Protestant minister, was the father of a former class-mate from school. I intentionally did not know his denomination. This was the best compromise I could make, given the religious sensitivities involved. Bill's family was Episcopalian, but he was alienated from that denomination. My mother, Genny, my brothers, and I were Catholic. My father said he was agnostic. He never went to church, and he never talked about religion. His sister Marjorie was Episcopalian. She looked down on Catholics; my father looked down on her. My cousin told me that our grandfather—my father's and Aunt Marjorie's father—had been Jewish. Bill said his mother's father had been Jewish, too. Everyone in my family knew not to discuss religion.

I'd been at the back door for a long time listening for the harpsichord when Bill's youngest niece came running toward me, looking worried. "They're waiting for you," she said.

"I...I...but I didn't hear the signal." After a moment's hesitation, I took a deep breath and strode forward.

When I reached the side of the house near the garden steps, I realized that the wind had been blowing the sound away from me; she'd been playing the harpsichord the whole time. Now its silver tones sparkled like lightning bugs in the air around me. Peace returned.

Slowly, deliberately, I walked with my father down the steps to the circle in the center of the garden. Bill, who had almost arrived first and had had to back up fast so we wouldn't collide, reappeared and took his place beside me. Bob and Bobbi stood behind us. Dr. Parker and Bill's nephew, Charlie, dressed in a red choir boy's gown and holding open a Bible Genny had given to me years before, stood in front of us.

My parents, Bill's mother, my brothers, and Genny sat in front of us on wooden folding chairs set below the pachysandra. The other guests sat on chairs arranged on the grass to my left, just beyond the garden. *I love that they're close: I'm glad we made it small.*

The minister had been speaking, I noticed a bit late. He was reading a psalm. "...lying and deceitful tongues." *What?* Bill and I had gone through the entire Book of Psalms and had chosen Psalm 23 specifically because it avoided references to sin, death, hatred, evil, or violence. He wasn't reading that. Bill's mother looked pale, as if someone had hit her.

Everyone else looked serious, but controlled, as if they were appalled but too polite to condemn us out of hand. *Charlie must have opened the wrong page.* As I listened, my stomach turned. *Not that one!* I wanted to scream. Bill wiggled his versatile eyebrows and gave me a look that said, "This is stupid, but I really love you." Like two woolly-bear caterpillars ensconced above his eyes, those dark, bushy eyebrows were always ready for action, just waiting for an accident such as this. With a deep breath, I inhaled perfume from lilies in my bouquet along with the roses. I resumed thinking about love.

The ceremony sped by. Suddenly our marriage promises were given—traditional but edited for absolute gender equality—and wedding rings adorned our fingers. The magnificent sweetness of Purcell's "Trumpet Voluntary" played on two flutes and a harpsichord transformed the grass into a magic carpet of music and light, as Bill and I proceeded up the steps and around the house to the front yard. In that grand wedding promenade I savored the most wonderful moments of my entire life. All my sorrows vanished into the golden train spreading out behind us.

A short while later Bill and I stood with our guests in a circle on the front lawn, each holding an empty wine glass. Daddy poured the champagne Bill had selected and paid for into our glasses—*Korbel Natural*: it was more expensive than *Brut*, but had an intense, robust flavor and a dryer, more sophisticated presence in the mouth. The chatter fell away as my father raised his glass; others followed when they realized what was happening.

"I'd like to propose a toast," he began.

"Toast? No toast! Vino. Vino!" an outraged child interrupted him. My cousin Jenifer's three-year-old daughter stamped her feet. She began to cry. Her face turned red. My cousin Jenifer's three-year-old daughter, India, stamped her feet. She began to cry. Her face turned red. India's first language was Italian, and the word "toast" had confused her: she was not to be left out. Our sympathetic laughter only fueled her rage.

Jenifer quickly handed India a glass with a token sip. We resumed our celebration.

Daddy's experience in his engineering societies had served him well. Despite his having taken issue with the champagne earlier ("I'm not paying to indulge that snob," he told my mother), he gave an elaborate and fitting toast to Bill, me, and our union. *Or did he?* As soon as he'd finished, I couldn't recall the words. I didn't have time to worry about that, because my brother Taylor was waving his hand, signaling his wish to go next.

I was impressed that my shy, teenage brother had chosen to speak.

"My congratulations to both of you," he began. I felt tension in his halting delivery. "You seem to be made for each other. May you enjoy a long and happy life together." Then he paused, and his face clouded over. Taylor's eyes narrowed. The veins on his neck stood out in dark lines. He stared long and hard at Bill. Tears filled Taylor's eyes, and his voice shook. "You," he said, jabbing his finger toward Bill, "You. Take good care of my sister."

Hairs on my arms and legs stood on end. For a moment my heart grew huge in my chest. *He loves me; he wants to protect me.* I flushed with joy. But I didn't understand what he meant. The thrill I'd read as joy took on a harsh edge. Icy fear rose from my toes to my scalp, spilling into my heart. I forced it away, focusing again on thoughts of love.

Our wedding reception consisted of three serving tables arranged on the front porch. Two held large platters of rolls and condiments, along with a hefty roast of beef or ham. Behind each of those tables, a plump, gray-haired caterer in a black dress and a white ruffled cap and apron served slices of meat she cut fresh from the roast. Guests could assemble their own sandwiches with various ingredients. There were white paper napkins and white plates available.

I was too excited to eat. My father walked around, refilling guests' glasses with Bill's champagne. I'd taken a sip of mine, but that also seemed to be more than I could manage. My stomach made plain it wouldn't like anything new. Besides, I was supposed to socialize with my guests.

"The cake will be ready in five minutes," my mother announced, appearing out of nowhere. "You and Bill need to be on the porch. Hurry."

I looked for Bill's hand-tailored white suit and orange-flowered tie, which would show up quickly among the denser colors and patterns of the guests. I knew if I scanned the top of the gathering I'd find him—he was the tallest person there. I felt grateful to have my mother in charge of the reception, and especially lucky that Bill had made all the plans for our honeymoon. I was content to follow orders.

Soon Bill and I were standing on the porch before a third, damask-draped card table holding a tall, white-frosted cake and a silver cake server. Guests crowded around us. This was one of those moments I'd looked forward to ever since becoming engaged: The Cake Ceremony. I loved the attention, yet now I felt unreal, as if the scene weren't happening, as if the present at any moment might disappear. I cut the first slice and lifted it to Bill's mouth. It crumbled as he bit into it, pieces falling onto the white tablecloth, some sticking to the lapel of his white suit. *I hope they won't stain. I hope I don't spill crumbs on my dress when it's my turn.* I negotiated a small bite without mishap.

The white-capped woman nearest to me took possession of the knife and began to slice the cake into pieces she moved onto plates for our guests. The other caterer started to serve coffee from the large table where the ham had been. The leftovers had been consolidated onto the remaining table. Near the coffee, neat rows of cups, saucers, and spoons, along with several sets of sugar bowls and pitchers of real cream, provided reassuring order.

I'd been smiling and chatting with happy guests when my mother arrived to tell me it was time to change my clothes. *You don't have to act so nervous,* I wanted to say. *I'm married now. You won't have to be responsible for me ever again.* But my angry thoughts passed quickly. The dream quality returned, less oppressive than before. I floated off to my room in a fuzzy, rosy glow.

The Finale: I'd dressed in my new beige going-away suit, a sleeveless dress and a long jacket with a Mandarin collar. Daddy's gift. As my mother and I were about to leave for the store, he'd announced with a smirky smile that we could spend one hundred dollars, surprising me with his generosity. Pinned to the jacket was the gold daisy brooch that Bill had given to me for a wedding present. A yellow diamond to match my engagement ring sparkled at its center. White gloves, purse, and shoes. *Fashionable, coordinated, and complete.* My suitcase was already packed into Bill's tiny sports car, all set to zip off to the airport a few miles away. I was nervous about the trip, although I acted brave.

Our guests had gathered in front of the house, waiting for Bill and me to exit together. My insides lurched at the thought of leaving, but I knew I couldn't let those feelings see air. *Think of them as bacteria that need oxygen to survive; don't breathe.*

I stood, dazed, but Bill grabbed my hand. "Hold tight," he said. "We go straight to the car. Come on." We swept out the front door and down the steps, my hand clutching his.

Our guests had formed two facing lines with a path for us down the middle. "Good luck!" and "Best wishes!" they called out, tossing rice as we ran between them. My stomach froze; I remembered hearing someone on the radio talk about the danger uncooked rice posed for birds that eat what they find on the ground after weddings. I hadn't thought about rice.

I smiled and waved to the joyful chorus of relatives. *Be happy; the man you adore is now your husband,* I repeated like a mantra. *Smile.* Suddenly I noticed the car: "Just Married" on the back window, cans and ribbons tied onto the bumper. *Cool!* Then I wondered how embarrassed I'd feel if we drove very far with that stuff. *Smile!*

Waving madly, Bill and I took off in the car, clattering down the hill until we reached the corner and turned out of sight. He stopped to take off the decorations that we guessed my brothers and Bob had tied on. For a few tricky moments I was afraid Bill was resenting that they'd messed up his car. "I love you," I gushed, hoping to distract him. Soon we resumed our trip, sharing observations about our guests and exchanging stories from the afternoon.

Right after the ceremony, Bill's mother had decided she needed a dog and informed everyone about her plan to buy a poodle the minute she returned to Cleveland the next day. "What'll your therapist say when he hears you're being replaced by a miniature poodle," I giggled. A glance at Bill's face and I changed the subject. Before long, we were back to painting besotted pictures of ourselves and our future, each one grander and more outrageous than the last, as Bill's blue sports car charged down the highway to the airport.

I lay beside my husband in the darkness of a Nantucket night. There was no light from street lamps, stores, or cities in the distance. Nothing. And it was cold. The house had been closed for the winter, and we were the first inhabitants this year. A neighbor had given us the key; beyond that, we were on our own.

We'd flown to the island in a four-person plane: pilot and copilot, Bill and me. I was embarrassed to be doing something so exclusive and expensive, but it was what Bill wanted, so I focused on the adventure of the trip and having married the man I loved so dearly. *You've come a long way from a shock table in a mental hospital,* I reassured myself. College, marriage, just being alive at twenty-six—all were more than I'd anticipated. Those thoughts warmed me again as I lay in the dark; they helped keep fear at bay.

But the blankets were thin; the house was downright cold. An earthy, damp beach-house smell accentuated the chill. The rooms open to us had been used originally for servants. Unable to find a double bed in the entire house, we'd tied two twin beds together with string we'd brought for our kites. We spread sheets and covers over both of them, to make it a bed for two.

Earlier we had dined on lobsters and champagne at one of the fanciest restaurants on the island. We returned to the house late, exhausted. For a few minutes, we lay close, arms clasped around each other. Then Bill fell asleep. I wouldn't have to deal with sex until the next day.

If I'd been normal, I'd have imagined sexual intimacy on my honeymoon as a beautiful ocean wave cresting throughout the day, then breaking at night on a splendid beach, drenching everything in the vicinity with love. But I wasn't normal—my wave would fit into a kiddy pool.

When we were sexually intimate prior to our wedding, I'd fought feeling smothered: lying on my back naked reminded me of waiting for shock treatment.

Sometimes we were successful, but I had rules. For instance, I preferred sex during the day. I avoided it at night. If he insisted, I needed a light on. If we coupled, I had to be on top. Bill seemed pretty healthy—which, for a man, also meant eager—but he seemed patient with my idiosyncrasies. I didn't tell him that the smells turned my stomach, and that I had to pretend I was somewhere else to make it work. When we were engaged but not yet married I'd felt self-conscious and afraid—as if my mother might burst into the room and disown me. Perhaps that was the problem. Now that I was married, sex would be officially endorsed. Maybe my feelings would change.

At least they didn't compromise my wondrous day.

More hours passed, and I was still awake. I wasn't surprised; sleeping had always been iffy for me. This time, the problem was that I couldn't stop worrying about the birds. *What if a bird eats too much rice and it swells up inside of her and kills her?* I hadn't known our guests would have rice. And I hadn't stopped them once I'd realized they were throwing it at us for good luck. On the most important day of my life, I was careless. I may have stayed silent when I should have made myself speak. I knew I needed to let go of those fears. *Bill reads encyclopedias for fun. He'll help me. Tomorrow I'll ask him what he thinks about the birds.* I snuggled close to Bill's warm body and curled my arm around his waist. At last, I felt the gentle fingers of sleep loosening my tangled thoughts, releasing me to the stars.

CHAPTER TWELVE

Modified Magic

Spring 1971

S ince I never knew how things might turn out, my policy had always
been: *keep trying.* Yet even I was amazed to see myself sitting on my
very own gray metal folding chair at the Class Day ceremony of Yale College, Class of 1971. I was an honest-to-goodness graduating Yale senior.

During the winter before our wedding, Yale had considered its first
female applicants. I knew that in planning an historic coed class, there
was no way Yale College would accept anyone from an adult-education
program, to say nothing of an ex-mental patient, although I didn't mention that. Nevertheless, I'd done well at General Studies, and, since I was
going to be living in New Haven, I applied.

My rejection letter arrived in late March. I wasn't surprised, but it
still hurt my feelings. By June, I'd arranged to be a "special student"—the
spouse of a Yale student whose college agreed to award their diploma
for work completed at Yale. I qualified, because Bill was going to be a
graduate student in sociology.

In September 1969, I entered Yale with the first female students. The women in the sophomore and junior classes were all transfer students, the cream of the crop skimmed from the top of the best colleges in the country. As a special student I lived off campus. I took the bus downtown. Sometimes I rode my bicycle, but the trip was long. I kept to myself. I smiled a great deal. I enjoyed my classes. And I did well.

Yet once again I was the new girl, looking in from outside. I was too self-conscious to make friends. I told myself I didn't mind, because to take Yale College classes at all exceeded my most grandiose dreams. In fact, I veered back and forth, sometimes grateful, sometimes resentful of what I considered to be my status as a second-class citizen. Because I could barely believe I was there, and because I had no undergraduate student interactions except in my classes, my experience was more like watching a movie than living a life: I was curious about the outcome, but I didn't feel much connection with what was unfolding in front of me.

Yale's transition to coeducation was difficult. A year later, many women had left, and Yale reopened admissions for transfer students. *Do I dare?* I thought. As a special student I was a sociology major earning honors in graduate as well as undergraduate courses. When I brought up the transfer possibility in therapy, Dr. Heller, a Yalie himself, encouraged me to apply. Transcript in hand, I marched into the office of the chairman of the sociology department to ask if he'd help me transfer from General Studies to Yale. He did.

When I doubted myself or felt overwhelmed, Dr. Heller bolstered my shaky resolve. My pride must have lit up half of New York City the day I showed him my acceptance letter from Yale.

A week later, I brightened the city again. Dr. Heller had brought a half-bottle of champagne to our session, and we toasted to the momentous occasion—a marvelous affirmation of my assertiveness and adult accomplishment.

Through all my years of therapy with him, Dr. Heller had been thoughtful and deliberate in his words and his actions. He was warm and funny. He was direct when he was displeased, but always with a calm, gentle demeanor that communicated security, a sense of safe control. He didn't have to elaborate that he took wholehearted pleasure in my success. That half bottle of champagne said it all.

For the final semester of my senior year, I was an authentic, legitimate Yale undergraduate. I secured a photo ID card, learned to play squash in the gym, signed books out of the library, and joined a college seminar for seniors, *The Troubled Adolescent in Literature*. Every Yale undergraduate belonged to one of twelve residential colleges, where they slept and ate and participated in certain activities—informal sports, chess tournaments, parties, things like that, or so I imagined. I chose Davenport College for my affiliation, because it had been Bill's when he was an undergraduate.

I stocked up on Yale stuff. I bought a Yale folder, several notebooks, and two T-shirts. The first T-shirt was white with "Yale" written across the front in big, dark blue letters. The other consisted of navy blue and white stripes with "Yale College" printed in the upper left corner, close to the heart. I stuck a Yale decal in the car's back window. (I removed the decal shortly after graduation; I wasn't ready to show off that much.) My being a Yale student felt like fragile magic. I needed to make the most of it while it lasted.

The semester ended with graduation. Determined to sample every dish offered at that grand buffet of privilege and prestige, I decided to attend the Class Day ceremony, which took place on Saturday of graduation weekend. I didn't know a soul. I was taking a chance that I'd look ridiculous, but I didn't want to miss my opportunity for a Significant College Experience. I wanted to feel cool.

I'd selected a seat on the aisle in a sparsely populated section among the vast sea of gray chairs filling the Old Campus. I listened to speakers I didn't recognize describe outstanding men and women to whom they were giving impressive-sounding awards. Between speeches, I caught snatches of animated conversation among groups of students passing by. They shared jokes and other references I couldn't understand. My heart ached with longing to be included. *It's not fair!* Yet I knew envy or resentment would undo me if I allowed them the tiniest entry. I kept shoving my feelings back. *It's enough that you're a mental patient who made good*, I reminded myself. *Who would have imagined this a few years ago?*

A group of girls passed nearby, laughing and chattering together, warm and comfortable with each other. I looked up and smiled expectantly, but they didn't see me. Envy whispered again. *I hate you*, I thought, glaring at them. Familiar waves of unreality rolled in to drown out that voice. How could I be envious, if what provoked me wasn't really happening? How could I be left out, if I didn't exist?

I was not cool. I wanted to go home, but I had an hour to wait before Bill would pick me up. I watched a few clouds float by in the otherwise clear afternoon sky of that lovely, late-spring day. I reviewed plans for the ceremony on Monday, wondering if my family would be proud of me. Would they be happy, or would my father use my graduation as another opportunity to diminish my mother and brothers? I still didn't know if my father understood that when he told my mother I was better than she was, he erased all goodness from whatever I might have accomplished.

However, I was a hopeful person at heart, so I soon forgot about my envy and my family problems. *Graduation will be spectacular*, I assured myself.

Fingering the thin, sheeny black gown covering my new dress, I stretched myself to stand tall. I was about to graduate from Yale College, the first graduating class ever to include women. Me, a once-terminal mental patient with no past and no future. Me, who had finished high school four years late. Me, who had been rejected by both New York University and Yale College the first time I applied. It was as if I'd bought a ticket to Albany and flown to Paris instead. I expected to be beside myself with happiness, celebrating this triumph of persistence, hard work, good luck, and excellent psychotherapy.

But instead of celebrating, I felt miserable. Right when I should have embodied essence of joy and delight, my entire being—from the soles of my feet to the top of my scalp—was bubbling with fear. Among the notices in my official information packet was a letter from the bursar's office that warned seniors, "Unless all tuition bills, residence, lab, and library fees are paid in full, the student will not receive a diploma at the time of graduation." What if the Department of Vocational Rehabilitation had not paid my bill and I was one of the students referred to in the letter? Among the multitude of letters, notices, and sets of instructions that clearly affirmed my identity as a graduating senior (some even gave me a specific number), my mind fixated on the one thing I couldn't verify.

Sunday morning I'd attended a baccalaureate service in Woolsey Hall, where I sat transfixed amidst its elaborate carvings, marble columns, Michelangelo-style painting on the vaulted ceiling, and gold leaf everywhere. I wondered if my parents were as amazed as I was to see me there. Beyond awe, the day blurred out of reach.

Now, Monday, I found myself seated in the beautiful courtyard of Davenport College, surrounded by lovely Georgian brick buildings landscaped with rich, green rhododendrons, laurel bushes, and hollies. The air was fresh; the sun shone. Grass underfoot felt lush and soft, and ivy really was growing along the walls. I couldn't count how many of us were in the large crowd. The Davenport seniors had walked here together from the Old Campus after the main ceremony, where the entire graduating class had seats in the place of honor, right in front of the stage. After that, everyone moved on to their residential colleges to receive their diplomas.

At first, I'd been distracted from my worry. I'd enjoyed being among the students flooding across the streets on our way to the Old Campus from Davenport, ignoring traffic lights, making cars wait while we crossed. I wished that the Yale clerical workers hadn't been on strike. A few edged the street looking angry when we walked by. Ordinarily, we would have had programs listing all graduating students and telling about the ceremony. The strike meant there weren't any.

I learned about this as I listened to conversations around me while I walked alone. But along the way I met a depressed man named Ed, and we began to talk. Ed worried that his parents were disappointed in him, because he'd been a Whiffenpoof and took five years to graduate.

Ha, I thought when he complained, *if you think being one year behind makes you feel out of place, try six,* but I didn't say anything. Although Ed's excuse was far better than mine, I knew we both felt that we didn't belong to this class; we wished we fit in.

"Your parents should be totally proud of you for being able to sing like that," I said, hoping to cheer him up. It didn't help.

All around me groups of beautiful young men and women talked, laughed, and hugged each other. Some had painted peace signs on their mortarboards. Most of the female students weren't wearing robes, but had dressed in long skirts and summer blouses, flaunting bright colors with patterns and ruffles. For weeks their photographs and stories had appeared in newspapers, on TV, and on the radio. As the first female students to graduate from Yale College, they were practically required to make a splash.

Obviously I didn't belong. Only one girl other than myself was wearing a cap and gown—a tall, attractive black woman. I guessed that this day meant too much to us for either to forgo tradition. Then again, I wondered if she had made a choice, or if, like me, she had never been included in the plan.

My parents and younger brother, Taylor, were sitting about halfway back in the chairs set up for families. Next to them were Bill's mother; Aunt Marjorie; her husband, Uncle Dave; and Genny. Richie and Bobbi were busy with their young family in Vermont. Bill and I hadn't told anyone that I'd received notification of election to Phi Beta Kappa, because we wanted to surprise them. Alas, I was the one taken aback: the thrill I'd anticipated was instead a dark hole, a crater of doubt. I couldn't stop thinking about the bursar's letter, "Unless all tuition bills, residence, lab, and library fees are paid in full, the student will not receive a diploma at the time of graduation."

You won't graduate; you won't receive a diploma; there will be no award. My stomach churned; my chest froze solid with fear of imminent disaster. Again I reviewed the pros and cons of my available evidence: *I was issued a packet, I received my cap and gown, no one stopped me so far,* said one part of me. Another interrupted, *DVR is a bureaucracy, it might not have paid, bureaucracies don't pay on time, maybe it never paid, why should it pay anyway?* No rational words I came up with were able to stop the avalanche of panic descending with increasing velocity and volume. Any fun, any pride in my accomplishment, any connection between myself and the momentous occasion were all buried deep and quickly smothered by my fear.

From somewhere far away, I watched the master of Davenport College indicate that the final ceremony was about to begin. A student delivered a speech about our historic class, but I couldn't hear it in a way that made sense. If I didn't graduate, what he said wouldn't matter to me anyway. The last act had started. In alphabetical order, in groups of three, seniors' names were read aloud, each followed by any honors they had earned. With every advancing set, my fixation on the status of my tuition bill and the problematic nature of my graduation increased. I tried to pay attention. I worked hard to look normal and to hide my progressive emotional deterioration.

OK, I said to myself with the concern of an executioner reassuring his subject. *You need to prepare yourself for the moment of disappointment. You won't receive a diploma and Phi Beta Kappa award. You will manage. You will cope. You will be OK.*

But I knew I'd be devastated.

You never expected to be here. How can you be upset about losing something you never thought you'd have?

I was about to crumple into tears when I realized the S's were being called. The light shimmered and the colors around me danced brightly—too brightly. They made me dizzy.

"Jeffrey Arthur Samson, *cum Laude*; Annita Perez Sawyer, *Summa cum Laude*, Phi Beta Kappa, Highest Honors in Sociology; Amanda Simmons...."

Did I hear that right? Are the honors before or after your name? On jittery legs I steered myself to the table where the Master of Davenport was presenting diplomas. He shook my hand, his grip firm. He looked me straight in the eye. "Congratulations," he said with a nod and a meaningful voice.

Back in my seat I continued to tremble, but I wasn't entirely uncomfortable. I realized that something dramatic and wonderful had happened. Instead of jackhammering fear, my heart's pounding now warmed my chest and made it feel huge, like a bass drum at the opera. Ever so slowly, I unfolded the dark blue case. I stared at the Latin words on the diploma inside. Enough Latin from high school and church had stayed with me to make out the authoritative graduation statement, written in elegant script. Below that, added by hand in darker ink, was *Gradus deletus summa cum Laude* on the right side and *Honores merites clarrissimis ornati in Sociologia* on the left.

My name was in the center.

CHAPTER THIRTEEN

Bat Radar

While I navigated undergraduate classes at Yale, I was also figuring out life at home. Aside from a cubicle mate in a mental hospital, Bill was the only person I'd lived with as an adult.

Bill and I shared far more interests than we'd realized. We were wildly enthusiastic about sociological theory, classical music, and Scottish country dancing. We both loved to read and to explore ideas. We loved birds and being outdoors—gardening, walking, backpacking. Also, we had both spent years in individual psychotherapy. Dysfunctional families had left us unprepared for competent adulthood, and we knew we needed help. Although we were well aware of who we did not want to be, when we inevitably discovered we were acting like the parents we disdained, we had little understanding of how to change that behavior. Often we each dug in our heels.

My falling in love with Bill was no accident. It was predictable according to an amazing intuitive navigation system, a human version of bat radar, in which wounded individuals are drawn to and cling to one another. No matter how much people abhor the idea of repeating destructive patterns, or how sophisticated they imagine the mate-screen-ing program they've developed, like radar for bats, the intuitive navigation system more often than not is the driving force behind human relationships.

Details of Bill's history are not mine to tell, but family references and repeated stories hinted at trouble. Bill's mother was his father's second wife. The youngest of five children, Bill was raised with two much-older half-siblings (a boy and a girl) and two brothers. His full brothers were six and four years old when Bill was born.

Not long after I married Bill, a sister-in-law passed on to me the family dynamic as she'd gleaned it from a deathbed conversation with his father. When Bill's parents conceived their first child, they had a plan: between them, they were sure they could produce a genius. By the time their first son, Sam, was two years old, they'd decided that he was bright, but not their genius, so they tried again. The next one, Baxter, fulfilled their requirements. He grew into an accomplished, eccentric scientist and individual. To round out the family, Bill was to have been a girl.

Bill struggled a lifetime to find his own path. A brilliant, multi-talented Renaissance man, albeit more artist than scientist, he expected perfection of himself and others and tended to scorn anything less. He fought to counter his mother's harsh, domineering voice, so omnipresent that Bill spoke of it to friends, at times even to mere acquaintances. He regularly mentioned her most indelible message, seared into his brain before he turned six: "You're as bad as bad as bad can be." (She'd caught him white-mustached after he'd sneaked sips of cream from the top of a milk bottle in the icebox.) As might be expected, Bill didn't respond well to criticism.

About a year into our marriage, Bill announced that he wanted to order some miniature roses. He showed me a glossy garden catalogue with photos of perfect blooms in lovely varieties of red, pink, and peachy yellow. I almost always found a way to justify whatever Bill wanted, but this plan was easy to endorse.

Ingenious as ever, Bill attached three rows of grow lights to cellar beams underneath the kitchen floor of our tiny house. This would be the nursery. After the plants arrived—all twenty of them—he lined up the green plastic pots on the cellar's uneven dirt floor, about four feet below the lights. I hadn't thought about where the roses would stay, but the fact that they were indoors and out of sight surprised me. That I had to stoop to visit them increased my disappointment.

Weeks passed, and many of the roses lost their luster. Some dried out; occasionally Bill forgot to water them. Few in the batch, if any, achieved the full-bodied blooms that had been advertised in the brochure. Several died.

One afternoon we had just arrived home from our weekly trip to Stop & Shop, when Bill proposed ordering replacements for the expired plants.

"I'm not sure I like the idea of growing flowers in the basement," I told him. "It feels to me like they're in a dungeon down there."

Bill didn't say anything, but his expression hardened. He grabbed the bag of groceries and strode into the house.

As we put away cans of soup and boxes of cereal, Bill banged the cupboard doors louder than usual. He said little, but his glare was unmistakable. I wasn't sure of my offense, but I knew there'd been one. I didn't address this directly.

Our house was so small that we couldn't really get away from one another. My efforts to avoid Bill didn't work. As the day went on, to show him that I was sorry for whatever I might have done, and to make clear that I had not meant to cause him distress, I was especially nice. I brought him tea. I told him he looked good in his shirt. He stared at me as if I were a pig with two heads and acne.

"You expect me to be friendly, knowing what you think?"

"What do you mean 'what I think'? I just paid you a compliment."

"Why would you serve tea to a jailer?"

"A jailer? Where'd that come from?" I raised my voice.

"You said I imprisoned the roses. If I'm that heartless I'm sure you can't stand me."

"I didn't mean you were heartless. I'd never say that."

"You made yourself quite clear."

No matter how much I denied it, Bill had latched onto the idea that I considered him a cruel jailer, the dead roses his victims. Days passed. He continued to smolder.

Maybe a week after my initial comment we were again in the kitchen unloading groceries from Stop & Shop. Bill didn't speak.

"You're still angry?" I asked, ever so gently.

"I'm just the local jailer."

Stupid baby. I thought. *Jerk.* Icicles like huge fangs encased each word. I was fed up with his sulky anger and his insistence that I'd devastated him. I wanted to bite off his head.

I said nothing out loud, however. I feared hurting Bill's feelings and wounding his self-esteem. Before I could formulate a tactful response, he banged a cupboard door. White noise replaced coherent thought. Infused with the rage that used to make me smash my head against hospital walls, I dashed into the bathroom and slammed the door. I clenched my teeth into my right hand. Red tooth marks grinned at me from either side of the fleshy pad above my thumb.

Awhile later I emerged with a sore hand, but I was calm. Pain had absorbed my fury. Hard as I tried, I couldn't remember the conversation that had set me off.

"What time did you say your class started tomorrow?" I asked, returning to the kitchen. Bill had put away the rest of the groceries and was about to feed the cat. "I was thinking I could make curly pasta and meatballs for dinner," I added, when he failed to respond.

Bill slammed a can opener onto the counter. "Do what you want," he said. Smack! An upended cat food can disgorged Friskies Seafood

Dinner Deluxe onto a plastic plate. Holding a knife as if it were a dagger, Bill stabbed the food into smaller pieces and placed the plate on the floor in front of Mumble, our loudly meowing brown cat. I ignored both Bill and the cat.

I'll need to start the water... We have a few fresh tomatoes for sauce...

I had a theory that if I enacted my fantasy of domestic harmony, it would come to pass. I was no longer angry, and when Bill saw this, he would appreciate me. When I served him dinner he would feel cared for. Whatever had come between us would no longer matter.

"I love you," I said, setting the dinner plate in front of him.

"You know I hate it when you do that!" Bill said and stormed away from the table.

I need to remember this doesn't work, I thought sadly.

CHAPTER FOURTEEN

The Other Chair

February 1975

During the early years of our marriage, money Bill had inherited from his father's business supported us. We paid $142 a month to rent our tiny house. New York State's DVR paid my undergraduate tuition, and a variety of government grants paid for graduate school. The Yale Health Plan, an early HMO, provided comprehensive health care. Beyond paying for psychotherapy, we had few financial demands.

When I thought that Bill was too grouchy or too picky, or that I was too weak or too anxious, I took comfort in my belief that if we had enough therapy it would change us. I didn't question the expense. I was stingy about eating in restaurants and bought few new clothes (and only if they were on sale), but diminishing our savings didn't phase me if the money was paying for therapy.

I looked to psychotherapy not only to fix our respective personalities; I also considered it an investment in my career. I was determined to become a psychologist.

The years following the student uprising at Columbia in 1968 and the rippling effect of Vietnam antiwar demonstrations on campuses across the country ushered in an era of student power in academia. For a while, flexibility and accommodation reigned. Fortunately, my senior thesis advisor from Yale College had been present when the psychology admissions committee had discussed, and then rejected, my application to the clinical psychology program in the graduate school. He told me about their decision right away, and I quickly transferred my application to the sociology department, where they knew me. It was accepted.

Although I was a graduate student in sociology, I managed to talk myself into a number of psychology courses; I needed only the professor's permission to register for a class. In that way I completed much of the coursework required for a psychology degree—Introductory Psychology, Abnormal Psychology, a Clinical practicum, Statistics.

Our sociology department was noted for its medical sociology scholars, including Bill's advisor, August Hollingshead, perhaps the leading medical sociologist of his day. Studying social psychiatry, epidemiology, deviance, and the sociology of mental illness, along with various theories of human social behavior, I developed a broad picture of medicine, and psychiatry in particular, within a social context. Years later these courses enriched my perspective as a psychologist.

At times I clamped my mouth shut and sat on my hands to avoid revealing my personal experience, especially in the face of generalizations I considered false—dismissive jokes about schizophrenics, for instance. I felt subversive, a former convict feigning ignorance of prison life. I saw myself as an alien among the other graduate students.

Gradually I moved beyond defining myself as a rebellious child or a nutcase. As the years progressed, fear of revealing my history diminished. The past simply didn't come up, or if it did, I fabricated vague references to commonplace events to make my childhood and adolescence sound ordinary. I focused on preparing myself to help others survive.

Perhaps because I was following my own plan—trying to become a psychologist in the midst of a sociology program—each step turned up complications I hadn't anticipated.

I learned that only students in authorized clinical psychology programs were eligible for internships, which were required for a license to practice. The Director of Psychology at the Veterans Hospital, site of one of Yale's best internships, explained this to me when he and I met the first time: he had no choice but to turn me down. However, he agreed to let me work as a volunteer with any VA psychologists who might need my help and were willing to teach me. I learned about psychological testing by apprenticing myself to a psychologist in Neurology. I helped in the Blind Center and on the Chronic Illness and Medical Wards. I assisted in group family therapy in Psychiatry. After I'd volunteered for a year, I applied again for an internship. This time they accepted me. "If she wants it that badly," the director reportedly said, "why stop her?"

My approved clinical psychology internship began in July 1974 on G-8 East, an inpatient psychiatry unit at the West Haven VA hospital. As one of two graduate student interns I was part of the staff. With my own set of keys I could come and go from the ward whenever I pleased. I met with all but the most unpredictable of my patients in my office, one of four off a short hall just outside the ward's locked metal door. Even after many months on the ward, using my key to open that door still gave me a thrill.

Unlike PI in the 1960s, when the psychiatry residents stayed on one ward for a year, the VA system trainees rotated every six months. So in January, our three psychiatry residents and the other psychology intern switched places with those from the Day Hospital. I was the exception. When another intern scheduled for this ward took a job in California, leaving them stranded, the director accepted my offer to stay for another half-year. I'd tried to appear altruistic, as if I were forgoing Day Hospital training to help them out, but it was something I urgently wanted to do. Now I wouldn't have to disrupt the relationships I'd developed with many of the veterans on the ward. I'd be able to advance to a deeper level of psychotherapy with my patients. And I discovered that my standing in the eyes of new residents increased, because I could explain how the inpatient system worked.

I wished I could tell them all I knew about inpatient systems.

Keeping my psychiatric history hidden felt like a full-time job in itself. I loved being called "Dr. Sawyer," but discussing restrictions, passes, and medications—or inhaling the antiseptic smell of alcohol when I passed the treatment room—reminded me of my own locked-ward days. Occasionally I became disoriented; for a second I'd feel terrified, thinking I was a patient again. I worried I was a fraud. Debating philosophy or Freud's theories with other trainees, in our nice suits, skirts, and slacks, was like riding a toboggan down a steep hill—the sweet joy of flying, coupled always with the fear of a crash. When I hung out in the day room playing pool with scruffy veterans, I felt much more at home.

Ironically, my secret knowledge also made me feel superior. *Transparent jerks*, I thought when I heard insecure psychiatry residents make snide comments about patients. Those were often the same doctors who wanted to make sure I knew that their status ranked higher than mine. They tried to show me how intelligent they were by using Latin terms for situations or procedures with ordinary names, or by correcting me in a condescending way if I mispronounced a particular term or drug. Some told mental-hospital jokes or mimicked weird things their patients had said, as if having contempt for disturbed thinking somehow proved they were sane.

On 8-East most of the young doctors treated me as an equal. We exchanged ideas and advice and helped one another. If rolled eyes or loud sighs from the arrogant ones sparked my anger, it passed quickly. Feeling respected made me more tolerant.

I'd watched even earnest trainees become frightened by patients who reeked, who stood too close, or asked bizarre questions in voices too loud. I wasn't afraid of craziness. Interacting with patients was easy for me. My problems showed more with the senior staff, where extreme shyness often made me act tongue-tied and feel stupid.

Monday again, it was time for our team meeting. I scribbled the last of my therapy notes, tucked the pen and notebook under my arm, grabbed my sweater, and slipped a loaded key ring over my wrist. With a single, well-practiced, one-handed move I lifted a square, chrome-colored key from the bunch and twisted it into the lock to secure my office. In the hall, I used the brass key to let myself onto the ward.

"Good morning!" I said smiling at an unshaven young man shuffling by. I listened for the lock click behind me before moving on. A few other patients ignored me as I hurried down the hall.

I'd soon settled into the conference room with my team. Dr. Balkan, our ward chief, and Dr. Brett, our psychologist, sat at one end of an imposing rectangular table. The rest of us—nurses, psychologists, and psychiatrists in training—found seats among the remaining chairs. Someone had written the date on a blackboard covering the wall behind Dr. Balkan. Across from where I sat, large windows looked into a blue winter sky. Morning sun shining on yellow paint made the room bright and a little too hot.

We were discussing Paul, a new admission. Unlike most of the young veterans on 8-East, Paul hadn't served in Vietnam. He'd been too disturbed to complete Army basic training. Before his admission he'd been seeing a private therapist, which was also uncommon in this setting.

Paul's mother had brought him to the Emergency Room after he'd told her that voices in his head were ordering him to kill himself. Our task was to evaluate his condition, then come up with a diagnosis and a treatment plan—a combination of psychotherapy, medication, occupational therapy, and group or family therapy—that would reduce his symptoms and help him develop better skills for managing his life. The fact that he had a private therapist meant we would try even harder than usual to prove our competence.

I sat quietly at the table, but my ears were ringing. Everything I looked at appeared exceptionally vivid and crisp. George, a smart, sensitive resident everyone looked up to, was reading aloud a preliminary report Paul's doctor had sent.

"He claims to be unreal," George read, "to inhabit a world of cardboard representations, absent any living creatures. And he wants to die. He believes his death will bring the world freedom and peace."

"That's not the end of it," Janine, our head nurse, piped up, almost interrupting George. She smiled as if she had salacious gossip to share. "Nursing reports that he hasn't spoken—hasn't answered questions, hasn't asked questions, hasn't said a word, nada, nothing—since he arrived in the ER Saturday morning." She raised her eyebrows while she stared at the stack of papers in her hands. Assorted "Wows" filled the room. Trainees groaned and exchanged nervous, whispered jokes. Senior staff sat composed in professorial silence.

"Who would like to interview this challenging young man?" Dr. Balkan asked, after a pause.

No one raised a hand, or moved, or made eye contact with Dr. Balkan. Why would anyone want to interview someone who refused to talk? Especially since our interviewing skills would later be judged and commented on, both in and outside of our meeting.

Yet barely contained energy roiled inside me. *I know about this. Let me do it!* I struggled to keep my face placid and hold my nervous fingers still. When no one volunteered for the interview, which would take place before the entire team, I waited briefly, then raised my hand. I enjoyed the silent gratitude I imagined from the others in training: *Thank God it's you and not me who'll be critiqued and skewered.* I was playing the reluctant student with skill born of much pretending. They had no idea what this opportunity meant to me.

Janine left the conference room to get Paul. Dr. Balkan and Dr. Brett moved to seats at the far end of the table. I slid the vacated chairs closer to the blackboard, where they'd be easier to see. A few people rearranged themselves to improve their view. Flushed with pride, I surveyed the room. *Can you believe I'm doing this?* I said to myself, and then, as the reality of the situation began to register: *Idiot, what were you thinking?* Still, eagerness to give voice to this stranger whose language I spoke overrode my fear. Seating myself in the first chair, I clasped my hands together as tightly as I could and waited for Paul.

At the door's opening *whoosh*, I snapped to attention as Janine escorted a disheveled, dazed, and lanky nineteen-year-old man into the room. "This is Paul," she announced.

I stood and extended my hand. "Hi, Paul," I said. "I'm Dr. Sawyer. I'm going to talk with you here so we can get to know you and figure out how we might help." Paul's trembling fingers barely touched mine. Unsteadily he lowered himself onto the empty chair. He turned his pale face toward me and stared as if I were a ghost. *Don't be afraid. I'm one of you,* I implored in eye language, aching to soften the brittle edges of his fear.

This performance, one of the ordinary chores of a professional medical education, embodied the extremes of my thirty-one-year-old life. No one present knew about all the times I'd sat in the other chair. For my audience I became an aware, caring doctor about to interview a frightened patient who believed he needed to die. I was a former mental patient who had just volunteered to demonstrate for her peers, the psychologists and psychiatrists of tomorrow, an initial clinical interview.

I glanced at my team seated around the conference table, waiting. *You have power. Don't screw up.* I straightened my shoulders and turned to the young man at my side. "How are you doing this morning, Paul?"

Silence. He sighed. A long pause followed.

Paul's body exuded a musty, cheesy smell that floated on the draft around our chairs. I recognized the odors of dirt, grease, and sweat accumulated in his blond hair and on his unwashed skin. I wondered how much time to give him to gather thoughts for his response to my question. I didn't want to rush him and turn him off, but neither did I want to appear foolish by waiting too long, if he was determined not to speak.

"You don't seem to be in a mood to talk."

He shifted in his seat, rubbed his hand through his hair, ignored me.

"You seem pretty nervous. I guess I'd feel nervous, too, in your position. It could feel quite intimidating to sit in front of a group of strangers and talk about yourself."

Still silent, he perked up slightly, sitting taller in his chair.

"Is that what's making you nervous—the audience?... Is it something else?"

Paul blinked and cleared his throat, his eyes on the floor. "You can't help. I'm gone."

"Gone how, Paul?"

Without looking at me he raised his head. Slowly, in phrases reminiscent of obscure poetry, Paul spoke, and in my own way, I translated. "I look for my parents. All's only cardboard." *He sees others outside himself as unreal. Like me!* My heart jumped. Here was a kindred soul who shared my experience. I pictured myself in the hospital, a skinny, terrified girl, unable to talk. Struggling to push aside that image, I focused on the clinical. *De-realization makes the object world around him seem fake, flat like cardboard. Nothing that happens seems to matter, because nothing is real.*

"They're gone," Paul continued. "I look for rest, but I don't exist." *And he's depersonalized; his own existence doesn't make sense, either. I know how each kind of unreal feels—profoundly, unbearably weird; it's awful.*

"You and your parents don't seem real, is that it? I can imagine that's difficult to experience."

Paul frowned. "Dark sky hides the snake. Kill it. Kill it dead. They don't want me here." *Does he feel guilty about sex? Is he worried about rejection?*

"You don't feel wanted?"

"Nothing to believe." He sounded despondent. *Then there's meaninglessness. Thank God I'm not still there.*

"A world where no one means anything to you and nothing is real sounds lonely, Paul."

"Uh huh." His face looked blank, but his eyelids twitched. I wished I could comfort him.

"How do you manage that?"

"Listen to music. Don't talk. I think poison."

"Poison?"

"Kill me."

"Kill you? Why?"

"Hell. Dudes find justice in Hell."

"Are you thinking killing you is connected with justice?"

From staring past me, Paul turned to look me in the eye. He nodded. "Yeah, yeah, that's it." His energy increased. "Voices say, 'Gotta go. Evil this boy. No supper for him.'"

"Do the voices tell you to kill yourself?"

Again he nodded his head vigorously, wrestling with a sticky tongue to form words, forcing them through crusty, white lips dry from anxiety and medication. "They give orders: 'Eliminate yourself.' 'Death is peace,' they say. 'Die, bastard,' they say." His eyes expanded, but they focused somewhere beyond the room, shining. Paul looked crazy, caught up in a world we couldn't see. *He's psychotic. Could I ever have looked like that?* I caught a whiff of sour sweat. I hoped it was Paul, not me.

"Do you have a plan? Is there a particular way your voices want you to do this?"

Paul slumped into his chair, and with a large sigh bowed his head.

"What just happened, Paul? You look upset."

"Bad drama. No one believes me," he said in a small voice.

"I believe you!" I blurted out, before I caught myself.

Paul didn't respond. After a while he sighed again.

"What is it no one believes?" I asked, deliberately calm.

Paul sat up. He leaned forward in his chair, facing me. "Plan is right. Life is nothing. Time to go."

This disclosure seemed to take the last of Paul's energy. He shrank into his chair, deflated, and covered his face with a large, bony hand. *Shit. Did I go too far?* I was worried for him.

Our twenty minutes were up. I had to bring the interview to a close.

"Those are pretty serious concerns, Paul," I said to him, now thinking more of the spectators beyond. "Poisoning, no value in life, nothing real, wanting to die. You sound very unhappy. Our job right now is to make sure you don't kill yourself and to give you time to figure out how to cope with these things. Do you think you could work with us on that?"

Paul uncovered his face. He hesitated. Then he nodded.

"Thank you for talking with me, Paul," I said.

Rising to my feet, I reached to shake his hand. He appeared confused, robotic from medication and his abstracted reality, but he pushed himself off his chair to stand. Then, for a moment he came alive. His eyes reached into mine; he smiled at me and gripped my hand. He held on tightly, even after I let my hand relax. I heard him mumble something—*Is he thanking me?*—before Janine guided him out of the room.

Happiness spread through my chest like warm tea. I felt profoundly touched by Paul. In a parallel space, as if time had been transmuted, I felt I'd encountered that lost girl from long ago and had reached out to heal myself. I thought back to Harold Searles. *I did it! How amazing am I?*

In the next second, I reversed. *Who are you kidding? He didn't say anything real, for goodness' sake. You looked like a fool, pretending you understood what he was talking about.*

Dr. Balkan cleared his throat as Janine slipped back into her seat. "Thank you, Dr. Sawyer. You stuck with Paul, even though at first he didn't appear to make sense." He paused to take a sip from his water glass. "I liked your easygoing attitude; it seemed as if you'd known him from the start. Your ability to be direct enabled him to trust you enough to speak."

I beamed.

"This is a very disturbed young man." The chief turned to address all the staff assembled in the room. "Her questioning allowed us to see his paranoid ideation. His delusion regarding being evil leaves him vulnerable to suicide. What's the diagnosis?" He looked around the table.

"Clearly, he's psychotic," one resident declared.

"Schizophrenic, most likely," another added after a pause. I recoiled. Reluctantly I wondered if, in Paul's case, schizophrenia could be correct.

The criticism followed. "She asked too many leading questions," the first resident said. "How do we know this is what he really thought or if he was just agreeing with her?"

I winced. He had a point.

"And don't you think some of your interpretations require a real stretch of the imagination?" he continued, looking directly at me.

"A fair question," I conceded. I thought of Searles again.

"I think the proof of an interpretation is in the patient's reaction," George asserted, defending me. "Hers obviously had some merit or he wouldn't have connected with her the way he did."

Janine raised her arm with a dramatic gesture and peered at her watch. "Time's up," she declared. She grabbed her stack of folders and left the room.

Amidst the sound of scraping chairs and the murmur of half-whispered comments, we gathered our assorted pens, jackets, sweaters, candy bars, clipboards, notebooks, and keys and headed toward the door and the hallway beyond. I was grateful for George's support, although by then I wasn't really listening. As I walked out of the room, nodding and saying, "Thank you" in response to several "Good jobs," I was focused only on myself.

In a small, quiet space, deep within my mind, I was thinking about the young woman I'd seen for so long as a psychiatric patient, wondering if I was ready to leave that perception behind. Could I call myself a psychologist now? Had I indeed become a psychiatric doctor?

I felt a hand on my arm. "…make time for it?" George and Dr. Brett were walking beside me.

Time? "I'm sorry," I said. "Could you repeat that?"

"Lunch," George said. "Would you join us for lunch?"

I tripped and barely caught myself. Blushing, I picked up my sweater and notebook from where they'd landed on the floor.

Who do they see? I wondered.

"Sure," I said.

CHAPTER FIFTEEN

The Next Chapter

June 1975

With my hands out of sight beneath the table, I rubbed the sides of my belly, which put me into a dreamy state. Our treatment team was in the midst of a debate about the merits of restriction versus a medication increase to control Jack M's worrisome behavior. Ordinarily I paid close attention to these things. I still felt it was my duty to make sure patients weren't shortchanged or given medication as the easy way out. But lately I wasn't caring so much. All the trainees would be leaving the ward in another month anyway. I pulled a parcel from my lunch bag and unwrapped my sandwich.

I was also less attentive, because I was pregnant with my first child. Patients and staff seemed happy for me. I was very pleased with myself.

As I bit into the thick brown bread, a slab of Swiss cheese, slippery with mayonnaise, dropped onto my soccer ball lap. Bill had made the bread himself with flour ground at home (the wheat berries came from a special farm in Ohio), organic yeast, and vitamin-rich walnut oil. I made a fuss about the mess, hoping someone would comment on the size of my sandwich. I wanted to show off what a great dad this baby would have and demonstrate what responsible parents we were, even before the baby was born.

Like many women in the 1970s, I planned to combine motherhood and my professional career, fully embracing both. I expected to give birth, pop my baby into a soft Snuggly infant carrier, take her with me to the library, and produce a dissertation in a year or two. I looked forward to natural childbirth and breast-feeding on demand—a perfect union with nature, family, and graduate school. *I can do it all*, I thought. *Look what I've done so far.*

Jessica's birth was difficult, but not long. After she burst into the world of bright lights and cool air, she cried for a few seconds. As the midwife handed me my tiny wriggling daughter, our glances met in one startling, world-stopping moment. She quieted, her round dark eyes fixed on mine. Laid onto my chest, Jessica straightaway began to nurse. I held onto the midwife's message: if I paid attention, my baby would teach me how to mother her.

I was sore and exhausted. In all my life I'd never been happier.

The midwife might have added that babies were not only miraculous but also messy and confusing. Complete responsibility for a tiny life could be terrifying. Paying attention to my infant was necessary, but it wasn't sufficient to achieve my goal of perfect mothering. I had to figure out what she was trying to say and what to do about it.

Bill and I didn't always understand our daughter's messages, and we often disagreed on the right response. I loved nursing Jessica, holding her, playing with her, bathing her, and changing her diapers. I looked at her for hours. Bill cherished her, too, delighting in her care. However, like many new fathers we knew, he had trouble sharing me. Bill's resentment of my time with Jessica, his feeling neglected when she wanted to nurse, stoked my guilt. Sleep deprivation left me crabby; hormones and history made me impatient and unreasonable. I fell far short of my goal. Perfection proved a cruel myth.

Delight, despair, pride, frustration, pain, exhaustion, disappointment, and joy beyond measure characterized our first year as we learned how to become a family of three. This was only the beginning of one of life's, and especially parenthood's, most profound lessons: I controlled so much less than I had anticipated.

By the time Jessica was eighteen months old, we'd outgrown our tiny rented house. Broken glass littered the street, and stray dogs roamed the neighborhood; outdoors wasn't safe for a child. We moved to our own home in what the local newspaper referred to as a semi-rural suburb of New Haven. My father lent us the money at 4% interest.

The day before our move, my beloved Genny died. Liver cancer was listed as the cause, but exploratory surgery had identified advanced lung cancer as well. Death followed her diagnosis by only six weeks. I had been able to tell Genny that we'd bought a house. My mother, Bill, and I, sometimes including Jessica, spent time with her. (Genny looked happiest when she was with Jessica.) More often than not, I sat with her alone, although she was often weak and didn't speak. One afternoon in response to a welcoming smile, I embraced my rigid, private, unemotional aunt and we both sobbed. No words. Just Genny and me, united in grief.

Bill, Jessica, and I moved as planned. It felt grown up to live in my own home, but I ached missing my aunt. I'd not experienced loss of that magnitude before.

Since marrying Bill, I'd rarely spent time alone with my mother. Now we spent several days together cleaning Genny's condominium.

"She was always Mother's favorite," my mother remarked one afternoon as we sat on Genny's bed folding pajamas and blouses. "Mother made me wait on her. I had to wash her underwear. Winter underpants were made like shorts in heavy wool. The wool's scratchiness hurt my hands, and they took forever to dry."

"How did you manage?" I asked, hoping I didn't sound like a therapist. I knew little about my mother's childhood, and this was the first glimpse I'd had of her resentment.

"I just did it; I was afraid to speak up to my mother." She paused, a blouse halfway lifted. "But I was Daddy's favorite," she said, and resumed folding. "Mother used to say, 'Rosanna, go see what your father's doing and tell him to stop it.' Daddy was always glad for my company."

Another day we talked about death. "Mother's death left a hole inside of me that's never gone away," my mother revealed. "She and Daddy are both buried in the cemetery in Valhalla, NY." Taking care to move slowly, I reached my arm around my mother's back, resting it lightly on her stooped shoulders. She seemed forlorn, so much in need of comfort, yet I feared that at any moment I might frighten her away. This emotional intimacy with my mother was new, and I felt grateful.

It lasted only a few months. When my father developed a suspicious lump on his neck, leading to a series of cancer surgeries, I was startled by her disdain for my sympathy. Words I hoped would help put her off instead. I made things worse. One evening, I'd telephoned to ask how she and my father were doing.

"I just this minute walked in. I had to put your father into the hospital again," my mother said.

"I'm so sorry. That sounds awful." I felt dismayed for her.

"Thank you for your concern, Madame Psychiatrist, but I am managing quite well," she replied with an icy tone. "I'm not dancing in the street," she said another time, "but we're managing. Just what did you expect?"

My picture of my mother as a sweet but passive mouse had been remarkably incomplete.

Along with school, Bill and I continued our individual psychotherapy. By the time the sociology department accepted my application to graduate school in the spring of 1971, I'd spent two years commuting to New York City every week to meet with Dr. Heller. I began to feel it wasn't reasonable to devote all of my Fridays to therapy. I also knew in my heart that I was ready to be an adult female, and eventually a mother, and I needed to learn from a woman. My undergraduate senior thesis advisor, who was a psychologist at Yale, recommended his friend Heather Sanders. With Dr. Heller's blessing, I made the transition to therapy in New Haven. He and I moved on to become colleagues and friends.

Dr. Sanders was lively, smart, and straightforward. In contrast with Dr. Heller's quiet reasonableness, Dr. Sanders was passionate, even impulsive. She said what she thought when she thought it. But like Dr. Heller, Dr. Sanders took me seriously. I began therapy with her shortly before I graduated from Yale College. We met two to four times a week for almost ten years.

Not long into my therapy with Dr. Sanders, our work was interrupted by a crisis in her family. One afternoon she arrived at the clinic more than half an hour late for my appointment. She glared at me as I hurried toward her. We rode the elevator to the next floor in silence.

"You looked really angry," I complained, once we'd reached her office.

"I'd been at a meeting about my very sick child," she said. "The way you rushed at me screamed neediness and reproach. I didn't need another problem."

To my surprise, I felt compassion for her. I could see the truth in her description of my behavior. Her honesty made me feel respected, as if we were friends.

"Sit up! You look like a mental patient," Dr. Sanders snapped one morning a year or two after that, when she found me huddled in the corner of her waiting room. The forthright way she objected to my self-negation provoked me to move to a new level.

Just as with styles of learning to read or processing math, patients in psychotherapy make progress in individual patterns. I seemed to struggle for months, sometimes years, then leap forward when I finally grasped some concept or achieved some insight that had eluded me. I spent a great deal of time mired in self-loathing. Tongue-tied in social situations, locked into my self-made box, I believed that others saw me as childish, stupid, and boring.

Soon after Dr. Sanders reacted to my miserable appearance, I had an idea: *Why not check out reality and observe the way people do relate to you?*

Since the winter before Jessica's birth, Bill and I had enjoyed singing in the New Haven Chorale, a local chorus. We rehearsed every Monday night and presented concerts two or three times a year. That night, at chorale rehearsal, I gathered data. People I knew smiled when they saw me. Some spoke to me during the break. Not even the choral police—the few fussy sopranos, often music teachers, who by training felt it was their responsibility to identify mistakes—corrected my singing or seemed put off by my presence. I was treated no differently than anyone around me.

The new perspective didn't end my insecurity, but it set limits on the emotional swamp I sank into. And I spent less time immersed.

Perhaps most influential of all was an exchange that occurred after I'd complained to Dr. Sanders about Bill for something mundane. "What else would you expect from a guy?" she wisecracked. We laughed together until we were exhausted. For those moments, I was just another woman; we were sisters. It felt glorious.

Dr. Sanders surprised me when she brought tea and cookies to our session during the blizzard of 1978. The state police had ruled all non-emergency travel on highways illegal; I had risked arrest by driving to her home office. Like Dr. Heller with the champagne, she followed her instincts and communicated affirmation for my assertiveness in a way I would always remember.

During that blizzard I was pregnant again. Jessica spent mornings at nursery school while I collected data for my dissertation.

I was still pregnant a few months later when Dr. Sanders gave me a hug that changed the course of my psychotherapy. (A hug was a very big deal in 1978.) We were planning for a home birth, and a visit to a new obstetrician had stirred up feelings about hospitals. In that session with Dr. Sanders, I'd become overwhelmed with grief as I thought of my mother giving permission to the doctors to administer shock treatment. (I don't remember exploring why I would blame my mother and not my father.) As my body shook with sobs, I felt my consciousness expand—I could reach deeper into myself. It was past time to leave when I finally stopped crying, still too shaken to move. Dr. Sanders offered a hug. Gratefully I soaked up her kindness and generosity. She recognized my grief; she intuited the rage I dared not consider. I felt that with her embrace, she had made her own commitment clear.

In response to my new openness, we increased my appointments to four times a week. I continued this schedule through the end of my pregnancy four months later. The intense therapy helped me feel more solid, more firmly connected with myself. I was also better prepared to deal with my family when my father's cancer worsened shortly after James was born.

CHAPTER SIXTEEN

His Tongue Cut Out

November 1978

While Bill waited in the car with our two-month-old infant James, I visited my father in Mount Sinai Hospital in New York City a few days after surgery to remove his malignant tongue. I walked in determined to be brave. At the sight of him, I wavered.

A flimsy hospital gown fell loose about his slight, bent frame, his bony arms and sticks of legs exposed against the harsh chrome of his wheelchair—I worried he might be cold. He stared at me, gray bloodshot eyes pleading, mouth agape, pink saliva spilling from both sides. A tracheal tube stuck out of a hole in his neck. IV tubes fed his veins with fluids dripped from bags on poles. A larger tube snaked from under his gown into another bag flopped on the chair beside his knee. Maybe that was the one connected to a hole in his stomach—access port for liquids pretending to be food.

I didn't register a bed or an individual room. There might have been other patients scattered at various medical stations in what I pictured as a giant space, much like a barn, although that would not have made sense. I remember the scene as dark, reflecting my emotional state or maybe shadows cast from over-bright florescent lights. Although my mother stood beside me, it seemed as though no one else was in the room. Only my father.

He looked so small.

He had brightened for a moment when he first noticed me, shoulders shifting back a little, hands lifting. I thought I saw his eyebrows raise before exhaustion, or despair, reclaimed him, and he shrank again.

"Oh, shit, Rosanna," he had said to my mother just before surgery.

Oh, shit, oh shit, I thought. My mind jumped from one image to another. My father, Lord of the Household, shrunken to a little boy. My dapper dad, a grizzled old man. Ousted from his powerful job, not a year into retirement, so soon laid low. A lifetime of vodka, Scotch, and cigarettes come to collect their dues. The picky editor, the sour critic, the Depression-victim-miser, all left without a tongue. It wasn't fair. He'd had no time. He might have softened, freed from deadlines and commutes.

Reduced to drooling, he would never speak again.

After watching me for a while where I stood frozen in front of him, unable to form words of my own, my father grunted. Keeping his eyes fixed on mine, he nodded his head toward a shelf of charts nearby. He labored to raise his arms in pantomime, as if spreading open a broad folder and peering inside. He tried to mouth words with his swollen, cracked lips.

"He wants you to read his chart," my mother said.

I didn't need her trembling voice to translate his request: *Tell me what they did to me. Tell me what will happen to me. Tell me what they really think.*

Find out how soon he's going to die.

"I'd like you to meet our daughter, Dr. Sawyer," my mother had said to my father's nurse the first time she came by. My left hand covered a nervous cough while I shook hers with my right. I wanted to explain that I hadn't yet completed my dissertation, that my mother's pride interfered with her grasp of the facts, that I would be a PhD, not an MD doctor in the end. An imperious glare commanded me to hold my peace. Within earshot of other staff my mother made sure to call me "Doctor," voice raised, diction impeccable. This was her mission, too.

In spite of all the progress I'd made on the emotional front, I was still in many ways a fearful sort of person. I did what I was told. The thought of being scolded made me sick. I didn't want to cross the authorities—charts were for professionals, not patients. What would I say to a nurse, or worse, a *real* doctor, who walked in and saw me, chart in hand, and demanded an explanation?

But my parents needed me. Like many of their generation, they distrusted psychologists and made nasty cracks about psychotherapy. I struggled to take a deep breath. My stomach quaked. *It's your chance to deliver. They'll be impressed and grateful. You have to do it.*

Thus, I agreed to become the family's private detective. Better to risk public chastisement than disappoint my parents.

The manila folders all looked alike. Patients' names weren't evident, and I wondered how I'd find out which one was my father's. I hated feeling forced. I turned to my father with what I'd later recognize as my version of my mother's *see how you're making me suffer; please don't insist* look—the expression I'd vowed never repeat. He frowned and pointed toward the charts, poking the air for emphasis. There was no going back.

I took another deep breath and decided that I was indeed a doctor, and that I had every right to read my father's chart.

As I drew closer to the shelves, I saw that the folders were not in any clear order, but were scattered along the countertop. I picked up the nearest one and opened it. A stranger's name appeared on the first sheet. An intimidated and inexperienced criminal, I studied a poster on the wall as I closed the folder and set it down. *See? I'm not actually doing this.*

The third chart was my father's. By then my ears were buzzing; outlines of objects around me shifted, refusing to hold still. I read as quickly as I could, but I stumbled on words I didn't understand. I knew some medical shorthand from the VA hospital internship, but many symbols and abbreviations eluded me. I blustered through.

A nurse walked over to the counter and picked up a chart. I intensified my studious doctor pose. She didn't notice me.

Ultimately, the detective-heroine-psychologist failed in her task to find new answers or uncover valuable secrets. Nothing was in the chart that Dr. Gilbert had not explained. He noted *squamous cell carcinoma* at the base of Henry Perez's tongue. He had removed it along with certain lymph nodes during the six-hour surgery. Post-operative condition, unremarkable. Blood pressure, somewhat high, but that wasn't new. Other vital signs, within normal range for post-op.

I replaced the chart on the counter and turned to confront my parents' frightened faces. "It doesn't say anything different from what the surgeon told you," I said. "That's good news. He thinks he got it all. Tests haven't come back yet. There's nothing about prognosis."

My father shifted as if to turn away, his body tense with pain. He gazed into barrenness somewhere far in the distance. I wanted to offer a hug for comfort, but his wraithlike appearance made me afraid to touch him. Despite the tubes and gaping wound in the center of his puffy face, he seemed made of the thinnest glass. I worried that he'd shatter.

My mother sighed and wrung her hands, "At least there's nothing we didn't know about." She forced a smile at her husband. He glared at her.

I wanted to cry for both of them.

A month after the surgery, Bill, our two young children, and I traveled to my childhood home in White Plains to celebrate Christmas Day with my parents. My father, wearing a handsome, tailored, navy blue bathrobe over ironed pajamas, sat as thin and unbending as a department store mannequin in an armchair in their modest living room. He'd stretched himself to be there. No one mentioned his condition, but from the way he moved and the lines in his face, I suspected that he was suffering.

Nor was mention made of the fact that for the second Christmas in a row, Genny was missing. Before she died, my aunt had spent every Christmas with our family since we'd moved back east when I was seven, almost thirty years earlier. At home in Connecticut, I sometimes wandered the house, calling her name. I still wept for her at night. My parents ignored the large empty space, so glaring to me, which broadcast her absence. Because a powerful, unseen hand refashioned me into a younger, timid-sheep version of myself whenever I crossed the threshold of my family home, I, too, said nothing.

The adults appeared stiff, our conversations stilted. Denying grief and fear sapped a lot of energy. But even at his best, my father's reactions to social gatherings hadn't necessarily been predictable. He'd been known to growl long before his current misery set in. New uncertainty compounded the risk of approaching him now that he could no longer speak. Should we try to converse? Hand him a pad of paper and a pen? Grunt, too?

For communication, my father could offer a nod or a slow, careful turn of his head. Grunts, singly or in slurs, in various pitches, pushed out of his mouth as he tried to shape words he could no longer articulate into vowels and consonants. Only three-year-old Jessica seemed unaffected by the tension in the room. She grabbed a cracker from the cheese platter and ran toward her grandfather's chair, holding it out to him with a big grin. "Here!"

Above his sallow, silly-putty cheeks, my father's eyes crinkled at the corners. Sunshine lit his sad, distorted face. He bent forward—hinting at a formal bow—and accepted the cracker. His skinny hand trembled as he reached to pat her arm.

"Hi, Gaffiger," she giggled, patting his arm in return.

When I was first pregnant and had asked my mother what she'd want her grandchildren to call her, she'd responded with surprising vehemence.

"I have no interest in answering to one of those cutesy nicknames like Nanna or Gramsy or BaBa," she said. Her voice dripped with scorn. "I'll be 'Grandmother.'"

Jessica's early toddler efforts to say her grandmother's special name came out "Gamburger," which charmed us all. "Gaffiger," for her grandfather, became its companion. Although Jessica's "Gamburger" soon turned into "Grandmother Rosanna", for the brief time her grandfather was in her life, his early nickname stuck.

After the cheese and crackers had been distributed and the children settled—Jessica on her daddy's lap; baby James asleep in my arms—we began the ceremony of Christmas presents. Grief added its own layer to the ambivalence that had dominated this ritual for as long as I could remember. Even as children, my brothers and I had been aware of our father's reluctance to part with money. He showed his distress with hostile silence or angry, sarcastic criticism of the purchaser as well as the purchase.

That day my father gave my mother two gifts.

The first package was heavy, and he labored to move the blue tissue-wrapped item toward where she sat on a striped couch behind the mahogany, Catholic Charities coffee table. He'd pushed it with his foot a few inches along the rug when Jessica ran to grab it.

"I'll help," she said.

Her grandmother quickly slid to the floor beside her, in front of the low table. "Let's open this together." Jess grinned and pulled her end of the bow at the top.

My father leaned forward. Anticipation brightened his eyes. A smile softened his cheeks and lips.

With curly ribbon untied, the paper fell away to reveal a dark red Maxwell House coffee can filled to the brim with pennies. My mother read aloud what he'd written in shaky script on the Christmas card he'd stuck into the can. *So you'll never run out of change. I saved this all for you.*

She blushed. "I'll put it to good use," my mother said. She tried not to cry.

Next, my father lifted a small package from beside him on the chair and held it up for all to see. "Oh - anh -unh?" he said. She smiled at him. He beamed. She unwrapped a handsome pair of dark green leather driving gloves, complete with black leather reinforcement strips on each palm and leather-trimmed oblong holes above the knuckles for flexibility and ventilation. *For your future journeys. So you can travel in style,* read the card.

My mother laughed. "Thank you," she said. "I've been doing a lot of driving lately. These will help."

My father's generous messages and boyish eagerness to please his wife with probably the most wholehearted gifts he'd ever offered anyone, shone in dramatic contrast to his usual attitude. My aching sense of his dependence on my mother kept growing. *What will become of them?*

On the ride home, Bill drove. The children, exhausted from a long day, slept. As we rode through villages draped with Christmas lights, snowy woods, and parkways in the darkness outside the window, my thoughts returned to a troubling incident from the past. I was back by the pool at the Brown's house on the afternoon my father had blurted out that he was in love with me before dashing back to rejoin his friends.

Perhaps Dr. Heller's shocked response had seared that scene into my memory. More than a decade later, it still felt fresh, unlike other, murkier times when my father had crossed lines he shouldn't have, which, at the time, I'd dismissed as bad dreams and brushed away.

On subsequent passes home that fall, if I was alone in a room when my father entered it, I exited. I didn't rush out in an obvious way, but my anxiety increased with each second he was near, compelling me to leave. In time, the pattern became clear. Once, after having left the living room to escape him, I returned soon after that to join my brother and my aunt, as well as both parents, who were gathering for cocktails. He took me aside and asked if I was afraid of him.

"A bit," I mumbled, feeling my face turn red. I didn't want to upset him, but I tried not to lie.

"Is that because of what happened in the summer, at the Brown's?"

I was stunned. *He's known what he did all along?* I'd excused him by assuming he'd been drunk and unaware of his actions. "Kind of," I said.

"Well, you don't have to worry about that anymore."

"Thanks," I said, unsure of what he'd meant or how I was supposed to respond. Fighting my impulse to flee, I remained standing beside him.

Nothing about his behavior or my reaction was mentioned again.

Through unsteady light from cars and street lamps glancing in the windows, I stared at Bill's solid profile and thought of the disfigured man we had just left. I didn't know what to feel. I hadn't questioned my safety since I'd married Bill. Should I celebrate that my father could never again wound my mother or my little brother with sarcastic gibes? Had some perverse justice been rendered? I felt sorry for the pain and humiliation of my father's condition, but it was a pale, washed out, generic sadness, cold and disconnected. *I believe he loves me, yet all I feel is numb.*

"What did you think of my dad?" I asked, hoping Bill might help me open a connection.

"He looked pathetic. He was hostile to everyone except Jessica. He hasn't changed at all."

Jerk. I never should have asked. Steaming, I turned my head away to stare again out the window. At least being annoyed with Bill produced a real feeling. Our ride continued in silence. Soon, we were home.

Six months after the surgery, my father, working at the dining room table, had almost completed his taxes. He was signing the last form when he started to choke. Unable to swallow saliva stuck in his throat, or to make sounds loud enough to reach my mother in the next room, he was unconscious by the time she found him. He died in an ambulance on the way to the hospital.

My father had long been clear that he wanted no part of any religion and certainly no funeral. When pushed, he'd identified himself as agnostic. In my childhood, on Sundays when my mother, brothers, and I went to Mass, he stayed at home and worked on the *New York Times* crossword puzzle. After he died, his body was cremated as per his instructions. Our mother arranged for a small memorial ceremony to be held at the funeral home.

Among those who attended the memorial were many prominent civil engineers—"the men who built America," he once told me. From the late nineteen forties through the nineteen seventies many of them had been instrumental in constructing the bridges, tunnels, dams, and highways that made up our country's infrastructure. He'd covered their work for his magazine; now they were old friends. In halting voices, red faces twisted in grief, one after another described a confidante and colleague they had loved—*smart, witty, loyal, fun*. While they wept, I sat solemn—respectful, but numb. Much as I tried to summon tears, they refused to come.

I thought about my father's drinking.

I'd been thirty-one, in the early months of my internship at the VA Hospital, when he had called to tell me that my uncle, my Aunt Marjorie's husband, had hanged himself. Uncle Dave had been taking Antabuse to control his drinking, my father reported. Without alcohol, Dave couldn't survive.

"I didn't know Dave had a drinking problem," my father remarked during the same call, referring to a man whose chronic inebriation my cousins and I had deplored for years. In that moment's denial, I grasped full force my father's own alcoholic condition.

I wondered how he had survived his own father's death by suicide. Had my grandfather also been an alcoholic? At home, my father had never spoken about his family; we knew little of his personal life. I learned the most controversial details of his history from my cousin Jenifer years after I'd left home. I'd never dreamed of bringing up my grandfather's death with my father. Secrets were to be respected.

In hindsight, I recognized the symptoms of depression in my father's grouchy manner, in his retreat behind newspapers and *Ellery Queen* mystery magazines. The icy wall he'd built around his past made sense; he was attempting to separate himself from emotional pain. But he had engineered his own destruction through his addiction to tobacco and vodka, where, eventually, my mother joined him.

A few months after my father's death, in the air that cleared following an altercation with Bill, I noticed that I wasn't anxious. My body had stopped vibrating; my stomach didn't churn. The change was remarkable. I was no longer afraid.

CHAPTER SEVENTEEN

Up the Hill

Early 1981

L ife with two children was busier than I'd imagined. Fortunately, we found a tiny, progressive school not far from our home, and the community of engaged, idealistic, likeminded hippie parents became our extended family. I'd always intended to rely on public education, yet this cooperative school embodied our values much more than the larger, and more geographically distant, local school. (Another parenthood lesson I came to appreciate: abstract, ideal priorities reorganize quickly in the face of concrete, real-life choices that involve and affect one's children.) Bill worked on the school finance committee and later served as treasurer. With what time I could find, I worked on my dissertation.

Although I'd been in therapy for all of my adult life, I knew I'd have to stop before I looked for work. I didn't want to lie or risk rejection when I filled out the employment medical history forms that asked about psychiatric treatment.

My car slowed as it climbed the long, steep hill. In winter's thin light, my surroundings took on the flat texture of a faded watercolor painting as I watched the familiar houses, driveways, intersections, and power lines emerge and retreat beyond the dry grass bordering the road. It was a cold Wednesday in late January. I was on my way to my therapy appointment.

When I first made this drive, Bill and I had lived only eight minutes away in our tiny flat-roofed house set between the projects and West Rock on the far side of New Haven. I'd traveled down my hill past the bleak public housing, crossed Whalley Avenue, and from there ascended into the increasingly prosperous neighborhoods of Westville and, finally, Woodbridge, where Dr. Sanders' office was attached to her house at the end of a long gravel drive.

Four years earlier we'd moved to a little town east of New Haven. My trip had expanded to forty minutes on a good day. Once in awhile I drove by our old house at the foot of West Rock, but as life became more demanding and complex, I lost interest in that part of my past.

I wouldn't be making the trip much longer. After almost ten years with Dr. Sanders it was time for me to complete my therapy and live life on my own.

I hadn't come close to analyzing all of my data for the dissertation, and ending therapy had been a theoretical concept, when Dr. Sanders proposed we set a date for termination. Although technically, the suggestion had been hers, she'd made it on the very day that I'd thought for the first time, as I backed out of my driveway, *I'm not sure I want to use a whole afternoon for therapy right now.* The idea had felt dangerous—I did what I could to erase it from my mind. But somehow, Dr. Sanders had sensed that the seed was there. When she asked me how long I thought I'd need to complete the termination, I picked the longest amount of time I figured I could get away with: nine months.

On the third day of April, early in spring, my true autonomy was due.

Some people might have considered nine months a ridiculously long time to bring therapy to a close. They would probably have been horrified to know how much therapy I'd had. If I counted only constructive, successful therapy—my work with Dr. Heller and Dr. Sanders—it was close to seventeen years. If I counted how many years I'd been treated by psychiatrists, including all the hurtful or incompetent ones and the good ones who had been wasted because shock treatment made me forget them, I'd been in therapy for almost twenty-one years—more than half my life. It was a formidable expanse of time, but I didn't regret my investment.

How could I question psychotherapy's value, when for years I'd assumed I'd be dead well before I reached thirty? Once I finished my dissertation, I planned to look for a job as a therapist. My goal was to pass on to others the healing that had made my own life possible, to express gratitude that I'd made it this far.

I'd received substantial psychology training in graduate school courses, particularly in my internship at the VA Hospital. However, the best training—and this was affirmed by many in the field—occurred during the experience of one's own therapy. Dr. Sanders had studied psychoanalysis. We agreed that my work with her had been an analysis. "Psychoanalysis isn't positional," she'd assured me when my father was dying and I wanted to look at her, not lie on her couch.

I'd come a long way in my therapy with Dr. Sanders. At the onset, I'd been burdened by a heavy, dark sorrow that sat on my chest and weighed me down like a mythical beast. I was convinced that I was a sinner whom no one could like. I overcompensated by being excessively helpful, trying to undo or at least make amends for my reprehensible condition, and making a fool of myself in the process. I lived in an ongoing swirl of anxiety, although that had diminished after my father's death.

During my internship, I proved I could be a good therapist. While far from perfect, I was a reasonable wife and mother, too. I often struggled with feeling as if I were a ghost or living in a dream, and I was still quite shy, but by then, I didn't worry about myself and other people so intensely. It was missing Dr. Sanders too much that worried me.

I was a thirty-eight-year-old adult woman with two children, yet I hadn't been on my own emotionally before. It wasn't that I didn't know how to take care of my family. Would I be able to take care of myself? Would I feel stable, or would I feel as though I carried a large hole inside of me where something essential was missing? Would I feel like a boat cut loose from its mooring, adrift alone in the middle of the ocean?

Don't be a wimp, I'd been telling myself. *You'll be fine.*

I wasn't always convinced.

On this particular Wednesday, however, I didn't feel like a wimp. Instead, as if I were under a spell, I felt my chest grow huge. There was room for all sorts of emotions inside of me.

I'd reached the steepest part of the hill, where I often thought the trip should be over, yet there was farther to go. After all those years, I should have known that it took longer than I expected at that spot. Perhaps I lost my perspective when the car slowed down. Yet as I drove closer, I felt exhilarated instead of anxious or frustrated. I wasn't worried about arriving late and risking a shorter session, my usual preoccupation. I knew I'd make it. I knew Dr. Sanders would be there waiting for me. And if she were still meeting with someone else when I arrived, that warmth would be sustained.

Something strange was happening to me as I drew closer. My fog had lifted. The day had come to life. Familiar mailboxes and utility poles shone with new intensity—they practically spoke to me as I drove by. The sky had turned so blue it took my breath away.

I pulled up behind a red Honda in the office driveway. It belonged to a person whose appointments often occurred before mine. I felt a surge of love toward the patient. What a remarkable change for me, who, even though I was close to forty, feared being unwanted if another patient was near, as if he or she was a baby brother or sister, and my therapist was a mother whose affection could sustain only one child at a time. I walked down the drive and into the waiting room, savoring every moment. I took my time. Nothing was going to disappear.

My heart pounded a joyful tune. "Can you see it?" I wanted to shout, "I am real. Do you hear me? I am REAL!"

Almost three months ahead of schedule, I had just been born.

A month later, Dr. Sanders cancelled an appointment. Her uncle had died and she needed to attend his funeral. When she refused to add a make-up appointment to those we'd already scheduled for the last three weeks before the end of my therapy, I reacted as if she had disowned me—the world had come to an end. Beside myself with rage, I jumped from her couch onto my knees on the floor. "I hate you! I hate you!" I shouted while I pounded my fists on the hard wood. In the midst of my tantrum, I observed that a shadowy Dr. Sanders, still seated quietly in her leather Eames chair, had become two figures. As if I were in a dream, I knew that one was evil and one good.

"You have to stop," one of the figures said firmly, without raising her voice. "I can't let you hurt yourself."

As I continued to watch, the two greenish figures resolved into one. A moment later the ordinary, familiar Dr. Sanders was back. My rage had disappeared. I knew she loved me.

The intensity of my reaction left me shaken, but not afraid. I'd read about termination's process of revisiting earlier developmental stages on the way toward consolidating wholeness. The integrity of that dramatic reenactment—my reliving a young child's experience—affirmed my belief in therapy's promise: I would be strong and feel secure, safe on solid ground some day.

After my final session, Bill surprised me with a gold pendant to honor my therapy graduation. Engraved on one side was the date: *April 3, 1981.* The other side read, *Yes!*

CHAPTER EIGHTEEN

Working Out

October 1981

"Guess who has a job?" I shouted, rushing into the house. Jessica flew down the stairs, her little brother right behind her. "Yay, Mommy!" they chorused.

Bill popped his head around the corner from the kitchen, his face all grin. "No kidding?"

"Yippee! Yippee! Yippee!" I could have been my six-year-old, jumping up and down. "McDonald's tonight. Just like I promised. Grab your stuff."

During the ride I filled them in. "I had two interviews. Then Dr. Mann asked me to sit in on a couple's session and a family meeting. I actually said something, so he'll start paying me as of today."

"Mommy, don't look in the dining room." James's dark brown eyes opened wide in his earnest, round three-year-old's face. "It's a surprise."

Jessica bustled back and forth from kitchen to dining room, stopping to exchange whispers with her dad.

"Five more minutes," Bill said to me. "Scram."

I returned to the bedroom upstairs, grateful for time alone. It was Friday, the last day of the first week at my new job, and my head was spinning. Exactly seven minutes later, as I headed down the stairs, Jessica appeared. With the confident air of a senior Sherpa, she took my hand and guided me into the dining room.

A blue and white linen tablecloth covered the table, set with our wedding china. White candles glowed in heirloom silver candlesticks. A small stack of boxes, gift-wrapped, sat on the buffet beside the table.

"Surprise!" Three shining faces beamed back at me as I whooped, then laughed, then cried.

Bill had prepared escargot with butter, garlic, and parsley—our family's official Very-Special-Occasion dinner. He'd even bought a cake.

After dinner, I opened my presents. Bill, who had worked as apprentice to a local jeweler in Cleveland for most of his adolescence, had helped the children fashion their gifts from silver. They had shaped each piece and hand beaten its surface. James had made a spiral ring that fit perfectly on my little finger. Jess had designed a small pin, shaped like a basket of flowers. Bill gave me a cotton sweater I'd ogled in a catalogue we'd looked at together a few weeks earlier.

For months we'd been living on savings, watching every cent. Now, not only would I bring us income, I could embrace the career I'd been dreaming of for much of my life. Bill said he was ready to take care of the chores at home, to shop and prepare meals, to pick up the children when I could not, to take them to the doctor and stay home with them when they were sick. He would water the plants and pay the bills and feed the cats.

It sounded easy.

In the summer of 1981, ten years after my college graduation, I finally completed my dissertation. The work I'd intended to produce in a year or two, with my baby nestled serenely in a baby Snuggli carrier, had taken me six to complete. It turned out that I couldn't do it all. Nurturing little children required most of my attention, even with a willing co-parent.

My dissertation, *The Influence of Professional Affiliation, Institutional Affiliation, and Related Clinician Attributes on Psychiatric Diagnosis*, grew from my internship. Our ward had been run by a psychiatrist who wrote books about narcissism. Our patients, who had been admitted with a variety of psychiatric diagnoses, were regularly discharged with a diagnosis of Narcissistic Personality Disorder. We prided ourselves on our sophistication.

My dissertation demonstrated that from 1975 through 1978, in southern Connecticut, the personal and professional situation of the diagnostician had a significant influence on the diagnosis given. In other words, different diagnosing clinicians often came up with a variety of diagnoses when assessing the same type of patient, and those differences appeared to be connected with things like the clinician's profession (psychiatrist, psychologist, social worker, or psychiatric nurse), where he or she worked, and where they had trained. Like my VA unit and our narcissists. Like my adolescent psychiatric hospitals and me.

My hypothesis was important to me beyond its intrinsic value as a medical and sociological observation. I had an emotional need to make sure my early diagnosis of schizophrenia could be understood as a reflection of the psychiatric culture as it had been then: a product of the times. I hoped to demonstrate that the diagnosis had little to do with me. That it had to have been a mistake.

Again, the next step proved more complicated than I'd anticipated. In the six years between my clinical internship and actual graduation with a PhD, the rules governing the practice of psychology in Connecticut had tightened. To identify oneself legally as a psychologist required a license. A license required a PhD from an authorized clinical psychology program; social psychology would not suffice. Although much of my coursework and all of my clinical training had been within the psychology department, my PhD was in Sociology. Nothing could change the graduate department granting my degree.

To my dismay, several interviews that had initially seemed promising ended in disappointment; days later an apologetic official would call and withdraw the institution's offer, citing my degree. My emotional state swung between joy and despair like a carnival ride, flying upward when I was thrilled, tumbling down when I was bewildered and angry. I was becoming deeply discouraged. Then Dr. Sanders recommended me to a friend of hers, a child psychiatrist who was expanding his practice. Dr. Henry Mann opened a professional door that made the rest of my career possible. We worked together for almost nine years. His partner, the psychologist Daniel Miller, became my mentor.

Spring 1986

My watch showed three o'clock. On Tuesdays, that meant it was time for Andrew's appointment.

Andrew's mother flashed a brief, ambivalent smile as I descended the stairs from my psychology office in the small professional suite tacked onto the side of Dr. Mann's Victorian house. Square-set jaw and padded shoulders emphasized her angular frame, a great statue incompletely chiseled from its block of stone. She stood in the waiting area, close to the door, as if she hadn't yet decided to stay or to go. Andrew weaved and bobbed beside her, uncharacteristically silent. On most days, at home, at school, or in my office, Andrew McNeal squealed, rumbled, and popped as if a TV cartoon soundtrack played out of his mouth. His high squeaky voice rose and fell to fit characters and scenes.

"Hi, Matey! Whatcha doin' with that slicer dicer on my watch? Clop clop clop. ZZZZZZing!" He spoke quickly and rarely paused. "Hands off me, you wisecrackin' worm. I'll serve you in twelve pieces if you aren't careful. Dooooooing! whoop. whoop. AAhhhh....Help! NO. Gotcha!"

With his large pale face, outsized hands and feet, unusual height, and mockingbird voice, this well-scrubbed, blond, blue-eyed autistic child often appeared closer to one of his characters than a flesh and blood eleven-year-old boy. His special education teachers and family friends, who'd been around him for years, loved Andrew, but he frightened other children and adults who hadn't encountered him before.

Sometimes without warning, Andrew erupted in tantrums for reasons no one could figure out. He'd pound his stomach or flail his arms, howling like a hound at a full moon. Listening to the Everly Brothers on his Walkman was losing its power to calm him—as were threats to withhold the tape for him to play. Andrew hadn't attacked anyone directly, but at school they worried. Eventually, in his flailing he was bound to hit someone.

Mrs. McNeal's mission was to forestall that dread day. When Andrew was five she'd defied the state's recommendation to place him in a home for children with limited IQs. An angry social worker had accused her of neglect. "We're watching you," the social worker had said. "Child Services has authority to take him away at any time." This terrified Mrs. McNeal. Although six years had passed, she still hovered over Andrew, fluttering her wings like a vigilant blue jay, ready to peck anyone who dared wander too close to her nest. I wished I knew how to comfort the grieving, traumatized woman, whose entire life had become compressed into protecting her son.

With two years of psychotherapy sessions behind us, I wasn't afraid of Andrew. I'd watched him grow; at heart he was gentle. In my office on good days he and I played loose games we made up as we went along. We might take turns at Connect 4 or race little cars. Sometimes we shared jokes.

"Look at the fire engine!" I'd say, pretending to be startled, wildly gesturing toward the window. While he peered through the glass I'd move a Connect 4 chip, and he'd catch me. We'd laugh together, knowing it was a game. Once in a great while he'd play the same trick on me. On most days Andrew bobbed around and talked to himself, while I listened to his sound track and tried to catch some meaning or a feeling he might be intending to express. My challenge was to engage him in interactions that felt satisfying, so he could see other people as being worth his attention. I hoped to help him identify what he was feeling and enable him to connect his behavior with those emotions.

"Hi, Andrew," I said as I reached the bottom of the stairs. Andrew ignored me. He continued to bob up and down, circling his mother without making a sound, an abstracted smile on his soft, round face. As he moved his lanky, almost-six-foot body, he could have been an ancient shaman performing a religious dance.

Andrew's principal had sent him home again.

"When Morgan tried to sit next to him, Andrew started pounding on the desk and wailing," Mrs. McNeal explained, her eyes tracking her son. Apprehension dominated her etched, gray face.

"On the way to school I'd warned him to watch out for Morgan. For what?" Tight angry lines now gathered around her eyes. Rage swamped her when she couldn't control her child. Andrew's mother blamed herself for his autistic condition and everything else that had happened to him. Perhaps my hardest job as Andrew's therapist was to help his mother forgive herself.

Andrew continued to bounce around the entryway, swerving his body this way and that, still silent. He appeared oblivious to his mother's distress as she added details to the story. This week Andrew had completely stopped talking, she told me. His tantrums had increased.

During our years together, I'd come to realize that Andrew lost control and was banished from school with increasing frequency every April and May. With crocuses and daffodils popping out of the earth and leaf buds on trees daily reshaping the landscapes, I wondered if spring might unsettle an obsessive autistic boy for whom familiarity and routine were important components of coping. He didn't deal well with change.

"Okay, Andrew," I said, in a matter-of-fact but cheerful voice. "Your mama's worried about your behavior. Let's see if we can figure out what's up. Come on."

Like a galumphing puppy Andrew followed me up the narrow stairs to the angular room that served as my office. Once inside, he wandered around the perimeter several times, touching toys on the shelves, looking out each window, fingering the leaves on the ficus tree in the corner, before he settled, cross-legged, on the floor. Slowly he began to rock. I seated myself facing him, also on the floor.

"What's upsetting you, Andrew?" I asked. "Kids don't have tantrums without a reason. Something must be making you very angry." I knew my chances of getting a coherent response, or any response at all, were close to zero, but I'd nothing to lose. I'd seen enough flashes of contact at unexpected moments to persist.

"My job is to help kids figure out what they're feeling. Maybe if we understand that, you won't have to have tantrums." I moved a crate of blocks, some flexible dollhouse figures, and a few matchbox cars to within Andrew's reach. "Can you show me what's bothering you?

At first he gave no response. I leaned backward, my weight on my hands, hoping my spine wouldn't hurt. I tried to be patient. *Breathe*, I told myself.

Andrew stopped rocking and stared at the crate, focused and serious. Reaching toward the smooth maple blocks, he selected a large rectangular one and placed it on its side in front of him. He picked out a similar-sized block and placed it beside the first, repeating this move until he'd set a line of blocks end to end in front of him. Beginning with another large block, which he centered over the crack where the first blocks met, Andrew added a second row above the first. He used shorter blocks when he ran out of large ones. I watched as Andrew slowly and deliberately added more rows of blocks. He'd constructed a barrier between himself and me.

"Looks like a wall between us," I said.

Andrew continued to add blocks.

"Maybe you're angry because of the wall."

No response. He'd stopped building. The barrier appeared complete.

"Andrew," I said. "Do you want the wall there, or would you like us to figure out how to help you get through?"

He ignored me.

I stayed on the floor but inched toward the wall. Taking my time, I carefully removed two blocks from the center of his structure, shifting a longer block above so it wouldn't fall. The wall now had an opening, in effect a large door.

Andrew stared at me but didn't move.

I leaned forward, my face almost on the floor. I peered at Andrew through the door.

Bending toward the wall, he stretched out his arm in front of him. With his thumb and forefinger, Andrew pulled down an imaginary window shade to cover the space I'd created.

I let thirty seconds or so pass. Then with my fingers I pulled up the pretend shade.

Andrew smiled and pulled the shade down again. I repeated my pulling it up. Back and forth we continued, down-up, down-up, three, four, maybe six times. Eventually we stopped. I'd moved last; the shade remained up. Andrew rocked, his hands on his cheeks, while he sat on his side of the wall.

Very gradually, I shifted onto my knees. I picked up one of the plastic dollhouse figures that had been lying on the floor nearby, a blond boy about three inches tall. I pushed him through the now open door and set him down on the other side of the wall.

Andrew watched. He didn't take long to move the toy figure through the door to my side. I sent it back.

After some time with this exchange—his side, my side, his, mine—I stopped. I left the doll where it was. Angled low on the floor, propping myself up with my left elbow, I reached through the open space with my right hand and part of my forearm. I waited. Andrew stared, a smirky smile flickering at the corners of his mouth. Very slowly, I withdrew my hand to my side of the wall. I held my breath.

After a long pause, Andrew bent forward and extended his hand through the door.

"Welcome!" I said.

He laughed. His blue eyes sparkled. We shook hands through the door in the wall.

A sly grin continued to play on Andrew's face as we released our grip. I stayed quiet. For several minutes, we sat on the floor in companionable silence.

A more experienced me would have waited for Andrew to make the next move, no matter how late the session had run. That day, reluctantly, I broke the spell. "I'm sorry, Andrew. It's time to stop. We need to clean up."

He didn't hesitate. We returned the blocks to their crate. Then we left the room and descended the narrow stairs to the waiting area below.

Hearing our approach, Mrs. McNeal looked up.

"Hi, Mama," Andrew chirped. He waved.

As his good mood registered and relief spread across his mother's face, it felt as if the waiting room were filling up with flowers.

When I worked late nights, I always called home at dinnertime. Squeezing into the office manager's tiny space to use the telephone, I needed a few minutes to collect myself before I dialed. Joan's office was the size of a walk-in closet, equipped with a counter, shelves, filing cabinet, and pocket door. Her swivel chair left barely room for one small person to turn around.

I stretched and breathed deeply, the way I'd learned in childbirth class: *in through the nose, one, two; out through the mouth, one, two.* My hands automatically rubbed the sides of my belly for comfort while I wrestled with images from the day. There was a large, angry firefighter determined to hide the frightened, battered boy I sensed inside of him. Initially he and his wife had come to discuss difficulties with her son. Now he met with me himself. A golden-haired four-year-old watched her mother enumerate the ways this lively child was a monster. There was a lawyer, powerful in court, speechless and compliant at home with a sadistic mate. I pushed aside the thoughts of those people, trying to make space for me in the present. I wanted room to be Mommy, in the real world, with my own children.

That evening I disliked the dark out of doors and the silence in the room. I resented Sharon and Elaine, the other therapists who worked for Dr. Mann, who were already at home. I assumed that Dr. Mann, too, was with his children in his house on the other side of the wall of the addition where we treated patients.

It's only once a week. You could have it so much worse, I repeated every Wednesday. I knew my reaction was out of proportion; I felt the separation as keenly as if I'd been an abandoned infant left on the side of the road.

As I prepared to dial the phone number, I stretched, then cleared my throat to rid all evidence of ambivalence from my voice. In my best dramatic style, I wanted to present the wholesome mother I longed to be, the one who was never away from her children.

"Hi, Pumpkin," I burbled when Jessica answered the phone. "How was your day? How did your report work out?"

"I'm OK, Mom. When are you coming home?" Her voice sounded thin, flat. I pushed on.

"I'll be there by ten at the latest, but you'll already be asleep. I left you a note. Do you have any homework?"

"No, I did my homework. We're eating, so I should go. Daddy bought lots of stuff for tacos, and we get to make our own. James wants to talk to you."

"Okay. Good night, Sweetie. Enjoy your dinner. Sleep well. I love you."

"I love you, too, Mom. Good night."

"Hi, Mom!" James sounded chipper. "I made my own taco."

"That's great. I love you, James."

"I love you, too. Are you tired?"

"Yup. But I'll be home later. Sleep well, okay?"

I can't fool anyone. I slumped into the chair and hung my head. *I hate this job.*

Any psychotherapy practice required late appointments. I wanted to meet with the couples and families whose schedules required evening hours, but it meant that I didn't see my children before they went to sleep.

Separation from them had always been difficult. I theorized that my painful reaction came from never really bonding with my own mother, coupled with the fear that developed from being alone in a mental hospital. *Cool it! The misery's about you, not them,* I told myself. But nothing softened the grating sense of dread that I was causing my children pain, that I was guilty of letting them down.

To help us all on those nights when I worked late, I drew pictures with notes on index cards for James and Jessica. Having just turned three and six, they hadn't yet learned to read when I began working as a therapist. A few years had passed, but every Wednesday I still illustrated notes I set on their pillows before heading off to work in the morning. (As adults, years later, each one independently showed me a box in which they'd saved all of their notes from those days.)

I tried to reassure myself. James planned to be a clinical psychologist and a deep-sea diver when he grew up. A short time earlier Jessica had announced that she would be a psychologist and marry a man who stayed home with their children. *See? The kids probably aren't the ones suffering from this arrangement.*

Ever since his summers on Lake Erie as a child, Bill had loved to sail. The year James was born, we bought a small cruising sailboat with money Bill had inherited. We named her Free Verse for the light, the sky, the salt sea air, the music of wind, waves, and snapping sails as she made her way through the water—poetry in motion. Although our savings and income, which were dependent on Bill's stock portfolio until I secured my job with Dr. Mann, were soon depleted by a series of bad investments, we still had a summerhouse on the water.

Every August, Bill, the children, and I spent a week or two living on Free Verse. We lifted our anchor in Branford and sailed to harbors up and down the coast: Nantucket, Cutty Hunk, Martha's Vineyard, Block Island, Mystic, New York City, Port Jefferson, Shelter Island, Mattituck, and more. We swam off the boat or rowed our red rubber dingy to shore. We licked ice cream cones on islands and downed cocoa in fog. We collected seashells and read books aloud. We sang songs at sunset and played *I Spy* in the rain. It wasn't always wonderful. Bill and I argued, sometimes the children were sick. But overall, I loved it.

Bill deserved time off from his work as househusband and chief childcare provider, I thought. I supported his sailing trips with friends. Once I had a full-time job, though, I needed help when he wasn't home. Free after my father's death, my mother stayed with the children and me during the weeks when Bill was sailing. When the children were older, they stayed at her White Plains apartment during the week while I worked.

One curious incident marred the last otherwise perfect stay with their grandmother. I'd come to pick them up, and as they dragged their suitcases to the elevator down the hall my mother confronted me in a way I'd never seen before. "You're supposed to help children, not ruin them. *Where Did I Come From?*" Her tone curdled with contempt. "How dare you read that to your children?" I realized she was referring to a popular children's book we'd left on the same bookshelf that held *Goodnight Moon* and *Horton Hatches the Egg*. My mother had seen it a week earlier, when she'd stayed at our house.

"How dare you put those ideas into their heads," she continued. "Sex feels like being tickled by a feather? What are you doing to them?" She was furious. I couldn't speak. The children returned and she dropped it. *Man, is she old-fashioned*, I thought, and dismissed her outburst.

In general, my mother blossomed after my father's death. She enjoyed many friends and busied herself with countless projects. Women who had become widows earlier offered guidance and support. She traveled to England and Scotland, France and Spain, China, and Israel. She began to paint again. She told me how decades earlier, before I was old enough to walk, she'd once become so engrossed in a canvas that she'd forgotten to feed me. Unable to trust herself not to do that again, she had packed away her colors. Two years after my father died, my mother sold the family house and moved to an apartment downtown. She resumed art classes and made many artist friends. For several years she directed a major art exhibit in her town.

In 1986, in what would be her last summer, my mother led me through the art festival's maze of paintings set up on sidewalks and parks in the center of White Plains, stopping to chat with exhibitors, introducing me along the way. I saw her welcomed as a friend and treated with respect. I observed her easy conversations and watched her offer thoughtful answers to difficult questions. This impressive public person was new to me. Fully-engaged, fully-present, she expanded before my eyes, no longer the constrained, anxious, emotionally elusive woman I'd known as my mom. I was excited. I felt proud to be her daughter.

CHAPTER NINETEEN

The Right Thing

Autumn 1986

The art festival had barely ended when my mother's persistent stomach pain was diagnosed as esophageal cancer. Her doctor prescribed intensive radiation, to begin immediately. The newly bright, full-blossomed flower faded, her petals drooped. The confident woman I'd witnessed only weeks earlier disappeared. This shrunken version of my mother seemed almost incapable of asking for what she needed; she'd become an extreme version of my own diffident self.

By then I'd been working in Henry Mann's office for five years. Jessica and James, approaching eleven and eight, had moved on from their tiny school nearby and were traveling to elementary school in New Haven. When I could, I drove to White Plains to take my mother to radiation treatments or to appointments with her oncologist, a grumpy, arrogant man who had kept one of her friends alive for ten years through a series of cancers. Although her chances of survival were statistically less than 25%, after the radiation she accepted his recommendation for chemotherapy. Bill and I drove her to the hospital for chemo, where she was admitted for days at a time. He visited her when I was at work and the children were in school. My mother loved Bill, and he loved her. She was the best mother he'd known. His caring for her was a great comfort to both her and me.

As time passed, and the tumor advanced despite the awful treatments, I despaired of being able to do the right thing. Dr. Mann was telling me I could no longer leave work so often. I yearned for more time with my children. I also knew that I had to care for my mother. Friends of hers sent letters telling me she needed me. Yet she would not ask me to come. "I'm managing. You don't have to.…Your children need you. You were here two weeks ago."

I hadn't learned to be direct and clear enough myself to explain how much difference it would make for her to let me know she wanted me to help her. My need to support the family, my responsibility to my patients, my own wish to be at home, and my fears of burdening Bill, of making him angry with too much childcare if I were to spend more time away, all fought with what I knew in my heart was a profound longing to help my mother when she needed me.

For both Bill and me, hospitals triggered old, unrecognized fears. My mother, who had never been a big woman, shrank before our eyes. Between unnamed worries and our grief, we fought often, overreacting to inconsequential things.

My mother died early on a Monday morning, one week short of a year after the initial diagnosis. She was down to sixty-four pounds and needed an oxygen tank to breathe. She and I had spent Friday and Saturday of that weekend together. We sat for hours without words, my fragile mother cradled in my lap. As I had during the time I spent with Genny at the end, I felt our peace with each other. In those precious hours, our earlier emotional disconnection no longer mattered. Our hearts touched.

July 1987

In a large, gloomy, pseudo-modern church with my brothers Richie and Taylor, Richie's wife Bobbi, my nieces and nephews, Bill, and our young children all beside me, I sat taking stock. I looked around at my mother's friends, scattered like bread crumbs among the pews, some young but most of them old, too few to undo the feeling of emptiness in that dreary space. During her last year, my mother had withdrawn from her community. A few of her most loyal and understanding friends had insisted on calling, but she refused to believe that even they would tolerate her if she complained, so she kept them at a distance while she suffered. Gradually she had disappeared, her body and her spirit consumed by the cancer.

Although I grieved my mother's death, I knew it was best for her. She wanted to be with my father—that was her dearest wish. My heartache was for myself, for my own bleak spirit. In the months before she died, my mother and I had spent more time together than ever before. We'd finally connected emotionally. Yet in the end I'd failed to live up to my ideal of a good daughter—I hadn't given her the attention I should have, the attention she deserved. And I grieved for all those earlier years, when I'd felt unwanted and alone.

Why can't I cry? I readjusted myself in the uncomfortable pew. I wished I were sadder at that moment; I wished my loss felt larger.

I thought about my father, whose death also had been a blessing, bringing relief from pain and the indignity of his disfiguring disease. I'd felt compassion for his suffering, yet I'd not mourned his passing. Eight years later, I still felt nothing—no anger, no regret, no sorrow, nothing.

The call for Communion interrupted my reverie. My brother's family headed to the altar. Richie and Bobbi were devout Catholics; their children understood Communion.

I stood. I sat. I stood. Jessica and James stared at me, confused. "Come on," I said. I would honor my mother by bringing my children to the altar and we'd all receive Communion. Halfway there I thought better of it, but it was too late to turn around. The kids had no idea what to expect, so I just herded them along. I showed them how to open their mouths wide to receive the wafer the priest placed on each extended tongue. They followed me back to our pew. Bill looked bewildered. I hoped he wouldn't be angry, or ask me to justify this later. He wasn't; he didn't.

I returned to pondering the nature of my relationships. Something large had been missing in my connection with my parents. Had they caused that? Had I?

In the dimly lit church, the priest droned on, and the children wiggled. I wondered about the lives my parents had lived before I was born. What other losses might each have struggled with? Had they hidden them from each other or reviewed them together? As a child I'd lived in my own world, accepting without question what went on around me. Even as an adult, how easily I'd fallen into that absence of curiosity when I was with them. Why hadn't I learned more about my mother?

Maybe because she wouldn't let you? Remember both parents taught you that asking questions was rude. My psychologist voice added some perspective. I smiled at Jessica, who was showing her brother how to mime patty-cake without making noise. I mouthed a large "Thank you" and bent to pat each one. The funeral mass was almost over.

After my father's death my persistent anxiety had significantly diminished. *What will change now that she's gone?* It was too soon to answer.

For several months, I'd telephoned each morning to make sure my mother had survived another night. Every day since her death, I'd begun to dial before I remembered she wasn't there to answer. Though she rejected the emotional comfort I tried to offer, my mother had been grateful when I checked in to make sure she was awake—alive and awake. I mourned that connection.

As adults, my brothers and I had been spread wide across the country. We kept in touch by phone, but beyond weddings and funerals we rarely saw one another. Although I'd have said we'd always seemed close, after our mother's death we grew much more so. Time spent together— making funeral arrangements, cleaning out her apartment, dividing her things, working out details of her will—reinvigorated our small family. We honored her best by loving each other.

CHAPTER TWENTY

Here for Today

Spring 1990

I'd been working with Henry Mann for nine years. I'd developed my professional reputation and was supervising less-experienced clinicians in the group. I felt ready for my own practice. Among other accomplishments, my mother had made successful financial investments and left me enough money to build an office. Dan Miller, my supervisor, supported my move. Heather Sanders, my former psychiatrist, agreed to be my medical partner until I qualified for a license. With the blessing of two of the most important people in my life, I left Dr. Mann's group and established my own practice. By using her money, I could think of my mother as blessing me, too.

A year later, my lawyer successfully argued before the Connecticut State Psychology Licensing Board that I met the license requirements that had been in place during the mid-1970s, at the time I had received my training. Seven years after qualifying for a license in Massachusetts, I passed the exam in Connecticut.

To keep an eye on my blind spots, and to learn all I could from a master clinician, I continued to meet with Dan for supervision through the next seven years, until his death. By that time, he had become my mentor as well as my friend and confidant. He had welcomed Bill and me into his family.

Autumn 1993

"My theory is that you're the daughter of leftist Eastern European Jewish intellectuals. I assume you grew up in New York City; I don't see how you could understand Montana."

The tall, wavy-haired woman seated next to me sounded pleased with her hypothesis, daring me to disagree. I was tempted to point out her misapprehension—and I was intrigued that her fantasy wasn't so far from my own, although it certainly differed from the narrow suburban reality I grew up in. I paused to consider my response.

"What comes to mind when you imagine these leftist Eastern European Jewish intellectuals?"

She thought for a moment. "It's what I wish for myself, of course," she said, "but that doesn't change the fact that you had it. I envy you. I want to belong to your family."

I sympathized. *You'd never believe how much time I've spent in your position*, I thought.

"I'm important to you, for sure," I said, running my hand through my hair. I was looking for the right way to tell her she had no idea what she was talking about. "But you've created this particular picture of me—my parents, where I lived, my culture—without actually knowing any of the facts. How come?"

She stared at her hands for a while, then looked up. "I think I want to believe you really do understand suffering," she said. "But you're so calm and together, it's obvious that you've had a good life. And good parents. But they must have understood suffering. I want that. I want to know that my pain is accepted and understood."

I didn't get distracted, I thought, pleased with myself, as the door closed about a half hour later. I felt excited about the session. *Dan taught me well.* My patient had worked her way by association from me to her first therapist more than twenty years earlier, and from there to her own family, her fears of persecution, and scary secrets.

I looked through the skylight and thought about my own New York City Jewish intellectuals. They weren't my family, not directly. But they had been my teachers and my emotional parents: they were my past therapists and Dan.

What would she think if she knew how I really grew up?

For as long as I could remember, I suffered through dreams in which I found myself mistakenly imprisoned in a mental hospital, powerless to persuade anyone in charge to let me out. Sometimes I was frightened, and the dream had an urgent, scary quality. Sometimes I was embarrassed, worried someone I knew would see me there. Sometimes I had joined the meeting as a psychologist, and later, mistaken for a mental patient, discovered I couldn't leave. I always awoke exhausted.

One nightmare, dreamed not long after my mother died, began as a perfect summer's day. My mother and I stood in a spacious garden engaged in lively conversation. She wore a red satin ball gown, reminiscent of a bridesmaid's dress she had given me after my father died. I'd worn it to a Scottish Ball when Jessica was five. In the dream, she seemed younger, maybe forty-five, but as skinny as the sixty-four pounds she weighed not long before her death.

Suddenly my mother collapsed. The cheerful garden turned into a mental hospital ward drained of bright color. Two nurses' aides appeared on either side of her, propping her up, while brown gibberish, like diarrhea, flowed from her mouth. I knew this meant that my mother was psychotic and beyond reach. Appalled, I watched life spill from her with her dark words, her head lolling to the side, eyes rolled backward. Then she shrank, wilting into a pile of flesh-covered bones on the floor. I knelt close to her crumpled form, laying my face on a cold hand.

Even as I longed to maintain that contact, I knew I was in danger. Torn, I couldn't bear to leave her, but I had to flee. I pulled myself upright. The aides grabbed my arms as I moved to leave. Too late. They thought I was my mother, and they would never unlock the door.

A recurring nightmare so vivid I believed that I was awake appeared throughout my adult life. In that waking dream, as I called it, I jolted from sleep to discover a strange man beside me. He wasn't Bill. I recoiled in horror and often profound disgust. Sometimes I jumped from the bed to escape. At other times I lay still, frozen in the terror of nightmares that made any movement an invitation to disaster. Urgently I talked to myself: I explained that the man in my bed was my husband, that he was supposed to be there, but the fear from the nightmare persisted.

I didn't discuss that dream in my therapy with either Dr. Heller or Dr. Sanders. I couldn't explain why, beyond a wish to avoid appearing melodramatic. As with so many aspects of my life, I dismissed those dreams as residue from my hospital experience and neglected to consider them further.

By the time I reached graduate school, psychotherapy had become my religion. I'd lost faith in Catholicism before I was married. I questioned the existence of God, and I angrily resisted anyone who presumed to tell me what to believe. Bill shared my religious disillusion. Cherishing our children, Scottish country dancing, singing in the chorale, harvesting vegetables and flowers from the garden, and experiencing the communion of wind, sky, and water that came with sailing as a couple and as a family nourished our souls. For years that sufficed.

We'd been married eighteen years when Bill and I attended a New Haven Friends Meeting for the first time. Jessica wanted to recapture her mood from a Quaker camp she'd attended the summer before. Officially known as The Religious Society of Friends, Quakers have no formal creed but rather a set of testimonies derived from the central belief that God resides in every person. Even the concept of God is open. Goodness, the Light, the Spirit, and God are words used to identify something beyond comprehension. Respect for all life is central to the community. Meeting for Worship is a gathering of individuals seeking to connect to this presence within, who sit together in silence, unless one is moved to speak. I enjoyed sitting among other people who were seekers like me. I loved the Quaker focus on integrity and peace. Most of all I loved their acceptance. Among them, I could be myself.

Standing fast in the Light and searching for truth in the face of impossible odds made sense to me. I couldn't find God for myself, but I found my place in a community of seekers.

Winter 1996

The trees outside the Meeting Room windows made silvery patterns against the late winter sky; their stark beauty seemed like an embodiment of the Light. Inside the room, thirty or forty people had gathered for Worship. Their silence wrapped me in sweet, hopeful comfort, like the stillness just before dawn on a mountaintop or a summer pond holding all the world in perfect reflection.

Motionless, I sat suspended to hear beyond what I knew. By setting aside my active consciousness—a feat I couldn't completely master—I made room for other kinds of awareness. Sometimes out of the midst of that place, new ideas, new ways of looking at things, and new ways of solving problems quietly emerged.

This stillness in the Quaker Meeting room matched a tear rolling down my cheek. It was a particular kind of silence. Alive, it moved, as my tear moved, making no sound but having an effect. Every now and then, a restless toddler in the corner where we'd placed the couches for families wiggled, making her jacket rustle. Her mother handed her a cloth book, which she'd taken from her purse on the floor. But even their exchange didn't disturb the moment. I marveled at the ability of small children to manage the room of quiet. *They must feel the peace,* I thought.

That peace left me without borders for my grief. It flowed out of me in tears that sprang from some deep crater beneath my ocean floor. I hadn't realized they were there.

According to Quakers, you never knew from where the word of God would come, so it was important to pay attention and consider with care anything spoken out of the silence of the Meeting. I couldn't anticipate what I might discover within myself when I was there.

I felt most like a reasonable, competent adult when I was in my psychotherapy office on the far side of the garage.

Winter 1998

My office chair showed years of wear. On the arms, a thin layer of padding between the twill and the wood had disintegrated and turned to a powder that felt lumpy and uneven under my hands. If I gripped the ends too tightly, yellow dust trickled out through the seams when I let go. The once-elegant striped silk—shades of blue, rust, and burgundy, dominated by silvery gray—appeared tarnished and dull. On the companion wing chair—a broader, deeper, softer version, set at an angle next to mine—colors both at the top of its arms and the edge of its seat had become indistinguishable from one another, a grayish blur growing whiter, like the edges of my hair.

My left hand ached. I was focused so intently on the woman seated on the couch across from me that it took me a while to realize that my tight hold on the chair's arms caused the pain. I moved my hands to my lap. I forced myself to inhale, then pushed the air slowly through my chest and arms, down into my wrists and from there to my fingertips. I was imagining Dan Miller, Stanley Heller, and Heather Sanders as part of me: fortification to make me strong. I was feeling intimidated, and I wanted to be able to hear, without preconceptions, what she was saying.

Tall and beautiful, Susanna reminded me of Grace Kelly, except she was too thin. An accomplished professional in her mid-forties, Susanna had sought help because, "I'm afraid I'm losing my mind." Overwhelmed by responsibilities at work and by her compromised personal situation, she could barely function in her professional world, although she continued to be admired and sought after. Susanna was addicted to OxyContin. "I'd die without it," she explained. She hadn't told me this when we started.

It had taken only a short time to see how desperate Susanna was, perhaps because she tried so hard to hide it. "I never thought of myself as someone who would talk to a therapist," she admitted in our first session. "I'm a very independent person. I expect to manage myself well."

Her chalky, thin cheeks and dark, haunted eyes belied her confident words. The forced cheer sounded hollow. She mentioned her concerns in passing, as if she were talking about the weather. "My boyfriend tells me I scream in my sleep and keep him up...They love me at work, but if I make another mistake there I'm out." *A few rain showers likely in the afternoon. Possibility of thunder.* She turned away from me to look out the window, running her fingers through her beautifully trimmed blond hair. "Not that I'd really mind," she added. "I could use a rest. Trouble is, large debts and no money. I'm successful, but then I blow it." *Isolated areas may experience strong winds and hail.*

By the end of her story, I knew that we would need to meet frequently to maximize any chance of helping Susanna save her job (she directed a geriatric clinic in our town) and maybe even her life. I worried for her.

Dan had taught us to treat every session as its own unique encounter, to attend to the process unfolding in each moment. I had never climbed a mountain or flown an airplane, but I had learned to approach therapy one step at a time, knowing that steps could take place on several levels at once. About a month into Susanna's therapy I took one of those steps.

"You hold many contradictions: an abusive father, a self-centered mother who abandoned you and your brothers, a grandmother who loved you. Your circumstances and your own resources forced you to take care of yourself and your siblings. You're still taking care of others." I paused. I spoke gently. "Who takes care of you?"

Her eyes filled with tears, but her tone was defiant, "I take care of myself."

"The drugs tell the same story," I continued, as kindly as I could. "You replay your early plight: you depend on them for survival. Instead of protecting you, they, too, are preempting your life."

In the long silence that followed, Susanna had turned again to the window, her face a mask I could see only in profile. Then she looked toward me, and for the first time we connected. "Can you help me?" Her tone was urgent. She pleaded with her eyes, before she lowered her head to stare at her hands clasped in her lap. "I can't go to a rehab program. If anyone finds out about this, I'll lose my job."

I waited before I replied.

"The most difficult part is more than detox," I said, speaking slowly to let the idea sink in. "It has to do with trusting me, when you have no experience with trust. You carry tremendous emotional pain, which you're trying to manage by yourself. This therapy process takes a long time; it's very hard work."

"I've run factories; I've created businesses and sold them for lots of money. I've managed large departments. I have a business degree and a medical degree. I can do anything I set my mind to. I've never asked anyone for help before. But I can't sleep. My job torments me. My relationship with my boyfriend is terrible. I have nothing left to lose." Susanna held her head in her hands.

Looking at her I saw a desperate child, all alone—*me maybe?*—and I wanted to cry. I caught myself. I looked again and imagined a landscape of life unfolding, an organic process within which change takes place. *Give her room to find her own way,* I thought. I waited.

Susanna raised her head. She looked straight at me, eyes bright, voice quiet but steady. "I'll make the commitment, if you will."

"Our work is cut out for us," I said, wanting her to hear the *us.* "And we'll need medical help with the detox. But if you're ready, I'm ready, too."

Gradually, the tension softened. After a long pause, Susanna smiled. I inhaled deeply and noticed my hand clamped onto the arm of the chair. As I released my fingers, yellow powder sprinkled onto the floor.

"I think we can stop here for today," I said, reaching for my appointment book. "I'll see you Monday."

CHAPTER TWENTY-ONE

Look What I've Overcome

During my entire twenty-one years of therapy that ended with Dr. Sanders, I did what I could to avoid the topic of sex. Regardless of who my psychiatrist was, I rarely discussed fantasies or my own sexual activity. I usually blanked at their questions; before long they'd give up. By the time I concluded therapy, I'd been married almost twelve years.

When Dr. Sanders did ask about sexual activity I answered with generalities. "We do it a lot...It's okay....He wishes I liked it as much as he does." I didn't tell her about Bill's frustration with my sexual passivity, or that he periodically stormed about, expounding on his disappointment and my deficiency.

Following Bill's sexual-misery outbursts, I would become temporarily more active. I initiated sex every day. I agreed to take my turn more often. I tried especially hard to satisfy him. Bill was not to be appeased, however, and, ultimately, he was right: my newfound passion flowed from a shallow well. I wanted to make him happy, but if I were honest I'd say that I especially wanted to avoid the hostile, petulant schoolboy his outrage made him become.

We enacted a similar pattern around our different language styles. Like everyone, Bill wanted to feel in control of his situation. For him, this meant that he knew exactly what was going on. When we were together, he expected to maintain emotional balance by managing the scene based on his understanding of my intentions. For Bill, it was simple physics: she moves here, and I move there, and the consequences will be predicable and reliable.

My style, on the other hand, tended toward poetry. I thought out loud in elaborate images. I spoke before my ideas were fully formed, meandering among possibilities, landing in places I might not have intended. If the initial effort failed to capture my emotional gist, I'd discard it without another thought and move on, or I might rephrase and approach it from a different direction.

When Bill thought I was clear but critical, he would seize my initial statement and react to the insult, even after I'd revised my account; he wouldn't let me take it back. On the other hand, if he didn't immediately understand where I was headed, he quickly became frustrated, because I left him with no bearings from which to proceed. He accused me of being elusive. I thought he was unreasonable. We struggled this way for thirty years.

Spring 2000

"What are you talking about?" Bill said, interrupting my barely begun complex, compound sentence. "I can't deal with your being so vague."

"Duh? If you'd let me finish you might find out. Your being nasty like this is why I dread talking to you," I replied, turning away from him. I never looked at Bill directly when I was angry.

"'Nasty,' eh. 'Dread'?" Then what are you doing here with me?"

"I didn't mean all the time. I didn't mean nasty as in terrible. I like our conversations most of the time."

"You said it. I didn't."

"I'm sorry. I really didn't mean to hurt you," I said, which had been true, although by then I was ready to hit him. I was careful not to say anything mean, however. I stifled my ugly comments—*Jerk! Idiot! F* you!*—holding my breath to contain the adrenaline's force. By the time I exhaled I'd forgotten what had started the argument and any points I'd intended to make.

Erasing my angry words erased unpleasant incidents as well. If you'd asked me, I'd have said that I had an unusually fine marriage. "Most of the time we're in love," I'd have said. "We have been since the early days." A walk down the street hand in hand lifted my spirits and warmed me all over.

It was discussing our children that sent Bill and me to marriage counseling. We couldn't agree on how we should understand them as they made their own lives away from home. In my heart they would always be children, in need of our attention. I felt privileged to grant their every wish, honored to be asked. Bill saw them as adults who made their own choices. When they didn't return telephone calls or take his advice, he felt abandoned and angry, insignificant in their lives. He resented my eagerness to serve them.

Sometimes, on visits home Jessica confronted Bill about the effect of his anger during her childhood. Instead of acknowledging her complaint, Bill's hurt turned to outrage, and he blamed her for their difficulties. As I saw it, we had raised our children to question authority. Like many in our generation—and most of the parents who made up our tiny school community in the early years—we valued assertiveness and autonomy of thought. We respected our children's intelligence; we encouraged their participation in family decisions, we gave weight to their ideas. Yet, in practice, Bill was devastated whenever Jessica questioned his authority.

Once Bill and I decided our marriage needed help, we made an appointment with Jacky, a clinical social worker recommended by a friend. "I know five couples who remain together today thanks to her," our friend had told me.

I could tell that Jacky enjoyed helping people from the way she gave details in her directions to her office before our first visit. "You'll see the stairs on the left, just after the fish tank and before the bathroom. They're steep, so take your time. There are couches upstairs where you can wait."

She was small and dressed mostly in black. She made decaf coffee for her *clients*. As a social worker, she felt it wasn't appropriate to call the people she treated *patients* the way I assumed most therapists did.

Jacky gave practical advice, eager to help no matter at what level, from brands of nose drops to how to listen better to each other, to where to look for a job. At the same time she was careful not to intrude or to give answers one would be better off arriving at oneself. She was modest about her work—"I just look at what's available to solve problems"—but she was well-informed and had a great deal of experience.

When she asked us each for a short autobiography, Bill and I both took Jacky's request seriously. We spent hours working on our stories. We carefully filled out the brief Meyers-Briggs questionnaire she gave us.

The autobiography I produced was well-written, I thought. It touched on my hospital history and shock treatment; it emphasized that Bill and I had a great relationship. Our only problem was talking about our daughter, who was having a difficult time in graduate school. I ended with something about how much Bill and I had loved Scottish Dancing together and that I hoped with Jacky's help to dance wholeheartedly with him again.

My picture of our relationship—and my life—was completely glorified. Bill's anger; my hidden rage; our sexual difficulties; and my passive, repressive, self-demeaning style had been edited out of consciousness. When I told Jacky that I was extremely fortunate because no one had ever mistreated me, I was utterly sincere. I had given it a great deal of thought.

Jacky could be direct in a way that sliced straight to the heart of an issue. "That's crazy," she said in response to my assertion of no mistreatment. Away from her office, Bill referred to Jacky as a clown, complete with red rubber nose and big orange wig. His description infuriated me, but when I protested he became indignant. He interrupted her in the sessions, correcting her vocabulary, asking her why she wasn't doing thus and so, as if he were the expert on marriage counseling and she were flunking her job. Afterward he raged that she and I ganged up on him.

Since Bill was critical of everything about Jacky, I became her apologist. I liked her coffee set-up, her style of therapy, her advice, her questions, her explanations. She was careful, respectful, and she was also direct. She asked us about sex. She brought attention to my dissociation—only at first she called it "dis-association," which many people did, but which was incorrect.

Problems with anger dominated our sessions. At home, Bill's hostility spilled over in ways he didn't recognize. For my part, I might be roiled by adrenaline in rage, but my thoughts and the angry feelings disappeared when I tried to speak of it. A couple can't resolve disagreements if one partner, in essence, vacates the scene. I began to understand how Bill might experience my emotional flight as provocative.

Jacky helped me see that I didn't lack anger; rather, I lacked access to it. She used the metaphor of a Magic Slate, the drawing toy we'd played with as children. I simply lifted the plastic film on which I'd drawn any experience of anger and erased it from awareness. However, she noted, the gel-filled cardboard bottom layer carried indentations from every line drawn. Eventually that made clear new pictures impossible.

My first twenty years remained a large blank in my mind, yet I had never felt angry at the hospital doctors whose treatment had obliterated my memory. I had an unrealistically rosy picture of my most important relationships. Clearly, I was stuck. Bill had had his own psychiatrist for years. We decided that in addition to our marriage counseling, I would meet with Jacky for individual therapy to see if I could discover those missing feelings. "I'm sick of being cut off," I told her.

My often dissociated, emotionally disconnected, "otherworldly" state in the sessions raised questions I couldn't answer. Not long into my own therapy with Jacky, we decided it was time to research my hospital records. "I need to know more about my past."

"You could look at this two ways," Stanley Heller replied when I called to ask his advice about how to retrieve my records. "On the one hand, they say, 'The truth shall set you free.'" I held my breath: this was what I was after. "On the other hand, many would counsel, 'Let sleeping dogs lie.'"

Darn! I hung up the telephone sensing that my esteemed friend was on the sleeping-dog side. *He probably doesn't want me to see what he wrote about me,* I supposed. *I'm not worried. That was a long time ago.*

"I've decided to send for the records from those hospitalizations when I was a teenager," I said to Malcolm, one of the friends at Quaker Meeting. "I'm ready to find my 'lost life.'"

"Are you sure you want to do that?" Malcolm had asked, looking worried.

"Yup. I'm too incomplete," I explained. "I don't remember my first twenty years. Before you know it I'll be sixty. And I still don't know who I am."

Even Bill's psychiatrist voiced concern, which annoyed me.

"If he thinks I sound reckless, then he doesn't understand how it feels to be missing a chunk of yourself," I said. I'd spent my adult life confabulating about childhood and avoiding any reference to my adolescence. That felt shabby, lacking integrity. As if I'd made myself up based on a character from a story I'd been told.

My children were grown, my professional standing secure. I felt strong and connected to my Quaker community. It was time to attend to my unresolved past. Years earlier, when I'd seen my high school transcript showing a Regents math score of 98% in my junior year next to a 54% a year later, I'd felt a surge of rage. Fearing resentment's ugly grip, I decided at that moment to move on. *What's done is done.* I sealed my lost years and the shock treatment into a vault and walked away. Now, with Jacky to protect me, I felt ready to unseal that door. Maybe I would never remember details of my childhood, but at least I could learn what went on when I was in the hospital.

My understanding was that I'd received fifty-four shock treatments—three sets of twenty, cut short by six when they gave up. Yet, this had to be incorrect. How could any hospital have allowed that many shock treatments, especially for a person so young? I intended to uncover the facts.

I also dismissed worries about the impact of the records, because I believed that my faulty diagnosis and consequent mistreatment had been mistakes of the times. "If it had happened thirty years later, we'd have had family therapy," I told close friends in whom I confided. "I never would have been hospitalized." The truth could only help.

I found others' fears that reading the records might disrupt my life insulting. *Not me,* I thought. *I can handle anything. Look what I've overcome.*

PART THREE
Lost and Found

CHAPTER TWENTY-TWO

One of Those

May 2001

The entry area was packed by the time I arrived, although people continued to stream in. Crowds of professionals and politicians, social and civic leaders, were gathering for a benefit conference to celebrate the fortieth anniversary of the founding of Fellowship Place, a community center in New Haven for people with mental illness.

Tables filled with hors d'oeuvres and wine rimmed the rotunda of an elegant oak-paneled Yale reception hall outside the auditorium. Two Fellowship Place violinists playing Mozart greeted enthusiastic guests, although chattering voices quickly drowned out the music. As we flowed into the auditorium, I met a social worker I knew slightly from Quaker Meeting. She and I found a spot together on the far side of the room where we could lean against a wall. By then all the seats had been taken.

Famed authors William Styron and Kay Redfield Jamison sat at a table onstage. They were there to discuss ways social stigma complicated identification and treatment of mental illness. Each gave harrowing examples of their personal experience with depression and bipolar disorder, describing the shame that made already heartbreaking emotional pain even worse. Then they turned to the stunned audience and implored each of us to consider our own psychiatric history.

"How many of you have recovered from depression, schizophrenia, and other disabling mental illnesses?" Kay Jamison asked. Self-conscious rustling rippled through the room. A few well-dressed individuals froze. Some sneaked sideways glances at the crowd. Except for a few Fellowship Place graduates, no one raised a hand.

"Fear of stigma keeps you silent," she continued. "Yet the example of your success stays hidden unless you speak up." If accomplished men and women shared their stories of recovery from mental illness, they told us, stigma and hopelessness could be modified, even overcome.

Inspired, I turned to the Quaker standing beside me. "I'm one of those," I whispered, barely inclining my head so she could hear. Clara spoke without moving, her face straight ahead. "Me, too," she said.

I'd taken part in several of those whispered exchanges over the years. I'd admitted to certain trusted friends or individuals with similar pasts that I'd been troubled as an adolescent, hospitalized even. Two or three decades after the fact, that didn't sound so terrible—a youthful indiscretion, not unlike my friend who crashed the family car the first time she got drunk, or the one who spent the summer after her freshman year of college at her boyfriend's apartment while her parents thought she was in the dorm.

Yet Clara and I never pursued our revelations further or mentioned our brief exchange again. I didn't tell her that I'd sent for my psychiatric hospital records a few weeks earlier, and that I was expecting them soon in the mail.

Even from a distance, I could identify the small white truck making its way down the narrow country road. Spring's afternoon light had drawn me out for a walk, and I was on the return stretch. Yellow primroses and multi-colored pansies brightened yards around modest raised ranches, colonials, and split levels scattered along the quiet street. I enjoyed my neighborhood. Children played hopscotch and catch in the road. Dog walkers stopped to chat. Most of the houses were around thirty years old, and several families had lived there almost that long. For Bill and me, it was twenty-five.

I tried to focus on the day, breathing in the color of the Japanese maples, which shone like red glass in the sunlight. Spirea bushes taller than I bowed with blossoms—they looked like they were covered in snow. But as the truck moved closer, I walked faster. I needed to get home. Maybe the package was already there.

The young woman who delivered our mail slowed the truck and waved when she saw me. She picked up a large gray envelope, which she held out the open door. I felt the scene jump, as if time had burped. *What does she want?* I thought. As the mail carrier handed me the envelope with "New York Presbyterian Hospital" printed in a corner, I recovered my presence of mind. I thanked her for the personal delivery. Ears ringing, I finished my walk, feigning calm. I smiled and waved as I passed two of my neighbors.

In the house, I ran straight to the sunroom, tearing open my envelope along the way. Breathless, I flopped onto the couch. Then I paused. Slowly I moved to sit upright, forcing myself to inhale. Heady perfume from fat pink and white peonies stuffing a vase on the glass coffee table suffused the air. The room glowed, lit by late-afternoon sun. With the fearful reverence of a midwife delivering her first newborn, I lifted the heavy folder from its package. I moved my fingers across my name and case number on the label. I held my breath as I raised the cardboard cover and confronted the first page. Awe quickly succumbed to voraciousness. I began to read.

After the admission note came the hospital's psychological assessment:

New York Hospital, Westchester Division
PSYCHOLOGICAL REPORT
June 7, 1960
Miss Perez is an intelligent, creative, and imaginative youngster who seems
to be slipping into a quicksand-like illness...deeply depressed with suicidal
preoccupations and fantasies. She has been able to maintain a facade of
functioning, but is paying dearly for it in terms of the energy consumed by
her obsessive patterns. On the Rorschach, there are indicators of catatonic
turbulence, deep depression, and suicidal concerns. The general picture
is one of an insidious illness made somewhat more hopeful by some still
remaining signs of vitality.
—J.D. PhD

Whoever wrote this sounds kind, I thought. *Although she's a bit overboard*
with the illness imagery.

 Insatiable, enthralled, I continued all day and night. Other than occasionally interrupting myself to pee, I didn't stop. Bill's concerns were
dispatched with a wave of my hand, "Don't say anything. I need privacy.
Please just leave me alone."

 Our little calico cat, Fuegito, kept me company. She tucked herself
under my arm. She climbed up my back to sit on my shoulder. When
I slumped into the pillows, she cuddled in the crook of my neck. She
never left me.

 Several psychiatrists had written detailed notes.

New York Hospital, Westchester Division
June 4, 1960
Since her admission the patient, as to the extent that that she was allowed,
spent a great deal of time by herself in her room and when she was asked
to come out with the group has furtively occupied herself on the outskirts

of that group in such solitary activities as reading. She has likewise, in the therapy program of the hospital, given minimal participation, protesting her gross lack of ability. In psychotherapy, she displays the same kind of passive resistance. Though obviously a girl of considerable intelligence, her productions, even in answer to specific questions, are of an obviously sparse and intentionally uncommunicative sort. Thus, although she obviously commands a superior vocabulary, she can only describe herself as "crumby" and it may be said that her participation in psychotherapy is, indeed, no more than a crumb of what it might be.

—*Dr. Ryan*

Dr. Ryan's frustration with my difficulty speaking and his lack of sympathy for the paralyzing fear he characterized as hostile resistance filled me with shame. I felt profoundly misunderstood. Despite all my professional sophistication, I couldn't separate my sense of my essence from his contempt. Mesmerized by stories that transported me directly into the early hospital years, I read and reread through to the last page, far into the night.

New York Hospital, Westchester Division
MENTAL STATUS
August 10, 1960
The patient was neatly groomed, fearful but cooperative. Voice was a barely audible whisper and there was much blocking. There was little facial expression other than a vague sadness. She kept her hands rigidly clasped. She looked much younger than her age and appeared to stare off into the distance as though unable to converge her gaze on nearby objects. (Arieti has described both of these physical characteristics as frequent findings in catatonic schizophrenia.) She stated that she was depressed and longed for death so that she could cease to be "a bother." Her feelings of worthlessness

amounted to an obsession to which she made continual reference...Judgment and insight were lacking.
—Dr. O'Connell

I dragged myself to bed in the dark early hours of morning.

With daylight, I returned to the sunroom. Wrapped in an old blanket, I huddled on the couch, shivering. Purple and white pansies, yellow begonias, and vivid pink impatiens fluttered in window boxes just outside the glass. Under a clear blue sky, the beautiful world around me seemed far away—unreal and meaningless.

What's happened? I wondered. *How can I be like this?*

Get a grip, another voice in me responded, not unkindly. *You have responsibilities, you have work to do. You've got to get a grip.*

But I had no answers and no grip. I sat, barely moving. Hours passed.

"How about some tea?" Bill offered. His face looked pale and tired. "Can I help?" he asked again. "Anything I can do?" he asked a few hours later. "Tea?"

"Tea is good," I said. I could tell he needed some way to feel relevant. Sometimes I could only nod. "I need time to process," I said, when I could speak. "I still need to be alone, if that's okay."

"Sure," he said. It wasn't really okay. He didn't understand why I was so upset or why he couldn't help; I hadn't found words to explain. I worried he was angry.

I pored through the thick chart several times. I recorded dates and the number of shock treatments received. I calculated the total. I double-checked. I checked again. The sum was eighty-nine. Eighty-nine electroshock treatments.

Eighty-nine shock treatments. For most of the week I walked around dazed and preoccupied, counting, counting, and counting some more. I made charts and diagrams and lists, which I arranged and rearranged.

No matter how I tried, the number didn't change. *Eighty-nine shock treatments.*

June 17, 1960: Has started on shock.

August 28, 1960: Course of 25 EST completed this month.

April 18,1962: Electroshock therapy stopped after twenty consecutive treatments.

November 18, 1962: EST series started and completed after 18 treatments.

April 17,1963: After a completion of a regular series of 20 EST treatments two months ago patient was placed on weekly maintenance EST treatments which were discontinued 2 weeks ago after a total of 6.

Once my stunned disbelief wore off, I sank into mourning. I grieved for what I might have been. Nevertheless, I had to bring myself to function in the present world among my colleagues, my patients, and the everyday strangers in the supermarket or on the street who had no idea of my situation. They couldn't see the hospital pajamas or the terrified girl. They didn't know what was missing, what possibilities had been burned away inside my brain.

A package from PI arrived exactly one week after the envelope from New York Hospital. PI was the hospital I had thought of as home. Its staff and patients had been my family—where I'd learned about the world. In a trance induced by what I'd already read, I consumed the next set as if I were a desperate addict, the words an irresistible drug. Nothing mattered but learning about my past.

Again I found myself sucked into a time warp, transported backwards, as if I'd become that twenty-year-old young woman who looked and acted like an early adolescent girl. I lost my bearings. At times I slipped underwater. I feared I would drown.

Another part of me merely observed. I was impressed with the detail in the handwritten records; no one I knew kept notes like that. As an experienced clinician, I could see troubling implications in the descriptions of my symptoms and behaviors. I appeared more disturbed than I had believed. My old explanation—that there had been a misunderstanding and I was in the hospital by accident—no longer sufficed.

For days after the records arrived, I rarely left the house. Grief weighed so heavily that I struggled to move from one room to another. I fought to pull myself together for my patients in my office, and afterward, I collapsed at home.

A few weeks later, Bill left for a week's sailing with friends. Initially, I'd felt relief: one less person to feel responsible for. And I enjoyed the quiet. I had no need of conversation. I liked eating whatever and whenever I chose. I fixed myself popcorn and ate ice cream straight from the carton while reading magazines and newspapers. I fried onions with peppers or tomatoes from the garden. Often I settled for cereal—I didn't have to cook.

Soon, however, harsh thoughts began to intrude, questioning my integrity, taunting me with images of dead animals and babies, calling me a whiner when I became upset. Before long, those thoughts had invaded every open space. As another Sunday arrived, I realized that I needed live voices to counter my own toxic internal ones. I missed the nourishing silence of Friends' Meeting, and I craved the company of good people I could trust.

The grim cloud that had enveloped me at home persisted as I drove to the Meetinghouse. I watched myself smile as I shook hands with the greeter at the door. Like a child who knew she should seek help from a neighbor when a hurricane threatened, and her mother wasn't home, I turned to those Quakers for the security and acceptance I could not give myself.

I found a seat in the farthest corner of the large Meeting room. *I'll be safe here*, I thought.

It was a beautiful June morning. Sun shone through the trees, making golden patches on the hardwood floor. The day's heat hadn't yet struck, and the various people assembled there—families with little children, elderly couples, widowed women, single adults of all ages, most familiar to me, some troubled, most accepting and caring—appeared comfortable in T-shirts and trousers, shorts and sun dresses. Although some of the children wiggled in their seats or pawed their parents, the peaceful quiet central to Meeting was settling over the room.

As the silence deepened, I felt myself sink into another reality–a scene barely formed, a memory just beyond reach. A foggy mist developed, surrounding me. Vague figures slowly, incompletely emerged. Whispery voices, auditory shadows, brought me to an old puzzle: it was almost twenty years earlier and my daughter was young, in elementary school. Her best friend's mother was dying….*Did I promise Catherine I'd take care of her daughter after her death, or had I only thought to promise? Did I give my word?* Later…voices in an unintelligible language, sounding like trouble, frantic exchanges between my daughter and her friend. Did these things really happen? I couldn't say. The figures had no faces, the words had no syllables, the gray cloud muffled everything, and it all seemed far away…

In the Meeting room an elderly man rose to speak. I adjusted my attention and half listened. "My back has been so painful I can barely walk. This morning I had planned to stay in bed rather than come to Meeting, but I thought I'd at least step outside for some sun. That's when I saw the bird. She sat on a nest she'd made in the eaves of my porch." He went into some detail about the intricacies of the nest.

"So today I bring hope," he said. "Her work inspired me to come."

Hope, I repeated to myself. *Hope?*

I slipped back to the memory of another summer: my family and I were visiting Cape Cod with friends during a vacation. We were taking a walk. My daughter, still young, listed for me all of her transgressions in life, as if expressing some profound anxiety about herself. *Why? Was she worried about going to a new school? Was there anything else?* My heart trembled. Was there something I hadn't seen? As my own mother did when I needed her, had I looked away? Fog rolled over me again, while on both sides and in front of me, the community of Quakers continued in silent worship.

Earlier memories appeared. The night was late. I was a child—maybe ten, maybe twelve—in my bedroom in White Plains. The house was quiet and dark. I heard the bedsprings creak in my parents' room, the shuffle of my father's feet on the floor. Suspended motionless in my own bed, I could trace his movements as he left the room. I heard my door shift and footsteps moving closer....

My thoughts refused to form coherent patterns. But fluttery convulsions made my stomach jump; my arms and chest were vibrating. I opened my eyes and looked around me. Nothing outward had changed.

Although I made no sound at all, tears flowed down my cheeks. I couldn't stop them, no matter how hard I tried. My nose ran. Liquid overspread the space above my top lip and landed on my tongue. I could taste the salt. Yet I couldn't sniff without drawing attention to myself. Even the *shish* of a tissue slipped from my pocket would interrupt the silence.

The realization that I was about to drown in a torrent of tears and runny mucus jolted me into the present. I felt like a person in a science fiction movie who had wandered in from another dimension. I was in

Meeting with a group of earnest people who had no idea that I was no longer one of them. At the close of worship, I rose and, without a word, walked out of the room and the building, while the rest of the community greeted each other with handshakes and hugs.

As I drove home from New Haven, fragments of thoughts whirled through my head. Stop signs, lane dividers, awareness of speed and route appeared and disappeared. Soon I found myself in my driveway, not sure how I'd arrived.

Distracted by the alternate universe into which I'd fallen, I was glad to be alone. Better not to have to try to explain all this to Bill.

I left my car and hurried into the house. Fuegito bounded to greet me, as she always did. I ignored her. The hurricane I'd tried to avoid had arrived full force. I set my purse on the kitchen counter, but I kept walking.

It really could have happened.

Of course not! You're a fool.

I paced, first back and forth, then circling the kitchen island.

I'm not the person I thought I was. My life is changed forever.

You're an idiot. This is self-indulgent rot.

I stumbled into the counter. I staggered away.

My stomach jumps at just a word, the merest thought. I can't be making this all up.

It doesn't mean anything. You are a desperate twit trying to get attention.

I'm not the person I thought I was. Could that stuff with my father really have happened?

Dizzy and exhausted, I sank into a sturdy kitchen chair, hunched in on myself. I rocked, wrapping my arms tightly around myself so I wouldn't break apart into pieces.

I understood what was going on. *My not seeing: that's dissociation. That's how it works. It makes you not know.* Identifying my own dissociation unlocked links to split off parts of my past. With each new piece of evidence, more tumblers clicked into place. I couldn't stop.

I struggled to comprehend for myself those things I saw so easily in others. Not only did I understand now how I could fail to recall my promise to Catherine or pay attention to my daughter and her friend, I saw how my mother might have unwittingly allowed bad things to happen to me.

Bad things? To me?

Once I accepted that possibility, my mind overflowed with fuzzy pictures, fragments of thoughts, fragments of body parts, powerful physical sensations I didn't understand.

You must be lying. You are a gullible, melodramatic fool!

Insults didn't stop the streaming images or calm my stomachful of fears. Yet, part of me was intrigued. From somewhere separate, I observed the process. I was a meteorologist measuring velocity inside a cyclone that was blowing her away.

I moved from the kitchen to the sunroom. I sat on the couch, staring, rocking. The physical sensations possessing me played on.

Thinking to harness the chaos, I decided to weed a garden Bill and I had started on a hill near the backyard shed. The space consisted of reclaimed woods that now included periwinkle, azaleas, wildflowers, and some old laurel bushes we'd moved from in front of the house. Our plants battled for dominance with an assortment of hardy weeds, including poison ivy. My task was huge. Even if I succeeded in clearing some spots, the weeds would quickly grow back. Nevertheless, I felt as though my survival depended upon making a positive impact somewhere, *anywhere*, and attacking weeds in a freshly-opened garden seemed like a reasonable place to start.

Weeding provided structure for my frantic energy. While thoughts spun helter-skelter through my mind, the quiet, methodical process of pulling up intruding, aggressive vegetation felt somehow reassuring. I thought of the testimony from Meeting. *Hope? Maybe.*

Soon, sweat was dripping off my chin. It ran down my arms and my chest. The blue tank top stuck to my back. My shorts were soaked.

Mosquitoes interrupted me, but I scratched or slapped at them and continued on. Eventually, I implored myself to stop, but I couldn't. *Just one more,* I said, the way children plead for cookies, or stories at bedtime. *Just one more.* Before I knew it four, then five, then six hours had passed. Dusk was deepening. The bugs were multiplying. I knew I had to return indoors. I had to eat dinner. I had to prepare for the week ahead. Yet, it was difficult for me to leave the haven of clearing ground-cover, making the space safe for periwinkle, and move to a new activity indoors.

You're acting like a kid who can't make transitions, Twit Face, I sneered.

Leave me alone. I'm doing my best.

You're a stupid crybaby. You haven't done anything today but think about yourself. The great psychologist can't deal with her own shit.

In that instant, I heard my mother's voice. I was appalled. I knew she had been a good woman, loved by many friends, but she had judged herself relentlessly, criticizing her own behavior even in the midst of a task. Whether it was taking her medicine, preparing a salad, calling a friend, or organizing an art show, she rarely acknowledged her own pain or forgave herself for imperfection. I'd sworn never, ever, to act like that. There I stood next to the shed, hot, dirty, exhausted, and stuck between utter disappointment in myself—almost despair—and a need to prove that I was not my mother.

You can't escape this fact, I observed with bitter calm, securing the door. *You have just demonstrated how, in essential ways, you have become your mother.* God, I hated that.

By then I'd made it into the house, and as I stood at the kitchen sink scrubbing off the dirt from underneath my fingernails, I found a small interlude of peace. For the time it took to watch an owl fly from one tree to another across my backyard, I felt sad for my troubled mother and compassion for her little girl, me, who couldn't make her darkness go away.

Then the wind picked up, and I was blown back into the storm.

CHAPTER TWENTY-THREE

Hanging On Backward

Summer 2001

"Sometimes I forget that you need me to avoid any reference to sex," Bill confided. He was speaking directly, without heat, just the way Jacky had coached us. But the word *sex* leapt from the sentence and headed straight for my face. My stomach flipped. Anxiety rippled down my arms and legs.

I tried to remember that he didn't intend to upset me. Bill's feelings were reasonable, I told myself. Yet, I could only turn and move away from him, swimming urgently against the current, fleeing a shark.

"What's that?" Bill asked the following afternoon as we stood in our kitchen discussing items to add to the shopping list he was preparing. He pointed below my waist to something that had suddenly caught his eye.

"Stop!" I screamed, as if his forefinger were about to stab me. I looked down. A piece of plastic wrap appeared stuck to the hem of my fleece shirt. I peeled the plastic off the cloth and placed it on the counter. I stiffened against my impulse to throw the ceramic mug next to it onto the floor. I wanted to hear the mug smash and watch its pieces fly all over the room.

"I didn't do anything wrong," Bill protested, raising his hands in the air. "Why do you treat me this way?"

He was right, but my rage at him wouldn't let go. "I'm sorry," I said, in a tone designed to kill. "You didn't do anything wrong." I ran upstairs.

For the next several months, a stunned preoccupation—physical, as well as emotional—overcame me. I barely functioned. Bill took care of me. He shopped and cooked; he brought me tea; he took responsibility for the cats. At times, he chafed. Mostly, he asked little in return. Our marriage counseling sessions focused on helping him understand why I was so distressed and finding ways we could help one another deal with our drastically altered relationship. I couldn't tolerate any intimate physical touch. I reacted viscerally to certain words.

Night's respite from interpersonal demands brought scant relief. A nails-scraping-the-blackboard sensation invaded my belly every evening when I climbed into bed. Vivid dreams left me exhausted. I traded one world for another and couldn't stop to rest.

I'm a little girl in a large car. I raise one foot and then the other, wiggling each in turn. Sturdy brown shoes stick out from the bottom of my tan wool leggings. They barely reach the edge of the back seat where I sit, my mother beside me. I lift my head to stare at my mother's smooth skin, her full, red lips and dark eyes, her soft brown hair gently waving around the edges of her face under a sloping fuzzy gray hat. She turns toward me and our eyes meet. She smiles. I sparkle all over. I know she is the very best mommy in all the world.

My happiness quickly turns into sad longing, a three-year-old's heartache: Mommy loves me. Mommy won't be mad. I won't hurt her. I can tell her...

Yearning swells into an ocean of grief as I awake and remember that my mother is dead.

Although Bill wanted to help, our misunderstandings increased. Dreading nightmares, I resisted sleep. Late nights and early mornings left me exhausted. I could barely complete a sentence without forgetting where I'd begun. I became more fragile and harder to comfort. Everything made me cry.

Sorrow infused much of what I encountered with an air of tragedy. This had begun months before 9/11, but it intensified thereafter. Bill and I had always left the radio playing. During the day, classical music on our public radio station filled the first floor of our house. Evenings, *All Things Considered* gave us the news, although we switched to CDs when we wanted to talk. Now most music brought me to tears. Bach or Mozart, Handel, Pete Seeger, Bob Marley, or Schubert—soft or loud, slow or fast—melodies seared my heart; I feared the pain would make me break. As seasons progressed, despite my contempt for canned tunes, I couldn't walk past a store playing Christmas carols without crying. When Fuegito climbed onto my lap to snuggle with me, I cried. If I thought Bill looked at me the wrong way, I became angry. When he was kind, I wept.

Only work offered relief. Interacting with my patients I rediscovered myself as a reasonable, if shaky, adult professional. I could focus on someone else, in the present. I was needed. I had value. My troubles paled beside those of my patients.

Slumped on my office couch, cushions and loose pillows gathered around her, Melanie had disappeared into her sweatshirt. A empty body marked her place. The poise she had shown when we introduced ourselves in the waiting room evaporated as she passed through the door to my office. Her shoulders drooped and her pace slowed. She struggled across the few feet of rug to reach the couch.

As I watched Melanie vanish, my energy drained away, as if I were suddenly struck with a bad flu. Maybe I should have said *no* when she called. Surely there were other therapists who could treat her. I'd agreed to see her only because Heather Sanders had asked me to do it; she said she'd manage the medication, and I'd do the therapy. I'd never say *no* to Dr. Sanders.

Half of me enjoyed the prospect of working with someone identified as a challenging patient. I looked at the referral as a professional compliment. The other half wondered if I was up to the job. What if I my ghosts interfered and I couldn't see Melanie clearly? We were both in our late fifties, both had childhood trauma unaddressed until middle age, our children were similar ages—Dr. Sanders had told me these things in our initial conversation.

And what if Melanie didn't like me?

I forced those thoughts aside. With a deep breath, I pulled myself together. "How can I help?" I asked.

After a long silence, a resigned, flat voice made its way from the farthest corner of my couch. "I don't imagine you can," the voice said. "I don't want to be here."

"How come?" I spoke as gently as I could.

"I'm not sure therapy does any good. I've had many therapists. I had a really bad experience with the first one. I guess I just don't trust any of you....Well, my last one, Emily, was helpful in some ways."

"How did Emily help?"

Melanie poked her head a little way out from the pillow-sweatshirt cave where she'd been hiding. She looked at me, tilting her head like a robin eyeing a worm. I waited, feeling exposed. Melanie's face had the pinched mouth and wide eyes of a young child trying to look brave. My first impulse was to comfort her. Then I remembered that she was afraid of me. I didn't want to frighten her further by moving too close. Nor did I want to be the worm.

Raising herself to a full sitting position, Melanie repossessed her body and regained some of her adult poise. "We both loved dogs. Emily had a dog, Katy, and Katy was always in the sessions with her. I could be friends with Katy and tell her things I couldn't always say to Emily."

"Katy made you safe there?"

"That's a stretch. I never feel safe anywhere. But Emily did more or less understand me after a while. Nothing improved until I was diagnosed bipolar. That was two years ago. Now at least I'm on the right medication. I don't know if I need more therapy."

"Who thinks that you do?"

"Well, I'm depressed most of the time. Sometimes I'm suicidal. And disorganized; I don't do what I need to do, like pay bills on time. I'm afraid to stop therapy. I've gone through quite a number of doctors. I'm not easy, I'm warning you. I've also seen a number of people who either didn't help me or made things worse—it's not all me." Melanie reached for another pillow, adding it to the moat she had built around herself. She didn't mention her medical problems, including asthma, allergies, and *systemic lupus.*

"I was fired by my first therapist," she added, as an afterthought.

Uh, oh, I thought. *Her therapist abandoned her?* Was the therapist incompetent, or might Melanie be one of those people who are so demanding and rejecting at the same time that some therapists do end up feeling like worms—poked at and then eaten? On the other hand, she seemed to have done well with Emily. Perhaps with Emily, Melanie had repaired some of her broken trust. "Would you be comfortable telling me about that firing?" I asked. "It might help me understand why you don't want to be here."

With a sigh Melanie began her story. "I'm not ready to tell you the whole thing," she explained. "Emily was supposed to send you a summary. Besides, I've said this so many times I'm really sick of repeating myself.

"Charlotte was my first therapist. After the first session I went home, got into bed, and pulled the covers over my head. I stayed there for most of three days. Charlotte encouraged me to depend on her. Five years later she said I was too much and she couldn't do it anymore. I'd used her up.

"You guys can give me all the advice you want, but you can only do so much. I don't think you have any idea how difficult it is to function when you're as severely depressed as I am." She stared at the last pillow she'd placed over her lap.

I didn't mind those sorts of comments. They gave useful information about how she was approaching me. But the poignancy of her isolation and her longing for help, even while she despaired of receiving any, greatly moved me. I couldn't help wondering about her childhood. I hoped I could keep her anguish separate from mine.

I lowered my shoulders and sat straighter in my chair. "How could you not be suspicious of me and wary of therapy, if your first therapist abandoned you?" I asked, lifting my hands to say *of course*.

Melanie continued, as if I hadn't responded at all, "Here's how I describe my past therapy experience: I'm in the ocean a distance from shore. I don't know how to swim, and the tide is coming in. I'm afraid I'm going to drown. My first therapist, Charlotte, stood on the dock and told me she did not want me to drown. She waved her arms and jumped up and down calling me to come toward her, like a cheerleader telling me I could do it. But the current was such that I couldn't move, and I wondered if I would die.

"My second therapist, Emily, worked by standing on the dock and giving me instructions on how to swim. She could see that I was having trouble, and she could teach me things, and I learned important stuff, but that didn't necessarily mean I could swim well enough to make it out, or that I would avoid drowning in the end. You can see why I don't have much faith in therapy or therapists," she concluded, sounding almost smug. "I'll always be in a different place from you."

"I'm wondering why the therapist stays on the dock and doesn't get into the water with you," I said.

Melanie did a double take. For a moment her eyes lit up. Almost holding my breath, I reviewed the implications of my metaphorical offer to join her. Could I do it? As if she were a movie of moods played too fast, Melanie's face moved from bright and open to sad, to dark, to flat; then the movie was done, the theater empty. I waited to see what would come next.

"I'm afraid I've left you speechless," I said, breaking a long silence.

Slowly, the projector's motor reengaged and Melanie perked up. "I...have to think about what you said. I've never considered anything like that before. I'm not sure I believe you."

"You've just met me. Why would you believe me? I'll have to prove myself to you over time."

"I've talked enough." Melanie was disappearing even as she began to move aside the pillows to reach for her jacket.

"Is Thursday at two o'clock still going to work for you?" I asked, trying to sound casual, worried that she might not return. We had scheduled this appointment during our first telephone conversation.

"I'll have to call," Melanie replied in a vacant voice. The traveler I watched leaving my office looked like a little girl running away from home, her worldy self packed into a wagon she pulled slowly out the door.

Melanie telephoned the next day. "Annita?" she asked in a plaintive, young voice. "I don't know if I can believe you, but I can't stop thinking about what you said...about...getting into the water. Did you mean that?"

Her tone was despairing. Melanie had endured catastrophic losses in her life, including a mother who had died when she was young. I pictured bodies piled one on top of another in a morgue. Next, I felt a surge of energy. We'd connected.

"Yes, Melanie, I meant it."

"I'm really frightened, but...I'll be there tomorrow."

"We can do this, Melanie," I said firmly. And for that moment, I was sure I was right.

CHAPTER TWENTY-FOUR

Rewind

Outside of my office, I clung to Jacky.

Jacky listened as I described flashbacks that invaded my limbs and trunk, memories my body carried without visual content—no coherent scene, no specific place or characters. I felt like a baby, complaining all the time, riddled with anxiety. I was afraid of the dark, afraid to leave home, afraid of going to bed, not able to breathe, not wanting to eat. Jacky insisted that she didn't see me as a drama queen. "It's how childhood trauma plays out," she reassured me.

My anxiety continued to increase. With growing urgency Jacky recommended medication, which offended me. I smoldered. She was patient with my refusal, until the day I arrived at my appointment unable to extract myself from a nightmare I'd dreamed the night before.

A toddler stood alone in a large barn, defiant, square feet set solid on the dirt. She stared at me with reproach and fear in her round, dark eyes. Her lower lip stuck out beyond the upper one, just as mine did. It gave her face a sullen look. A thin rope fell from the hayloft down to a noose draped

*loose around her neck. I knew that I was the child, and that she was about
to die.*

The dream's shadow of suicide followed me all day; I was frightened. Although I hated the idea of *taking drugs*, as I contemptuously described it,
I agreed to ask Dr. Sanders for help. She prescribed an antidepressant and
medication for anxiety. I felt grateful for her kind, immediate response,
and I welcomed the relief the medication provided. Nevertheless, shame
made me secretive. I told no one. I hid the bottles of Celexa and generic
Xanax. I made sure that even Bill never saw me swallow a pill.

"Of course you don't like medication," Jacky said. "It reminds you of
being in the hospital."

"No duh!"—an embarrassingly obvious connection once she noted
it, yet I hadn't put it together myself. There were countless links to the
past like that one, which I missed on my own, that helped me make
sense of what I was experiencing. Jacky saw them and explained them
in a reasonable way. Her solid, steady, accepting presence contrasted
with my haphazard comprehension of what was unfolding. Some days I
made progress. Others were lost.

Broken, deformed, abandoned infants and young children littered
my dreams. When the toddler in the barn appeared, Jacky gave her a
name. The inner child I raged against became Anni.

Shame about my condition and about being in psychotherapy
again meant I kept Anni secret, too. I never mentioned her outside of
a session. Yet nothing captured my dilemma of shame and secrecy, the
self-contempt I struggled with, as succinctly as my relationship with
Anni. Jacky said I wouldn't have access to passion until I connected with
my anger. And I wouldn't be healed until I could feel compassion for
Anni. I would have to love her.

The Anni I pictured came from an old photograph taken when I was
perhaps two years old. It had sat, unremarked, with other old photos on

my bureau for decades. Yet now I rarely imagined her without becoming adrenalized with rage. I saw myself smashing her body against the floor, crushing her skull by stamping on her head, spitting on her limp remains in disgust.

"What would you say if one of your patients reacted that way?" Jacky asked when I described my violent fantasies in her office. I hated when she did that, but it was fair.

"I'd remind her that little children try to keep their parents good, because they love them and depend on them and need to feel safe." I watched myself divide into two people, a frightened little girl and a wise adult. I still wanted to hurt the child, but not as much. "They attack themselves as bad, because they know something is terribly wrong, and their rage has to go somewhere." I felt like I was reciting a script, but maybe the reality check helped. What reached me was the pain on Jacky's face as she listened. *She really believes I was hurt.*

With Jacky, I read abandonment into every conceivable message. At times I lashed out, furious because she had ended a session a few minutes before I thought it should be over—surely she was letting me know she wanted nothing more to do with me. I didn't know what she thought in private, but in front of me, Jacky seemed to take this in stride. She helped me put my thoughts and feelings, my impulses and my dreams, into context. I learned to look at the metaphorical and symbolic meaning in my behavior.

I'd always assumed that my lack of childhood memories was a result of all the shock treatment, although experts insisted that amnesia caused by shock treatments was temporary. Now, after decades of being reconciled to the loss, I was suddenly remembering: reading my hospital records, while informed by my own clinical awareness, triggered a significant amount of memories.

The lost memories returned by various routes. Some developed as conscious thoughts, some came in dreams, and some arrived intact in an instant, provoked by ordinary things—a color, a smell, an action—that I might have overlooked or dismissed in different circumstances.

One night, a few months after receiving my hospital records, I gathered sheets and blankets around me in the usual way as I snuggled down to sleep. In the process, I must have upset a spare pillow. Fortified with my army of covers, I turned off the light and curled onto my side. I stretched out my arm to pat a sleeping Bill's shoulder.

A moment later, before I could think, I was standing beside the bed, terrified. I realized that the loose pillow had fallen onto my head, but I couldn't explain my extreme reaction. Reluctantly, I returned to bed. Eventually, I slept.

The next morning, summer light filling the room before five o'clock awakened me. I reached for my black cloth sleep mask, as I often did, and hooked the elastic over my ears. When I lifted the mask into place on my face, I felt a hand reach from behind me to cover my eyes. Again I reacted with terror. I tore off the mask, vowing never to wear one again. I must have imagined the hand.

"What was going on last night?" Bill asked a few hours later. "Your screams made my hair stand on end. Twice. Should I wake you up next time you do that?"

By evening I felt that I'd found an explanation for my panic the night before. I'd recalled a scene in our bedroom at my grandparents' house in Yonkers, just outside New York City. I would have been barely two and a half years old. My parents, my baby brother, Richie, and I had returned to my mother's childhood home when we left Florida, soon after Richie was born. It was during WWII; my father was in the Navy at the time.

Autumn 1945

It's the middle of the night. Everything is dark.

"Leave, Rox," I hear my granddaddy Dick say to my mommy. My new brother Richie is sleeping in his crib next to the bed. My daddy is away at the war. My grandmother is asleep in her bed. My Genny is sleeping nearby. "Leave, Rox," he says again. "I won't be long."

And she leaves. My mommy does what her daddy tells her. She hangs her head down and slumps over like she doesn't want to do it, but she gets out of bed. She leaves. I'm all by myself with my granddaddy. He says not to worry, but I'm scared. I want my mommy.

If I hold real still and don't make a sound I can make this not be happening. It's hard. Even thinking makes noise. I have to stop up my thoughts so they don't move and don't make noise. I have to hold so still I'm invisible. Quieter than when Richie needs a nap. I have to make this not be happening. I'm not here. I'm not here. My granddaddy is not here and my mommy will come back. If I'm real still, and air stops, my granddaddy can't be doing this. I'm not here. I stopped air. I can do that. I can....

I wake up. Mommy is crying. I fall sleep. Then I wake up again. Mommy tells me I had a bad dream. She says she's sorry. It's still dark. Now I'm floating on top of the room. I can take care of my mommy. I can. I don't want her to be sad. I'll stay awake and make sure no one hurts her. I'll watch my baby brother, too. Until it gets light and my daddy comes home. Maybe by Christmas. Mommy says everything will be fine when the war is over and my daddy comes home.

As new memories arose, I seesawed between stunned grief and contemptuous doubting. *Oh God, please no* versus *It couldn't have happened; you're making it up.* I read and re-read the records. While the doctors' interpretations of my thinking and behavior often seemed limited, even blind, the records' basic information supported the picture that was emerging. In this way, the notes helped quiet my cruel inner voices, at least for a while.

Psychiatric Institute

REPORT OF PSYCHOLOGICAL EVALUATION

August 12-13, 1963:

The acute character of her psychosis, its late adolescent onset, and the specific repressions noted make it possible to speculate that the patient's disorder may be related in part to early traumatic events possibly associated with a primal scene, as a result of which sex and aggression remain unconsciously fused.

—G. Fried, PhD

CHAPTER TWENTY-FIVE

The Body Knows

Summer 2001

I thought everyone knew this, yet increasingly it caught me off guard: *Just because you can't remember something, don't think it doesn't affect you.*

I hadn't yet learned to drive when I married and moved to Connecticut from New York City. I depended on Bill for transportation. He drove a nifty Volvo sports car with seats low to the ground and seat belts that crossed your whole body, one over your shoulder and one for your lap. This was quite advanced for 1969.

Not long after I'd settled into the routine of married life, I noticed that each time we drove anywhere, as I clicked my seat belt into the catch, I was overcome with intense dread. I believed I would be killed in a car crash during the ride. My heart pounded; my head became light and dizzy. I was sure I was going to die.

I knew there was no justification for my reaction. Bill was a good driver. I'd never been in an automobile accident. My fear was irrational.

Even at twenty-six I still honored my first rule from the psych hospitals: *Never say anything that might sound crazy.* So I didn't tell Bill that I feared death when we drove off in the car, and I certainly didn't bring it up in my sessions with Dr. Heller. I never discussed it with anyone. After we'd been married for about two years, Bill taught me to drive. Once I mastered driving myself, the fear disappeared. I forgot all about it.

More than thirty years later, a few weeks after I'd read my hospital records, I remained stunned by the doctors' descriptions of my personality and my behavior. The number of shock treatments dismayed me. I was explaining this to Jacky, when the car terror suddenly reappeared. I hadn't thought about it for decades—why now? Although I was mystified, the answer was obvious to Jacky and to almost anyone else who knows my adolescent history: buckling the seat belt in the little car reminded me unconsciously of being strapped onto the table just before delivery of the shock treatment. Bill would kill me by crashing the car—not intentionally, but by accident—in a process that replayed the original drama of my anticipating death at the hands of the hospital psychiatrists, whom I also knew did not intentionally plan to kill me.

Once I grasped the meaning of my reaction, further intriguing possibilities appeared. Most likely none of my apparently inexplicable idiosyncrasies occurred by chance.

Whenever I left home for more than a day, I made sure before leaving that my effects were in order—mail sorted, underwear tossed into the laundry basket, computer logged out, personal notes hidden. Longer trips involved telephone calls to my children, my brothers, sometimes my closest friends. I needed to say "I love you" in case I never returned. The possibility of sudden death colored every day of my adult life. I was always prepared to die.

My detesting the smell of alcohol on a man's breath no longer seemed unreasonable, once I realized it was connected with my father's inappropriate intimacy. I'd reacted that way for as long as I could remember. Earlier in our marriage, on occasions when Bill had indulged in excess drinking, I'd responded with a fury I couldn't explain. Until this insight I'd given it little thought.

Hypervigilance would explain the startle response that still adrenalized me when the phone rang or a door slammed. I had always been easy prey for anyone who wanted to make me jump or shriek. What about immediate, violent rage if my arms were restrained, even for an instant? As obvious as it appeared in retrospect, before my conversation with Jacky I hadn't recognized the role of the restraining cold wet-pack that preceded each shock treatment or the strait jacket I was forced to wear in the quiet room.

I took another look at my restrictions around sex, like the rules about no sexual activity at night or in the dark. Eccentricities I'd tried to hide, because I thought of them as shameful, began to make sense. I reacted violently to unexpected sexual touch. I had access to orgasm only by dissociating to sexual fantasies in which I was a young child. Although I knew that sexual behavior carried important information essential to understanding past as well as present relationships, I'd never described these reactions to either Dr. Heller or Dr. Sanders. They were much too embarrassing.

Jacky's straightforward, unselfconscious manner seemed to take the tension out of discussions about sex. She made it ordinary. Eventually I would learn to look honestly at my sexual fantasies and impulses, although so much had been repressed or dissociated that this would take many years to accomplish.

Another morning, close to Father's Day, I sat again in silence among Quakers. Gentle sunlight warmed the simple room filled with a quiet assortment of men, women, and children who had come together in the early minutes of Meeting for Worship. I'd been there many times before. Yet, in the weeks since I'd read my hospital records, everything in my life seemed to have changed. This sanctuary, my refuge of spiritual nourishment and peace, was changing, too.

In the silence of the Friends' Meeting, as I looked around me at the people gathered there, despair erupted unexpectedly from deep within the stillness and washed over me. It was about fathers.

I was with men and women I imagined to be connected with their fathers. They cherished them. They visited their fathers and called them on the telephone, they asked them for advice. They named their children after them by choice, out of love. I saw the men and the children, fathers and grandfathers, comfortable, caring. Although ordinarily I felt numb when I thought of my father, I was filled with longing.

Then, as seemed to happen often during the silent time of Meeting, a scene emerged. I was a young child living with my family in my grandparents' house. The day was just beginning.

Summer 1946

Daddy used to be away at sea, but now he's back. He goes to work at night and comes home in the morning. Mommy says he helps fix big boats at the Brooklyn Navy Yard. I wonder if he's afraid in the dark.

I'm standing at the top of the stairs, between the bathroom I've just come from and the bedroom where we all sleep. I'm three. That means I'm a girl who can go to the bathroom alone and wipe herself after, and I just did. When I close my pajamas by myself it makes a loud snap. That makes me feel big, like Mommy says I am.

I'm supposed to be going back to bed with Mommy. But I stop outside the room. I turn toward the stairs. Then I can't move. I just stand still. I turn around again. I head for the bedroom door. I stop. I move from one foot to the other and back again.

Is my daddy waiting for me downstairs? Sometimes when he gets home and everyone's asleep he sits in the kitchen by himself. At the table by the window he smokes his cigarettes and drinks his yellow juice in a tall glass. It stinks, but I don't say that, because I don't want to hurt his feelings. I like it when he smiles at me. My daddy is tired and mad a lot, and I get scared, but when he smiles I'm happy.

Sometimes he's only in his underwear. He tells me he likes me there. He says girls like me are supposed to help their daddies. Should I go downstairs now? Should I stay here? What if he wants us to do that thing? It makes me sick. But it makes him happy. He likes me. He'll be sad if I don't go. He wants me to be there. He says I'm his girl. He needs me.

Mommy won't mind. She won't be mad. Mommy is asleep. Richie is asleep. Mommy will be glad if I make Daddy happy. I won't make noise. I won't tell.

"What are you doing up so early, young lady?"

"Yikes!" I jump. Genny scared me. She laughs, but it's a little one, because we're supposed to be quiet. Genny lives here, too. She has a job at the Yonkers Public Library. She goes to work early in the morning.

When I see it's Genny I'm happy. Genny always smiles at me.

"Get back to bed. Scoot! It's not time to wake up," she whispers. "I have to go to work. Your father isn't even home yet." She gives me a little push toward the bedroom and walks down the stairs.

Now I'm back in bed. Genny has gone to work. Mommy is still sleeping. What will happen if I go downstairs when my daddy comes home?

"What's the matter?" Mommy asks. By mistake I woke her up. Her voice is loud. "I said no crying, remember?"

I know I make Mommy sad when I cry. I try not to, but it happens anyway. Bad girls make their mommies mad. Bad girls cry when they're not supposed to. More tears keep falling and falling out over my hot cheeks. I can't make them stop.

Cathy next door says there's monsters in the dark. They catch bad girls. My tummy hurts.

Psychiatric Institute

REPORT OF PSYCHOLOGICAL EVALUATION

August 12-13, 1963

The patient's TAT stories yield a clue as to the reasons for her inability to accept sex and assertiveness. In one story a man approaches a seated woman and announces that he is going to kill her. "She is not married or anything and he came up and said that." Aside from the inappropriateness of the story to the stimulus properties of the card, it is clear that sexuality is equated with violent aggression—in fact, with murder.

—G. Fried, PhD

September 2001

I sat across from Jacky on her couch, picturing a man, my father, confronting a small child who stood naked in front of him. He was about to sexually abuse her. I stared in horror, while my body twitched with primitive anticipation.

"I hate you," I said, raising my arm.

Jacky looked worried. She also seemed to be encouraging me. "Use a pillow," she said, pointing to a cushion nearby.

I smashed my fist against that man with all my force. A rocket exploded! I doubled over. Engulfed in pain, I crumpled in on myself, cradling my wounded hand.

"I was aiming for the pillow," I said, as soon as I could speak. I didn't want Jacky to think I was self-destructive. She retrieved a cold can of Coke from her refrigerator to serve as an ice pack. We wrapped a towel around it.

"I'll be all right," I reassured her, swallowing the three ibuprofen tablets she offered. Jacky's mothering made it almost worth the pain.

My fury had vanished with the blow. I couldn't think of much beyond my hand, but I didn't want Jacky to be upset. I especially wanted to make sure my condition wouldn't make her think she should end the session early. I tried to pick up from where I'd been diverted, "What was I saying about the man?"

It didn't work. I'd lost interest in the naked girl and her father.

"Poor, poor, Anni," Jacky said, genuinely distressed. I knew she was trying to remind me that the abused child was innocent, but I was unmoved. Anni was stupid, and my hand hurt like hell.

The next day, the pain had intensified. Bill said I needed to see a doctor. My internist nodded sympathetically when I told him the story I'd created to explain what had happened—there was no way I wanted anyone to know the truth.

On the night before my session, President George W. Bush, responding to the 9/11 attacks, had given a nationally televised speech regarding Al Qaeda and the new War on Terror. "His attitude outraged me," I said. "Without thinking, I banged my fist onto the arm of the couch where I was sitting. I missed the cushion beside it and hit the sharp edge instead." At least the couch detail was true.

The blow had indeed broken a bone in my hand. Other doctors in the practice smiled in a friendly, maybe conspiratorial, way when I returned with x-rays from the radiology group down the street. No one questioned my story—anyone there could have done the same thing. The surgeon who operated two weeks later, the hospital staff, my friends who asked for details, all accepted my explanation.

With one move, I'd coupled rage at someone I loved and crippling pain, branding them together into my brain. Looking back, I marveled at how succinctly I'd demonstrated my childhood belief that anger was not only sinful but dangerous; mine would always cause harm.

I suffered no guilt with my fake story, perhaps because it wasn't entirely false. I theorized that my outsized reaction to certain political figures, ones I identified as hypocritical exploiters of vulnerable citizenry, sprang from that disconnected rage. A politician's betrayal became a metaphor for what I had imagined in that brief moment between my father and me. Yet political emotion was considered normal. Partisan outrage could be shared with like-minded friends, safely removed from intimate personal experience.

Years later, the fury at my father's exploitation hadn't reappeared. I had yet to connect with the hatred and rage that had to exist somewhere beneath my awareness.

"Have you forgiven him?" people often asked after they'd heard my story. "Did you confront him?"…"What about your anger?"

"Not yet," I'd explain. "I'm working on the anger part. I'm still numb. When I think of my father, I don't feel anything."

Sometimes I'd point to the edge of my right hand. "There's a metal plate holding together the bone that was broken. It's small; it doesn't set off sensors at the airport."

Dealing with anger had been a problem all of my life. In my family, no adult expressed it directly. I never heard my parents shout. I almost never heard them swear—"Damn!" meant serious trouble. My father was grouchy much of the time—sour and disdainful—but he was quiet. We could feel his hostility, but we didn't identify it by name. I avoided anger. If I felt it stir, my mind and body blanked out. I disappeared. As I grew older, this dissociation prevailed.

I rarely spoke in anger. I hardly ever raised my voice. In high school, its volume had significantly diminished. My handwriting became so small that my teachers threatened not to read my papers. My words, my actions, my physical being all shrank as I strived for invisibility.

I recalled my mother's taut description of the years when I was young and we lived with my grandparents in Yonkers. Conflicting work schedules and emotional agendas made for dramatic tension, which reverberated throughout the house. Genny ate breakfast and left for work while my father finished his "dinner" after returning from his job in the early morning. He slept during the day. My grandmother demanded quiet for her afternoon naps.

My grandfather worked for the Nestlé Company as an engineer. He had invented a process for sterilizing milk in cans that made possible condensed milk and similar products. These brought impressive benefits—probably billions of dollars by now—to his employer, who owned the patents. At home my grandmother treated my grandfather as if he were stupid. She frightened me.

Genny was a bossy big sister to my mother, Rosanna. Although my mother had married and was raising two children, Genny treated her as if she, too, had little intelligence or common sense. My father also treated my mother this way. I never saw my mother protest or show anger at them. She only sighed and shook her head. Often she seemed overwhelmed—fragile and insecure.

My self-appointed job as older child and grandchild was to take care of everyone and to protect my mother without provoking their anger at me in the process. Decades later I still played that role.

During those early years I did have tantrums. According to family stories, repeated in the hospital records, those tantrums were often around the issue of food, when I was expected to eat things I was absolutely determined to refuse. No one understood why I overreacted to being told to eat broccoli or old, overcooked potatoes. I hated to drink milk. Sometimes it was just too much, and I erupted in passionate outrage. My baffled parents responded with "zero reinforcement"—the toddler tantrum management method advocated by Dr. Spock. They ignored me. I screamed, and cried, and kicked, and carried on. Apparently, no one noticed.

By the time we moved from Yonkers two and a half years later, the assertive, spunky, tantrum-throwing two-year-old had become a compliant, fearful, obsequious shadow of a four-year-old. My mother theorized that her dismayed reaction to my anger had provoked this transformation.

"One Sunday you refused to change into your play clothes after church, so I sent you to the bedroom. Working in the backyard awhile later, I noticed you watching me from the window. When you saw me looking at you, you stuck your tongue out at me. I felt so guilty, I burst into tears. You never showed anger or disobeyed me again."

The most dramatic examples of anger—and my disconnection from it—come from the two psychiatric hospitals that served as my homes for many years. In Bloomingdale's, initially, I stayed quiet. My behavior showed nothing overt that might seem angry. By the time I was transferred three years later, however, I'd become violently self-destructive. At PI, I raged by cutting, burning, and scratching myself. I bashed my head against the wall with force that required x-rays and stitches in my scalp. I broke a front tooth by punching myself in the face. I held my breath until I collapsed in a dead faint. I bit my hand and drew blood. I spent days with straight pins stuck in my thigh.

Although my fury should have been obvious, I didn't recognize anger in the physical sensations of rage that surged through my body. I responded to my impulses as if I were a toddler again, without conscious thought, reenacting tantrums provoked by a desperate, frustrated need for emotional reassurance, inchoate terror at the prospect of being abandoned.

Because I'd been raised to think of anger as an emotion that harmed others, that would lead to being unloved and unwanted, I felt ashamed of being angry. When the doctors and nurses around me insisted that I was enraged, in an understandable effort to increase my self-awareness, I felt harshly criticized and deeply misunderstood. I withdrew into my own world, mortified by my misbehavior, alienated from those I needed to help me.

Sometimes I dealt with those impulses quietly. I cut or burned myself in secret. The resulting pain absorbed the oppressive energy overwhelming me. However, once the rage was soaked up, I was left with a gash or, more often, a painful and ugly burn—guilty evidence that engendered more shame.

I'd learned very early that the world was safer if I kept harsh emotions at bay.

Spring 1948

I'm five, and I look before I say anything now. I see what my Mommy's face looks like, and Genny's, and especially my Daddy's. I see if they are happy or sad. I take care of them. I cheer them up. When I was little, I didn't do that. I wasn't careful; I talked too much.

Sometimes I don't pay attention. I get in the way. "Look out, girl. Look what you're doing," my Genny says. When Grandmother says, "Look here," I stop what I'm doing no matter what, because she gets mad at me and Richie, even if we aren't being bad. "Look, missy," my Daddy says when he's playing with me. "Let's be special."

They know I have to look.

Once I was mad at Richie because he didn't let me play with his trains. "I don't care about your stupid trains, because it's just me and Daddy in the morning," I said. "Daddy loves me better than anybody."

Then I saw Mommy's head go down, and Daddy's eyes got tiny, and his whole face squished into tight lines. Genny coughed and started drinking her cocktail. Then she walked into the kitchen to get more. Mommy stood up and said it was time for Richie to go to bed. Grandmother and Granddaddy Dick were already upstairs. I got hot and sweaty, while my Daddy just stared at me with his tight face.

Next time early in the kitchen, Daddy said he knows I love my Mommy and I don't want her to die. "If you tell anyone what we do, just me and you, it will kill your mother," he said. "You can't talk about this. You'll end the family."

So I'm careful. I don't talk much. With grownups, I never talk if I don't look first. I'm going to kindergarten after we move. I'll be good there.

CHAPTER TWENTY-SIX

The Little Annita

Reading my hospital records prompted months of travel into the past, where I searched for my lost self, the child Jacky called Anni. The journey began with cold facts, an official map of my history: *you were born here; we moved there; your father's work was this.* As I wandered into those landscapes, early scenes began to take shape. Each new memory engendered others. In the midst of old stories, if I stayed open to Anni's voice, I discovered the girl I had been.

March 1951

Even though I'm only seven, I've lived in lots of places. Mommy keeps track. When I was born, we lived in Yonkers with Grandmother and my granddaddy, Dick and my aunt, Genny. There was The War, and Daddy was in the Navy. While he was on ships Mommy and I moved to Virginia, and Alabama, and then Florida, where Richie was born. Then we came back to Yonkers and then Newport and then Yonkers again, and then Long Island and then Chicago—Park Forest and Chicago Heights. A few months ago, we moved again. I live in New Jersey now.

Since November we've lived in an apartment above a large garage. The garage belongs to a beautiful stone mansion that looks like a castle, high on a hill. I go to second grade at a school down in town. Although at first some girls made fun of me, because I was new, by Christmas I had a few friends. Not long after that, Gail Lucarelli started her Hate Annita club. Now most girls in my class don't talk to me.

I should like weekends, because there's no school. Yet Sunday is my least favorite day. There's the morning fuss about church—getting scrubbed and making my brother get dressed up, arriving on time to kneel and think about sin. Then every other week there's the family trip to visit Daddy's mother, Grandmother Annita. We drive to her apartment near New York City—Mommy, Daddy, Richie, and me.

In stories, grandmothers are soft, kind old women who give children candy and take them on trips to the zoo. Neither of my grandmothers is like that. I don't think either one likes children. Daddy's mother is especially grouchy. Because I'm named after her, I worry that I'll turn out like her when I'm old—skinny, fragile, and very easily annoyed. In case I forget I'm connected, my Aunt Marjorie, Daddy's sister, calls me "the little Annita" when she talks about me.

I suspect Mommy doesn't like this grandmother, either. If my parents are talking and her name comes up, Mommy gets stiff, and her face clouds over. You can almost feel a cold wind.

The drive to my grandmother's is usually quiet. Once we're there, Daddy parks the car in front of her building, and, with Mommy carrying a bag of groceries, we walk—well, sometimes Richie runs—past large fake potted plants to the elevator, which we ride up to the third floor. Her apartment is #2.

Daddy rings the bell and right away opens the door. "We've come to visit, Mama," he shouts. We aren't allowed to say it, but she's extremely hard of hearing.

The front door opens directly into the living room. Even on this sunny day the apartment seems pale and dusty, with cream-colored walls turning yellowish brown, like the underside of pancakes when it's time to flip them over. Curtains on the two small windows match the walls. A couch made from carved wood, with old cushions covered in red silk stripes, takes up most of the wall next to the door. In the corner across from the door, on the far side of the room, stands a tall brass lamp with a whitish lampshade. Underneath that shade is my grandmother.

She sits in the middle of a worn, green armchair, her cane resting against its side. Grandmother's eyes match the green of the chair. She wears her faded yellow hair in long, thin braids wrapped like a crown around her head. Even though she is tiny, pale, and shriveled up, and even though she scares me, I can tell that my grandmother once was an elegant, beautiful woman.

Daddy hurries to Grandmother and kisses her quickly on the cheek. "How are you today, Mama?" My father pronounces the second *ma* of *Mama* louder than the first, which sounds like he's royal.

"You know better than to ask that," she says, frowning. Daddy squirms. Her thin quavery voice sounds fancy, too.

"We only have a few minutes, Mama. We've brought you some soup and those cookies you like," Daddy says.

"I don't have much appetite. I hope you didn't spend a lot for them."

My father tells her the latest family news. How last night Richie found our dog, Beagle, after he ran away again. We tried to keep a muzzle on him after the last time he came home bloated beyond belief from having eaten garbage all night. This time, not only was Beagle bursting from eating garbage, but all sorts of disgusting food was squeezing out from the muzzle's edges. Grandmother smiles a little hearing that.

Then Daddy tells her I'm in the second grade play at school.

"Last week your cousin Jenifer performed a flute solo in front of the entire school," she says. Mommy leaves the room. *I wish just once Mommy would stick up for us.*

My grandmother looks at me. We're supposed to have a *conversation*. Although I can hear my parents putting away groceries in the kitchen, I feel completely alone. I tell myself not to be afraid of an old woman, so thin from arthritis she could just break. However, to me she seems huge, and she grows larger as we talk. When Grandmother asks me to tell her about myself, my brain dries up. I can't think what to say. Then I remember about the play. "It's *The Princess and the Pea*. I'm the princess," I say, feeling proud.

"Speak up," she yells, "Speak up, will you?" I become more flustered, trying to force my mind to produce an idea. "I know you have something interesting to say," my grandmother insists. "I expect more from you than this."

I've run out of possibilities. I know I shouldn't cry, but my eyes fill with water. Soon tears are running down my face.

Daddy hurries in from the kitchen. "I didn't realize you already had onions, Mama," he says. "We'll just take these home with us. Will that be all right?"

"It doesn't matter to me."

"Do you have all the medicine you need, Mama?" Daddy continues. Now my grandmother starts telling him about her terrible pains, and I can leave the room. I think he said that to rescue me.

Since my brother is only six and a boy, he doesn't have to go through a conversation with my grandmother. As soon as we arrived, he disappeared into the bedroom at the end of the hall. In a large closet behind the door, there's a box of old toys he gets to play with.

I join Richie, but I don't feel like playing. I'm ashamed to be a crybaby who can't talk to her grandmother.

But I do like Daddy rescuing me.

Annita Taylor, my father's mother, had grown up in southern California, a cavalry officer's daughter, the eldest of his four children. At twenty she fell in love with Henry Fridenberg, an engineer and entrepreneur from New York City. They had met while each was vacationing at Lake Tahoe that spring. When her parents refused to let her marry him, presumably because he was Jewish, Annita and Henry eloped. Her mother and brothers didn't speak to her again.

My father didn't discuss his parents's family situations or why my grandfather and Uncle Bobby, one of his nine siblings, had changed their name from Fridenberg to Perez. "It was during WWI," Aunt Marjorie told me years later, as she approached her 100th birthday. She had agreed, uncharacteristically, to speak about her past. "It wasn't good to have a German name. It wasn't because we were Jewish." By then my cousins, brothers, and I saw it differently: among my grandfather's numerous siblings and my father's cousins were noted physicians, a Metropolitan opera singer, and a United States senator, many of whom had proud Jewish families.

My father, Henry Taylor Perez, was six years younger than his sister Marjorie. During the 1920s their parents made a glamorous New York City couple, working and playing with the political and cultural elite. From the time both children were young, they left my aunt to take care of her brother, an arrangement both siblings resented.

Life changed drastically with the stock market crash and the Great Depression that followed. The family suffered severe financial losses.

My father was sixteen years old, a senior in high school when his father, my grandfather, hanged himself in a New York City hotel room in 1932. He forfeited a full scholarship to Stanford when his uncles in California, my grandmother's brothers, who had agreed to give him a car and a place to live, reneged, insisting he stay home to take care of his widowed mother.

My father attended Cooper Union, which was tuition free. He slept in the Bowery. After his death many years later, my mother told me that during those impoverished years my father had kept a tuxedo in a rented locker. He wore it to society functions, where he filled his pockets with food to sustain him on the street.

I knew that my grandmother had suffered in her life and was still in distress. I could see it in her eyes, which looked more desolate than vicious when I had the courage to look directly into her face. She was proud. She had lost a great deal, and she lived with significant physical pain. Staying alive was hard work.

Once I no longer feared turning into her, my grandmother faded away, like the residue of a melancholy dream. Long after we were grown, I asked my brother Richie what he had thought of her. He paused for a moment, then laughed. "She was a real dog," he said.

Spring 1952

Our landlady in the stone mansion, Mrs. Hughes, is tall and speaks with an English accent. Her gray hair sweeps up into a wavy bun fixed with silver combs. She could easily pass for royalty. Everyone in my family, except maybe Richie, is very impressed. Her grandchildren, Katie and Chippie, live with Mrs. Hughes. Katie goes to boarding school, so I don't really know her or see her much. Although Chippie and I go to different schools, we're making our First Communion together.

First Communion requires a long time of study. Every Sunday I've been going to Sunday school and memorizing the Catechism, a book of questions about God and sins. The Catechism teaches that we are born sinful. Our sins made Jesus die.

I regret in my heart that Jesus suffered and then died on a cross because I have evil in me. Sometimes I slap or pinch myself to help pay for my part in killing him. It's hard to do on purpose something you know will hurt, but if I concentrate I can do it.

When you climb the steep stairs from the Hughes's garage up to our apartment, the first thing you'll see is the kitchen. A sink and a little stove sit on one side of a green linoleum floor. A refrigerator, a few cabinets, and a dark green table with a bench built in beneath it take up the other side. Some light comes from a small window in the center of the outside wall. A bit more comes from a dim bulb in the center of the ceiling. Daddy insists that we use low watt bulbs so he can keep down the cost of electricity. He worries about cost a lot.

A narrow hallway leads away from the kitchen to the living room, the bathroom, and my parents' bedroom. A wall separates Richie's and my room from the kitchen. It's in the corner of the apartment, with one of our windows facing the hill behind the Hughes's house. The other looks out over the driveway. My side has the driveway window.

Before my baby brother, Taylor, was born last Christmas, Daddy built a partition dividing the room almost in half. We don't exactly have separate rooms, but I can lie in my bed against the new wall and think I'm alone. And I can still read to Richie on Saturday mornings, so our parents can sleep late.

I love my room most when I have a fever. I'm hardly ever sick, so it's a very special treat. I stay home from school, in my bed, and Mommy brings me lunch on a tray. I read and listen to the radio. I love the radio. I listen to Stella Dallas: "What happens when a girl from a small mining town out West comes to the big city to seek her fortune…?" And the Shadow: "Who knows what evil lurks in the hearts of men? The Shadow knows!"

Last year, I had a real medical problem. Taylor was only a few months old. Richie was seven and I was almost nine. At my regular checkup the doctor noticed that I had a large, pimple-like bump on my chest. It was on a corner of my right nipple.

He asked my mother to come into his office, speaking in that soft voice adults use when they they're worried but they don't want to let the child know something is wrong. He told me to stay in the waiting room until they were done. Was I scared!

A week later, in a bed in the children's section of Englewood Hospital, fuzzy from anesthesia, gauze and tape bandages covering my chest, I heard doctors' voices outside my white curtained cubicle. My doctor had removed the lump, which turned out to be a tumor. He hadn't received the report yet, he was saying. He needed to be certain regarding a question of malignancy.

Malignancy. I didn't know that word's proper meaning, I only knew it meant I might die. With that idea, fear disappeared and peace flowed into my almost nine-year-old heart. After years of trying to make up for my sinful being, I could rest. I would die a painful death and undo my sins.

I imagined myself receiving sad visitors come to say farewell. I listened to their sorrowful messages with kindness, despite my suffering. Mommy sat beaming beside my bed. She was proud of me.

The tumor turned out to be harmless. A week later I returned to school.

CHAPTER TWENTY-SEVEN

Opera with Genny

Autumn 1952

Although both of our grandmothers want Richie and me to call them "Grandmother," and my father's sister is "Aunt Marjorie," in my mother's family, we call our grandfather "Dick" and our aunt "Genny." As if we're friends.

Now Genny works in New York City at Time-Life in the research library, gathering information for their magazines. She's always kind to me, although she's pretty bossy with most people I've seen her with. I think Genny and Daddy clash because they both think they're the boss of my mother.

Because she works, Genny has money for vacations all over the world. She brings me souvenirs. I have little dolls from Peru, and Italy, and Scotland, a bracelet from Arizona, a ring from California, even an Indian doll with a papoose from Texas. From Mexico she brought me a beautiful red skirt with all sorts of colors woven into a pattern at the hem. I have a necklace from Egypt, along with a framed photograph of Genny on a camel.

Genny's best friend, Dot, usually travels with her—they're always together. Genny bosses Dot the way she bosses Mommy, and they tease each other like Richie and me, bickering but not serious. Dot's a secretary at Union Carbide.

Seeing me makes Genny happy. Her teeth shine and her eyes sparkle. I never wonder if she misses me. Genny's my godmother, which I understand to be a sort of backup mother. If my real mother died, Genny would have to make me go to church. What I like is that she takes me to special things in New York City. We've been to the circus in Madison Square Garden. I've seen Russian folk dancers, the Moiseyev Ballet, and the Scottish Black Watch Highland Band. She gives me records of the music for my birthday, so I can listen to it whenever I please.

When I grow up I might become a ballerina. This comes from watching ballets with Genny and Dot, where dancers in beautiful costumes and toe shoes fly in gorgeous patterns across a stage, while the orchestra plays magnificent music. When I'm home, listening to my records, I pretend I'm one of the dancers on the stage. The music fires me up. I kick my feet high like the Russians. I speed around doing pirouettes and arabesques. Dancing flows out of me when the music plays. I'm happy.

I especially love when Genny takes me to the opera. She and Dot have had subscriptions to the Metropolitan Opera Saturday matinee series since before I was born. I first went to the opera when I was seven, shortly after we moved to New Jersey. I've seen *Aida* and *Don Giovanni, Carmen,* and *La Boheme.* Sometimes I'm invited because Dot is busy that day. I saw *Faust* with Dot, because Genny doesn't like that one. Today we'll see *Madama Butterfly.*

On opera days I take a bath and dress before noon. I clean my room early, but there's not time for other chores.

I'm wearing my best dress, which I got last Easter. It's yellow satin and comes with a crinoline slip, puffy short sleeves, and a big sash that ties into a bow in the back. My shoes are black patent leather, and my socks have little ruffles on the edge where you fold them over. Last night after we washed my hair, Mommy put it in curlers to make my pageboy look just right.

I wish I were prettier. My front tooth is chipped where Richie hit me by mistake with his metal toy gun. My hair is thin and flat and my lower lip sticks out. I suck it in for photographs.

Genny will be here any minute. With today's weather on the chilly side, I'll need to wear my coat from last year, which is too small. Some of the girls at school say the brown is a yucky color and that I look silly wearing it. I'll take it off once we're in our seats at the opera.

Going to New York with Genny lets me forget my problems at school. "There are always mean girls who pick on new kids," Mommy told me when she first heard about the Hate Annita Club. "It isn't your fault."

Last year in third grade, I had only two friends. One was Eleanor, who still plays with me. The other was Michelle. Michelle and I were friends the way you are when nobody else likes you. We tried to help each other. Kids made fun of Michelle, because she was fat and she couldn't read.

One day, without any warning, Michelle was gone. Her family had moved, so she could go to a different school. I didn't miss being too afraid of the bullies to talk back and defend her, but I missed Michelle.

In school I'm quiet and keep to myself. At home I spend most of my time helping Mommy take care of my baby brother Tay Tay. He can sit up and crawl, although he can't walk yet. He says Ma Ma and Da Da. I think he says Nee Nee for Nita, but Mommy isn't so sure. I know he likes me, so I don't care about being unpopular at school. Or so I say.

I've explained to Tay Tay that I'll be gone today until supper-time. I don't want him to be frightened when he doesn't see me. I know babies can't understand regular talk, but I figure it's better to tell him anyway. I don't want him to think he made me go away, as if it's his fault.

"Hi, there." My beautiful Aunt Genny has arrived. "All set?"

"Yes," I tell her, jumping up and down while she climbs the stairs. Everything I ever worried about disappears when I feel her friendly arms around me. She lifts me and holds me tight, close to her heart. I can't tell if it's hers or mine I feel beating.

Genny sets me down and steps back. "Don't you look gorgeous," she says. I feel as if I have a halo all over. We head down the stairs. I wave good-bye to Mommy, who looks sad, and my glow flickers, but we're soon outside. I dash to Genny's car and jump in.

To solidify my good mood, I stare at Genny. I notice her big brown eyes and her wavy brown hair. Her eyebrows are smooth. She has red lipstick on lips that are just the right size, not too thin or too fat. Her dress is black with white dots on it, a red belt in the middle. Pearl earrings are clipped to her ears. A matching pearl necklace shows just below a red scarf with little flowers on it tied around her neck. A black coat rests on her shoulders, leaving her arms free for driving.

I look at Genny so I can fill up my mind with her beauty, and fill up my feelings with love for her. That leaves no room for feelings I hate: wondering if I'm making Mommy unhappy or being a selfish, spoiled-rotten type of girl, who skips her chores and goes out to have fun while the rest of her family stays home.

My love plan works. Before you know it we're at the George Washington Bridge. From the middle of the bridge I look over at the endless Hudson River dividing New York and New Jersey. The tall buildings of the city move closer and closer. Under a shining sun and blue sky, great cliffs on the New Jersey side vibrate with bright-colored autumn trees, and the vast river points downtown, our destination. I can't imagine anyone happier than I am.

"Shall we stop for lunch at Schrafft's?" Genny asks.

I clap my hands and wave my feet: it's my favorite place. We start to plan our order. Usually I ask for a BLT on white toast. Genny goes for ham and Swiss.

The real reason to eat at Schrafft's is their ice cream sundaes. A Schrafft's sundae comes in a large, tall glass. Through the clear sides you can observe details of the ice cream—individual scoops' curves and wrinkles, shades of strawberries or different nuts' textures—and watch the syrup as it slides down the edge. With a special long-handled spoon you can reach syrup settled way at the bottom without getting your hands sticky. Because I can't decide between butterscotch and marshmallow on my butter pecan scoops, Genny lets me order both. I top it off with whipped cream and a shiny red cherry with a stem.

I'm so busy imagining my sundae that I hardly notice we've parked. It's a short block to the restaurant. Inside, long red tables with bright chrome edges and legs stand between red-cushioned benches. Large mirrors decorate the walls. Everything around us is big, beautiful, and shiny. The waitresses wear starchy white aprons and ruffled caps, so you feel like a princess with your own maid.

Genny explains that we're going to the opera and we have to be on our way by one o'clock.

"That shouldn't be a problem," the friendly waitress says, winking at me. Then she asks for my order. Suddenly, I'm so shy I can't talk. I force out words about a BLT, but she can't hear me. Genny orders for both of us. She asks that it all be served at once, so we won't have to wait and risk being late.

Then we do wait. And wait. Genny begins to get angry, because the order is taking so long. I start to not be hungry anymore. Genny says she'll speak to the manager. I worry she'll upset the people working here. Just before she stands up, our waitress approaches our table carrying a tray with all of our food on it. When Genny sees that, especially those big sundaes, she smiles at me. The sun comes out again.

After lunch we hurry back to Genny's car and drive further downtown. We end up in a large garage. As Genny hands the attendant her keys, she jokes with him as if he's an old friend. I'm a little embarrassed. My parents never talk to people like that. But Genny looks like she's having fun, so I decide not to worry.

With Genny holding my hand we head for a door on the side of an old brick building. The door is crammed with people waiting to get through. I'm glad she's holding tight. I could become mixed up in the pile of bodies and not find my way out, but Genny is strong; she doesn't let go.

Soon we're packed into an enormous, elegant elevator. It's made with shiny brass sides and a door that folds like a fan to open. When it's closed, you can see through the hinged metal bars. It's a little nerve wracking because it lifts so high.

"Family Circle," the elevator man announces. The lacy metal box slows down and creaks to a stop. Everyone rushes out. After climbing steep, thick-carpeted stairs, Genny shows her tickets to a short, round lady dressed in a black uniform with dark red trim. "Good afternoon." Genny knows this lady, too. The lady nods and hands us each a program. She gives me a big smile as I walk by.

Our seats are in the middle of a row, and we have to slide past several people already there. Genny stops to chat along the way, so it takes forever, but eventually, we reach our seats, remove our coats, and settle in. The stage looks like a tiny toy far below. Box seats made of carved wood painted gold extend from the high edges of the stage. Everything here is elegant, from the dark red and gold opera house to the dressed-up ladies' jewelry. Genny even has binoculars with gold trim and white mother of pearl circles around the top to help see the stage. She lets me look when she's not using them.

During the drive, Genny told me the story of *Madama Butterfly*. She had brought a libretto, but I wouldn't have time to read that before the performance. I feel quite grown up, knowing so much about opera.

I'm reading about Richard Tucker in the program, when suddenly the atmosphere changes. Lights dim. Voices turn to low murmurs and then fade. The conductor appears; everyone claps. As he raises his arms, a breath-holding hush fills the hall. As he lowers them, the first notes sound. The opera has begun.

Genny and I are squished into the elevator returning to the street. Around me people are talking about who they liked, who they didn't, who was better at singing some of the arias. I'm holding Genny's hand, so I won't become lost, but I'm not thinking of Genny just now. I'm still upset about Madame Butterfly killing herself, and her little boy no longer having a mother.

I'm having trouble managing my sadness. At first I cried. If I hadn't known that Genny hates crying, I'd probably have cried more. I don't show it, but I'm still weeping inside. How could Cio-Cio San just kill herself and abandon her own child like that? How could Pinkerton marry her and then leave and forget about her? Those thoughts fill my mind.

We don't talk much on the car ride home. I enjoy being still and listening to the music as it continues to play in my head. Genny is probably doing that, too. I'm grateful she didn't complain when I felt sick during the last act, close to the end. My head tingled and I began to sweat. I thought I was going to faint. We had to walk down all those stairs so I could drink some water from the fountain in the hall. I was embarrassed to disturb the row of people in the seats between us and the aisle, but Genny didn't act annoyed. She didn't seem to mind at all.

The sky glows golden red with the sunset. It will be almost dark when we get home. Probably Mommy will invite Genny to stay for supper. Genny will say, "No, thank you. I have to get back to Mother and Daddy." But she'll join them for a drink. My parents and Genny will sit for a while with their scotch and sodas or vodka on the rocks and have a couple of cigarettes and talk about how good I was at the opera. I don't think Genny will bring up my feeling sick, but she might talk about lunch. I'll say how much I liked everything, and I'll say to Genny, "Thank you so much for taking me." I'll also thank Mommy and Daddy for letting me go. After that I'll leave to change my clothes.

I wish I were already alone in my room. I need a quiet place where I can think about Madame Butterfly dying and her little child without his mother. Later, I'll think about the exciting ride and the big sundaes and the wonderful music I can still hear in my head. I'll think about how lucky I am that Genny is my godmother. Right now, I have some crying left to do.

CHAPTER TWENTY-EIGHT

Ghost Dreams

A few months before my tenth birthday, my parents, brothers, and I moved from the garage apartment we'd rented in Englewood to our own house in White Plains, New York. It was the fourteenth move for me and the first time my parents owned their home. The old Tudor style house looked somewhat run down, but with a porch, three floors, odd-angled rooms, closets large enough to hide in, and lots of stairs, it seemed like a wonderland to Richie and me.

Huge old lilac bushes, rhododendrons, and early azaleas ready to bloom decorated an expansive front lawn—what my father called "the lower forty." Glossy pachysandra thrived underneath large oak trees. The small backyard, in contrast, had been neglected. Much of it was overgrown with weeds.

Spring 1953

Kneeling over a tray set on the lumpy ground, I hold a teapot midair between us.

"May I offah you some tea, my deah Lady Lynn?"

"Chahmed, I'm shuah." Lynnie lifts her cup.

"Please be so kind as to pahss the petti fingahs," I say, once I've poured each of us some tea. We wave our pinkies at each other, giggling. I love my new friend!

A week later, mommy gasps and throws up her hands when she sees my bleeding, blistered skin, although that doesn't keep me from scratching—once itching starts, you don't think of anything but how to make it stop. It seems that Lynnie and I had been sipping our tea in the middle of a patch of poison ivy.

Pink lines up my arms mean I have to see the doctor. I know Mommy's worried. "We're going to the hospital," she says, coming out of Dr. Ridley's office. "I'm really sorry." She looks away, as if she's done something wrong. She explains that getting rid of a poison ivy infection like mine will require a few days of medicine delivered directly through an IV. "They'll take good care of you there. Don't worry." The word *hospital* gives me shivers. I remember the tumor.

We park behind a redbrick building with a sign that reads, "St. Agnes Hospital." By now my face feels as if its skin has been ripped off. A hundred engines roar inside my head. Approaching the front door I reach for Mommy's hand, but she pulls away. A scary cavern opens inside me. Then I remember that you can't touch a person with poison ivy. Mommy apologizes again and tells me to walk ahead.

One look at me and people move out of the way fast. Some startle as if they've seen a ghost. I try to make my face blank so I won't scare them.

Inside, Mommy talks to a lady dressed in a nun's habit. It's white, not black. "In a Catholic hospital nuns are the nurses, " Mommy explains. The lady leads us onto an elevator that stops at the fourth floor. I see children at the end of a long hall. On our way to where I'll stay she points out a playroom with a large dollhouse.

When the nun-nurse shows me the room with a bed where I'll sleep, my stomach turns over. My face throbs. I feel as if I'm little again, all alone and wanting my mommy. Another nurse tells me to come with her. I can't speak. There's no voice to tell her I don't want to go. Mommy stands in the hall and looks sad. She doesn't say anything, either.

"Cheer up, dear," the nurse says in a bright birdie voice. "Your mother will be back with your things. We'll just get you into this nightie for now." She starts pulling off my clothes. My ears pop. The room looks strange, as if I've been in it before. She holds up a flimsy hospital gown that doesn't close. I let her dress me as if I were a doll; my arms do the job but don't feel like they're mine.

"My, but you are a mess!" she squawks. "You must have been rolling in the stuff."

She thinks I did this on purpose? The idea horrifies me. *It was a mistake!* Itching takes over. I want to tear off my arms.

"No touching that skin, dearie." The nurse grabs my hands and holds them away from my arms. "We'll cover these so you won't scratch," she says. "Scratching makes it worse and spreads it around more, you know."

On a metal stand above my bed a jar hangs upside down. It's attached to a thin tube that runs to a needle stuck into my arm. Gauzy strips wrapped around my hands make it look as if I'm wearing fat mittens. Other strips loosely tie my hands to metal bars on the side of the bed. I don't know what will happen if I have to pee.

I don't cry. I know Mommy wants me to be brave. My face doesn't hurt. I don't feel anything. As if I'm looking at myself from the ceiling, and I'm not real.

When Daddy gets up in the middle of the night, his bed creaks and his slippers shuffle on the stairs outside my room on his way to the kitchen for a drink of whiskey or vodka in a little glass with ice that clinks. He steps quietly on the way back and sometimes he opens my door but I lie still pretending I'm asleep. He stands at the side of my bed and slowly opens his bathrobe and his pajamas and I feel my stomach jump. My heart shakes and I make myself not know what's happening. Sometimes he whispers I'm his girl and he loves me but often he says nothing and I keep pretending I'm asleep but I feel that squishy velvet fluttery feeling in my stomach. I'm in a foggy dreamy place where there's no telling how anything happens because it's all a dream I can't remember and even if I do remember it changes if I try to see what it was. I forget because it was a dream and dreams disappear.

When morning comes, I wake early. I'm glad to see the light. But my teeth chatter, and I'm scared.

My parents want me to be happy. I smile, but beneath my skin is putrid dirt; my bones are filled with poison. I'm an evil girl who should be hated and killed. When I'm alone, I cry.

Mommy says I've always cried at the drop of a hat. Even when I was little, like maybe three, and we lived with Grandmother and Genny and Dick in Yonkers. When I wet my pants in kindergarten, I cried. In Park Forest, when I was six, Mommy told me that after we saw *The Wizard of Oz*, my best friend, Shanshee, and I cried so much we had to go to the doctor for shots. Both of us thought the Wicked Witch of the West was coming to get us. For weeks we sobbed during the day and screamed in our sleep at night.

My brother Richie likes to make me cry. He forces me into it, then makes fun of me. He steals my favorite doll, Frances, and holds her over the toilet, threatening to drop her in headfirst. He'd do it, too. When I beg him to stop, he laughs, so I scream for Mommy. I want to tell her what he did, but my eyes fill with tears and I can't speak. She shakes her head and leaves. "You two wear me out," she says.

Psychiatric Institute
REPORT OF PSYCHOLOGICAL EVALUATION
The phallic area on Rorschach Card IV is included in a "monster" percept,

but when the patient was asked to identify it anatomically, she said, "It's just a part of him," illustrating her refusal to deal with sexuality despite a frightening acknowledgment of its existence.

Again, in the story told in response to card 13MF, in which a husband wishes to go to bed with his wife, is refused and strangles her in retaliation, sex and murder are inextricably intermingled....Sex is taboo because, in association with aggression, it, too, can lead to murder. Moreover, she is threatened both by her own unsuccessfully isolated aggressive impulses and by those which she projects onto the people in her milieu, so that her percepts take on terrifyingly vivid intensity. On card V for instance, she saw "A man creeping up; you know, he's got a costume on; sneaking." Also her refusal to touch the Rorschach cards except to turn them over when indicating she was finished, attests to her phobic loss of distance.

—G. Fried, PhD

Summer 1955

I'm weeding the front lawn, close to the ground, searching for plants I have to eliminate. Sweat drips off my forehead. My knees are wobbly from crouching. In the patch I'm checking at the moment, the weedy culprits are definitely thicker and greener than the frail-looking proper grass they're competing with.

Daddy says that owning your own home comes with serious responsibilities. Everyone has to help. Over the two years I've had weeding as my Saturday chore, I've become expert at zeroing in on the particular shape and the particular color of dandelions and onion grass. I don't see much of anything else.

Onion grass is a darker green than regular grass. Its stem comes in just one or two pieces that stick up from the ground. They're round, not flat like blades of lawn grass. If the air is still and I concentrate, I can smell when I'm in the presence of onion grass. It's sad that I've come to despise that oniony weed. I think real onions are delicious.

Dandelions spread from the center, forming a circle. When they're blooming, you can't miss the bright yellow flowers on top. After they've turned into gray dandelion puffs, it's easy to see them, too. Daddy tells us not to blow puffs the way little children do, because that spreads seeds around. So there goes the only part of this chore that could be fun.

To remove the entire plant, including the root, you have to dig deep under a dandelion. Sometimes I don't concentrate, and the root stays in the ground. I pretend not to notice, but I know the dandelion will grow back if I don't do it right.

My brother's chore is worse. Most of the time, while I survey the lawn for weeds, my father mows the grass. Richie has to walk beside him, or a little in front, and pick up any sticks or rocks that might be in the way. Daddy doesn't want to run over them with the lawn mower and dull the blade or risk a flying rock that might hit someone. If Richie misses a twig or a rock, Daddy shouts at him to pay attention. Richie acts like nothing bothers him, but I'd be upset if Daddy yelled at me like that. I'm guessing that his yelling gets to Richie, too.

By now sweat is also pouring off my nose and down my shirt. I'm boiling. I decide I love sweltering in the heat, which I don't, although some days I can almost make myself believe that I do. I concentrate on the weeds. *Ah ha!* I notice the circle of dandelion leaves interrupting the regular line of grass. "Take that, vile weed!" A knight with my weed digger sword, I have to kill the villain fast, before he kills me. There goes a dandelion. "And that!" A stalk of onion grass. And another.

I stab and pull and stab and pull and stab and pull, and then, through the sweaty blur, I discover even more dandelions and more onion grass than before. No matter how much I dig, no matter how much I check, when I turn around to look in another place there are dozens of them. I'll never get rid of them all.

In some ways I'm pretty smart for twelve: I know my job is impossible, yet I do it anyway. With my father, I'd never think to say *No*.

Just when my last scrap of energy is used up, Mommy calls us for lunch. She has made baloney sandwiches, which I like. Daddy's has two slices; Richie and I each have one. She spreads mayonnaise on the bread and mustard if we want it. My father likes special mustard called Grey Poupon, but I don't like the way it feels on the top of my mouth. I choose yellow French's. Tay Tay is napping upstairs. Even though he's three and a half, he doesn't eat regular food.

After Tay Tay wakes up, we'll drive to the beach club to swim. I'm not keen on this, because I don't know people there, but Mommy has women she likes to talk to, and Richie always has friends to play with. He knows lots of kids, but he'll even play with someone he doesn't know. I wish I were sociable like that. I help Mommy take care of Tay Tay and hope nobody notices I'm too shy to make friends.

CHAPTER TWENTY-NINE

Are We There Yet?

Spring 2002

Fumbling awake from troubled sleep, at last I could see morning. I'd been checking for daylight through much of the night, like a child whining in the back seat of the car, "Are we there yet?"

My right hand had clenched into a fist so tight I needed the left one to peel open its fingers. As I lay in bed gathering focus, I reviewed the night. I'd dreamed about a child with a bandaged arm pushing her baby brother in a carriage. It brought to mind an old photograph of me at two years old holding onto my grandfather Dick's hand. We were standing beside an infant Richie in a baby carriage. When I thought of the crowded bedroom in Yonkers, my stomach started jumping. Those shuddering contractions, just under my diaphragm, had become a fact of life, set off by a word or an image connected to the past. I sighed and began to analyze the dream. *If I'm all the parts—the carriage, the damaged child, the baby…* But remembering the haunted look in the girl's eyes added chills to my body's intensifying twitches and jumps.

I leapt from the bed and rushed into the bathroom, wanting to leave night under the covers.

The dream followed me. I hadn't found a way to elude that ambiguous, fuzzy state between night and day. I pulled on the frayed, purple fleece bathrobe we'd bought at REI during a visit with Bill's brother and his wife in California five years before and stuffed my feet into wool slippers Jessica had passed on to me after college. Hugging the soft robe around me, I exited the bedroom, heading down the stairs and out the front door, shuffling up the steep driveway to our mailbox on the street, where I grabbed the newspaper.

I stopped—*just for a moment*, I promised myself—to pinch wilted blossoms from the tops of early daffodils lining the space between the drive and the mailbox. On my return I grabbed a plastic bag with a second newspaper, and carried them both into the house.

Warm smells of pumpernickel bread toasting and Lapsang Souchong tea brewing greeted me. Again I'd lost myself in the process of morning newspaper retrieval. Bill had almost completed preparing the tea and breakfast toast we'd eat in our sunroom. He hadn't yet started when I left the house. *Was I gone that long?*

Dodging dismay, I flopped onto the couch to devour the news while sipping tea and eating crunchy toast. Bill indulged my request that we not converse. No matter how bad the world outside might have been, no matter what concerns sat unresolved between Bill and me, I counted on that peaceful interlude to help me dissipate the nighttime ghosts still cluttering my consciousness.

As the mist dissolved, I could see the day ahead. Now Bill and I shared plans. While I worked in my office, he'd begin to rototill a patch of garden where he wanted to plant peas. In the afternoon, after his therapy appointment, he'd take the cat to the vet, pick up dry cleaning, and shop for dinner. I left the couch and headed upstairs to shower and prepare for work.

Yet by the time I'd reached the top step, I'd become again an anxious child, my fragile tummy fluttering just below my heart. Later that day I'd meet with at least three women who had struggled for years as I seemed to struggle now. I knew how to comfort them. Why couldn't I help myself?

I'd been standing in front of my bureau, debating far too long which pair of earrings best matched my mood and my dress, when a loud buzzer from the office door sounded in the hall at the bottom of the stairs—my own private butler announcing a visitor. *Saved,* I thought. *My patient's here.*

Deciding the earrings I was wearing would do, I gave my hair a quick brush, grabbed my appointment book, and headed for the office. I left my cluttered bedroom, hurried through the narrow hall lined with photographs, past Bill's room, the bathroom, and the children's rooms which, since they'd left home, were filled with various boxes of stuff. At the bottom of the stairs, I turned right to the front hall, zipping past the bright kitchen into the family room—crowded, too, and filled with plants—where I opened the door to the garage.

With deftness born of long practice, I squeezed between an old freezer and a four-year-old white Saab, past three aging, plastic garbage cans, and a broken recycling bin. On my right, after the Saab, I passed space for a second car now filled with piles of empty boxes awaiting a trip to the recycling center. In my hurry I hit one by mistake, starting an avalanche. *Damn.* It wasn't the first time. I shoved one box back into place, and another fell down. I tossed that up into the pile. More descended. I grabbed and tossed, and grabbed and tossed, until I realized I had worked myself into a frenzy. *Stop!* I screamed in my head. *Get a grip.*

Moving gingerly, I lifted the last few boxes onto the top of the pile, holding my breath until I saw they were balanced.

With a sigh, I resumed my trip and soon reached the far side of the garage. I was facing the wall where the house had ended before the office suite was added. Two short wooden steps led to the first door and into a tiny entryway. Storage shelves lined one side. A second door opened to the office itself.

Once inside I set my appointment book on the ottoman in front of my chair. I paused a moment to catch my breath and reset my attitude.

As I opened the waiting room door, a friendly, "Oh, hi," greeted me from the couch. *I'm okay, she's here,* said the look on Luke's face.

"She" was I, however. For a moment I stood there, paralyzed—an anguished child, an angry young woman, a grief-stricken adult on one side, across from my mentors, therapists, and other believers in my possibilities. *Grow up! This drama is a luxury you cannot afford.* Hearing my mentor, Dan Miller's quote, I snapped into action. As I smiled back at that brave, hardworking young man, warm energy bloomed like a flower within my chest. I found myself in the present. That must have been what "take heart" referred to: our meeting smiles awoke my heart.

Throughout the busy morning, my darkness ebbed and flowed. It could vanish in an instant as I opened the waiting room door to greet a person with whom I had a powerful emotional connection. Yet just as quickly, fear could envelope me as I walked the short distance through the garage into my house.

In the house, between appointments, I might drink a glass of water, or make tea if time allowed. I collected the mail and checked my telephone messages. I fixed lunch in the kitchen.

This time I paced around the kitchen island while deciding what to eat. Back and forth, I debated the merits of each choice. Complicating my task further was the fact that anxiety smothered my appetite. I settled on some leftover pasta, which I heated in the microwave oven. Emotional nourishment came from reading *The New Yorker* while I ate.

Fuegito hopped onto the island and tried to sit on the magazine, right on top of the story I was reading. Using cat body language, I showed her that I didn't approve of her being on the counter: I turned my back to her, while I grabbed the magazine and held it out in front of me. Believe it or not, that worked. She jumped down. Pleased, I moved all my stuff to the couch and coffee table in the sunroom. Now Fuegito could sit close to me and not walk where she shouldn't. The cat's constant need for attention reminded me of myself, which brought more sadness, but her warm, furry softness and her sweet purring as she snuggled against me reassured me that we'd worked this out.

There was time to return one phone call. A harried sounding woman had left a message saying she was looking for an appointment for her six-year-old daughter, who was having nightmares. *I'd like to treat a six year old*, I thought. *What's she like? What's going on in the family....* With no available appointments, I'd have to disappoint another mother seeking to help her child, so I postponed the call.

But thoughts of a six-year-old girl suffering from nightmares bedeviled me.

I'm abandoning a child who needs therapy.

You haven't time. You shouldn't make a commitment you can't fulfill.

Maybe I could find space.

Other therapists can help her. You're not indispensable, you know.

The buzzer signaled my next patient's arrival. I traveled through the garage still warring in my head, wondering if I would ever sort myself out. Again in my office, I stood still. I looked at the blue sky and the hemlock branches framed by the skylight. The fluff of a white cloud blew by way up high, lit by the afternoon sun. I hitched my sadness to the cloud and willed them both to move on. I had to find a way to let go of my dismay, so I could be the doctor while I worked.

Inhaling a deep breath, I paused midair, then took another. This time I didn't think before I opened the door. I was thrust into the moment, in spite of myself.

There she sat, like a fruit tree hit with ice—freezing the buds, disrupting their bloom—all that promise drained of color and hope. Karen dragged herself into my office, her body bowed inward, sighing as she sank into the large armchair next to mine. I could feel my energy start to drain away.

Was I this hard? I wondered. *Probably.* I doubled my determination.

I waited for Karen to collect herself, using those moments to settle myself as well. She stared out the window at the white pines, which had grown at least six feet since I'd first sat there more than twelve years before. Little patches of blue from the sky formed a peaceful backdrop behind them. The carved tops of posts marking a fence set between the trees and the yard beyond showed through here and there.

A blue jay was building a nest in the pine tree that was most visible from where I sat. The jay gathered twigs and long pine needles from the roof and gutters and carried them in its beak to the nest, almost hidden, close to the trunk of the tree. The bird's busy work, flying back and forth, contrasted with our motionless silence. What could I say to a depressed sixty-year-old woman who was so angry with her family that she wanted to die, while at the same time she refused to talk about it?

Karen often appeared cold and withdrawn. While sometimes I discovered a gracious, gray-haired grandmother, that day I sat beside a rigid two-year-old determined to hold her breath until she passed out. I was about to share this impression with her, when something made me pause. *Hold it,* I said to myself. *See what happens.*

"Look," Karen said. "I think that bird is building a nest." Rising in her seat, she leaned forward, pointing toward the tree. "That's what I like about coming here," she turned to me, her face crinkling into a smile, "There's hope."

CHAPTER THIRTY

Balance, Moderation, Peace

Jacky was knowledgeable and experienced working with adults confronting childhood trauma. Every week she met with me alone and with me and Bill as a couple to help us manage what had become a major disruption in our lives.

The marriage counseling could be unpleasant. Sometimes when Bill felt criticized, his personality changed. He would lose his ability to see our difficulties as products of misunderstandings between us and recognize only that he was being humiliated.

My flashbacks made sexual intimacy untenable. Similarly, I developed an urgent need for privacy. Fear bordering on terror at the idea of a man in the room prompted my request to sleep in the master bedroom alone. Bill moved into the guest room next door. I had no answer to his understandable anger. My elaborate apologies didn't stop him from feeling rejected, which, in turn, set off painful feelings from his tumultuous childhood. His rage drove me farther away. My dissociation was maddening. He felt as if I were withdrawing on purpose, to hurt him. He wanted to hurt back.

When I met with her by myself, Jacky's office became a safe place to reveal what for me were outrageous and unbelievable thoughts and feelings. Certain statements—*This can't be true. It was my fault. I must be lying. It couldn't have happened. I made it happen*—recycled almost nonstop. Explanations I offered so confidently to others sounded meaningless in my own ears. Yet in Jacky's voice the same words made my symptoms and my distress understandable. "Young children see everything as about themselves. Those are flashbacks. Your body remembers it all, even before words."

Proximity to Jacky comforted me. However, the possibility of losing her—of her becoming tired of me, deciding she was done and abandoning me—was terrifying in equal measure. Most of the time her presence allowed me to get in touch with profoundly disturbing aspects of myself. For better and worse, I was discovering the reality of incest along with traumatic hospital treatment and the ways those events and relationships still colored my behavior and my sense of who I was.

As the clinical professional at work in my own office, I could usually pull myself together. At home, most of the time, Bill helped me where he could. Trouble arose when he felt powerless. This frequently occurred around sex, since I was not only unavailable, but he couldn't even mention it without freaking me out. There were also times when my evident distress couldn't be mitigated no matter how hard he tried. I feigned good cheer so Bill wouldn't feel inadequate, to soften his anxiety or anger, which might be provoked if he felt ineffective. He saw through this, of course, and felt insulted by my pretense.

When I was at my wits' end, I took refuge in writing.

Summer 2003   Some Thoughts on a Very Bad Day

How do you find peace? Do you sit under a tree and wait? Will it come by if you are quiet enough, like a deer or a hermit thrush invisible in the scenery, eventually revealing itself with a rustling that leads you to it?

I have not found peace. I am angry, frustrated, aggravated, pissed off. I have old hurts unclaimed and unhealed, and they rattle around inside of me like loose bolts in a car, source unidentified, always beyond reach.

Sometimes my anger exceeds frustrated and pissed off. Deep rage foams and bubbles like boiling sewage, fouling the air, distorting the view, putrefying everything in the environment.

Perhaps today I am suffering the ultimate hubris of the therapist patient. I must face in myself those symptoms, defenses, and mental distortions brought forward from twisted childhood that I spend my days witnessing in others. I am the surgeon who must perform an appendectomy on herself. If I don't act, my damaged organ threatens to spill its poisonous contents and destroy me, even while I hold my breath in pain, gathering courage for the incision.

I know this. My vocation is healing others, bearing witness to painful injustices in their lives. I stand by them, hearing their cries, calming their terror, all the while aware of their innocence and the lessons learned by children who have been exploited. I tell them to hold on. I point out inconsistencies, the way children think, the way loved parents can betray, the cost, the loss, the damage, the pain, the consequences in awful repetition, the rage, the abuse, the disconnection that allows our own children to be hurt.

Oh yes, I know it all. I can talk a good story. I understand. I care. But here is the awful truth about me: I am that innocent child. I am the trashed treasure, the broken dream. My challenge now is to face this news in a different way from every earlier time. I have to be a vigilant therapist to myself lest I revert to easy violence. The sewage is ready to overflow, the bloated organ about to burst. I must perform surgery while resisting the impulse to excise my own heart.

I have seen it all, and now it is in me. I see the man with broken bones who knows he courts more while he still rages. The one who is terrified that if she lets me help her, she'll need me, and then I'll be gone. I see the heartbroken parent whose child has disappeared. I see lives in terrible pain and people who would prefer to die. They endure with my help.

And what help is that? What kind of hypocrite am I to help when I could as easily die myself? Who am I to call on others to stand fast when I am sinking? To be calm when I am driven and relentless in my turmoil?

I used to starve myself and feel power in that deprivation. I used to burn myself and feel stronger with that pain. Now I sit here on my bed ferociously chewing gum. I'm using my jaws to pound and crush the pink and purple and green bits of sugary dough rather than destroy myself. I've made my mouth into a dragon and put my regrets into bubble gum. How ludicrous is that?

I think about the work I should be doing. There are bills to pay, flowers to be picked, soup to be made. I could be sorting old mail and old junk, mending clothes, writing reports, eliminating decades of worthless stuff I have accumulated because I don't know how to say *no* and can't bear the idea of wasting something that someday might have a good use. Sort of like myself.

It's strange, isn't it, how everything comes down to oneself? I identify with the unwanted old clothes, the unread newspaper articles, the flowers and vegetables that flood the garden at this time of year. I would give them to someone else in an instant. Yet neglecting them feels wrong.

At times like this I'm possessed with an unceasing restlessness, because I feel I have no place to go. My shame, that signature of self I've carried from before I learned to talk, drives me, even as I glory in my objective liberation from all childhood demands.

My heart is stubborn and uncomprehending, clinging to old certainties of evil and rejection. My intellect, my pride, my strength in life stand banging at the gate, while that young part of me refuses to let them in. What would my neighbors, or my colleagues, or my patients think if they were to see me now? Whither balance and moderation?

Balance means I have found a way to stay on life's tightrope without falling off. It means the scales of justice can firmly hold my childish innocence and my good heart, even as they weigh my self-serving obliviousness, my need to avoid conflict at almost any cost. It means that when I want to die, I remember why I want to live.

Moderation means that as I do that living I hold the big picture, the blue sky and the flowers in the garden beside the dark forest and the hurricanes. When I look both ways before crossing the street, I am being moderate. I hold back my angry impulse to crush the frightened Anni, and I speak to her with kindness. This is moderation.

Balance, moderation, peace? I think they mean I forgive myself when I'm the patient.

September 2005

I had returned to the sanctuary of my office on a sunny afternoon, after a week away. I felt invigorated, not only by seeing my patients, but also by experiencing this room. I loved the warm, honey color of the oak floor, the more or less matching bookshelves, the oak desk, and the trim around the windows. One of my mother's watercolor paintings, a peaceful assortment of small sailboats anchored in a cove, hung on the wall across from where I sat. Over the desk a lovely sketch of a thistle reminded me of the giver's message: *cherish goodness, expect prickles.* My Yale diplomas hung in a corner, unseen by most, but I knew they were there. Above all was the skylight through which I watched the clouds and the birds and the seasons.

I'd seen buds on the trees grow fat and turn into leaves, then watched them change color and blow away a few months later. I'd watched snow falling till it covered the window, then disappear the next day under bright sun in an azure sky.

Therapy had its own seasons, in the sense that there seemed to be a reliability and integrity supporting the process, a pattern that remained true and unfolded even while feeling like chaos—too hot one day; too cold the next—on the surface. What my patients saw as my calmness—"How can you be so sure of yourself?"; "You obviously think this will work"—was my belief in the process.

I'd watched the sky through that window in anguish and in delight. Only a few years earlier, I'd been close to despair, wondering if I would survive. Yet in that room I'd found relief. In the sanctity of the therapy-session exchanges, I rediscovered each day a part of myself that could be serene and in control. I could leave my demons behind and find my voice in the present.

Slowly, over months, then years, those periods of calm increased and expanded beyond the office. I recovered perspective. My resilience grew.

My perspective on Anni changed, too.

For a long time I'd been unable to think of the abused child I imagined within myself without wanting to hurt her. I hated her; I felt contemptuous of her; I wanted to destroy her. When I was an adolescent, it was Anni I felt obligated to kill.

Yet a time came when I would picture her and reach for her hand, or I stooped down gently and quietly so that I didn't frighten her, and I said, "Hi." This wasn't because I felt sad for her, or pitied her, or even thought she had it so bad. I just didn't hate her. I was willing to help her without being ready to like her.

Progress was uneven, but the direction was right.

Gradually I was able to comprehend that the behavior leading to my hospitalization, as well as my behavior in the hospitals, had been my teenage effort to communicate urgent information I was otherwise unable to know or to pass on. I spoke and acted out in metaphor. Because the doctors didn't understand this—and I offered them little help, not grasping it myself—they defined me according to what they were familiar with. They looked at my insistent self-loathing, my suicidal depression, my abstract adolescent language and apparent inability to speak directly, at my dissociated condition, and they decided I was suffering from schizophrenia. From this flawed diagnosis flowed the recommended treatment. In the early 1960s that was electroshock therapy. Shock treatment in many ways compounded the message that I shouldn't speak, reinforcing silence by erasing my memory and by inadvertently punishing my efforts to communicate. In certain concrete ways it mimicked the abuse itself. My hospitalization was so extensive—and the first one so futile—because I'd fled to the hospital from home. By looking only at my symptoms, the doctors failed to see that they were repeating the abusive pattern I was trying to escape.

Childhood trauma and its effects are much better understood now than they were forty or fifty years ago. Many of the symptoms attributed to Schizophrenia, Bipolar Disorder, Major Depression, and Borderline Personality Disorder are also associated with complex Post Traumatic Stress Disorder (PTSD). My symptoms sprang from sexual abuse, not schizophrenia.

When I bashed my head against the wall; I was not only protesting painful thoughts, I was also enacting lessons learned from home and from the hospital: that my mind held something dangerous, that I should keep my secrets hidden. Although anyone reading a description of my behavior could tell that I was desperate and furious, the subtle meaning within a particular action was missed by everyone. Attacks on my face, swallowing glass and poison cleansers, the rage I expressed with my mouth, the way I used my eyes for pleading, my various efforts to disappear all reflected aspects of my early experience.

Pay attention, I tried to say then, and I want to say now. Pay attention to every gesture and to each moment. We humans show more than we think.

CHAPTER THIRTY-ONE

Reunion

May 2011

The first announcement arrived more than a year in advance: *Reserve May 14-15, 2011 for your White Plains High School, Class of 1961 50th reunion.* I ignored it. I remembered so little. I'd been so disturbed. However, Jacky told me that healing from my trauma required that I return to that unhappy scene. I needed to redefine my relationship with my past—take control and stand tall where I'd tried to disappear. I knew Jacky was right. With almost no memory of high school, it made sense for me to return, to see what I could learn. Nevertheless the sullen teenager with haunted eyes I recognized in the hospital records photograph still frightened me.

"Let's keep it on the agenda," I told Jacky. "I can't decide now."

Months passed. Encouraging mailings increased. My resistance softened.

We were clearing the table after dinner when I told Bill I was thinking I'd attend the reunion. "Sounds right," Bill said. "When do we go?"

"Would you mind terribly if you didn't come?" I said, loading dishes into the sink. As Bill handed me another dish, I turned to scan his face, alert to signs of anger or disappointment—*eyebrows raised? jaw set hard?* "I need to prove to myself I can do it."

Bill's whole body relaxed into a smile. "Oh, good," he said. "I'd much rather support you from here." I'd been in touch with Sara and Sue, my two closest high school friends, several years earlier. Sue had come to New Haven on business, and we met for a lively lunch we both hated to see end. I'd visited Sara once. She had welcomed me, but while we sat sipping tea and sharing bakery cookies on her couch, I drew a blank on every incident she recounted from our past, one after another. A terrible emptiness spread between us, like spilled ink. For me, the loss of all we had shared felt unbearable. For Sara, it might have been worse. Neither of us pursued a serious connection after that.

Sara wasn't coming to the reunion. I'd recognize Sue. But what if something intervened and she couldn't be there? What if I didn't recognize other people? Worse, what if someone asked me directly about events I'd participated in but couldn't remember? Well, at our age many people complained of memory lapses. I could probably get away with using that explanation.

First, I had to confront the biography: the reunion committee wanted a half page statement from every participant. What would happen if I told the truth? Why go at all if I had to hide it? I was sick of pretending, weary of the loneliness that came with secrets.

I began with accomplishments: the Yale diplomas, my psychology practice, so they'd assume I was now more or less normal. I spent hours honing the rest. I didn't want to frighten or alienate anyone.

I left our class at the end of junior year (May 1960) when I was admitted to a psychiatric hospital. A year later I returned to school, but in the middle of my senior year I was hospitalized again. I spent more than five years in two hospitals. Eventually, with skilled psychotherapy, I recovered.

I met my husband at the School of General Studies at Columbia. After we married I joined him in New Haven. We have two adult children and two grandchildren.

Except for close family and a few friends I kept my psychiatric history a secret. Shock treatment administered early in the hospitalization had left me without many memories of my first twenty years. I avoided everyone from my earlier life, ashamed of being unable to remember them. A decade ago I read my old hospital records, and this triggered memories I had assumed were lost.

Most of the dramatic symptoms that overwhelmed me when I first read the records had receded, although not all had disappeared. Many years of slow recovery proved a far cry from the months I'd allotted when I made my original plan, oblivious of what was in store. "I figure I'll have the summer to process whatever I have to," I'd explained to Bill before the hospitals' packages arrived. Now I chuckled at how far-fetched that timeline was.

Headaches, nightmares, intrusive images, and destructive impulses no longer bothered me. I didn't grind myself down with self-loathing. The disabling anxiety was mostly gone. Although dissociation remained a factor in my everyday life—perhaps embedded in my personality—I lived in the present more than ever before. I might always be disorganized and a bit obsessive, but my self-confidence had grown as I made peace with those quirks. I'd made progress with shyness. I awoke optimistic more often than not.

Yet at times I succumbed to an ancient grief: the seasoned professional, on a mission to change the world, could be swept away by the terrified woman who was sure she'd wrecked her career and possibly all her adult relationships by exposing her vulnerability. Shame, the legacy of incest and psychiatric hospitals, blindsided me and brought a fear that felt ineradicable. It stuck to my bones; it took root in my cells; it lay so deeply ingrained that sometimes I questioned whether I'd recognize myself without it.

The caller ID read *Florida.* Another telemarketer, I figured. "Hello," I answered in a cold, *you won't get anything out of me* voice.

"Hi, Annita. Are you the one who went to White Plains High School?"

Stunned, I ran a hand through my hair a few times before I realized I should speak. "Yes," I said, still thinking the person was calling to sell me something. "Who's this?"

"It's Peggy from high school, only I'm Meg now. Do you remember me? I read your bio. You're a brave girl!"

"I think I remember; I certainly know your name." I struggled to get my bearings. With my reunion information online now anyone could find me. My life was exposed for all to see. "How great that you called," I said, not sure if I meant it. "You're the very first one." I began to pace.

"I wasn't smart like you and your friends in all those special classes. But, I wouldn't have survived that first year at the high school if I hadn't had you to confide in," Meg said. "We slept over at each other's houses. I'd never have guessed about you being in hospitals. Your mother was so nice, although I have to admit your father was scary—are you okay with my saying that?"

Meg filled me in on her life since high school, her marriage, her husband's early death, and the painful years that followed. She described her misdiagnosed hip problems and visiting her grandson. She asked me to deliver a message to a friend whose name I didn't recognize. "Make sure that you tell Al his friendship meant the world to me," Meg said.

We'd been talking for more than an hour. Chores called, but I was torn. Her story was engaging. I longed to find out more. "I hate to hang up, but I have to stop."

"Come visit me, sweetie," Meg said. "There's always a place for you here."

The call calmed my worries about telling the truth. I was grateful for a sense of who I'd been for Peggy, as I'd known her, and disappointed that I couldn't remember anything she'd referred to: the sleepovers at her house and mine, her parents' painful separation, her trusting me with her secrets. I'd always remembered Peggy's name. It hurt not to remember our friendship.

I approached the White Plains Crowne Plaza midday, distracted and anxious, wondering why I'd agreed to join the lunch that a former classmate had arranged. Days earlier, I'd looked forward to my reunion, but that morning, when it was time to leave the house, I'd wished I could cancel the whole trip. Standing outside the hotel, I wanted to flee. *Remember, you're an adult now. You can do this.* I took a deep breath and opened the door.

Men and women in desert camouflage, along with other adults and children, packed the entrance. B Company had just returned from a tour in Iraq and were enjoying a picnic lunch with their families. *All those beautiful young people,* I thought as I threaded my way through the mustardy cold-cut smells and friendly party din. My anger flashed. *All that trauma.* I shook my head hard, as if that would jettison the unwanted thoughts.

Beyond the lobby I found a dozen or so well-dressed older men and women talking in a group. Not one looked familiar. I didn't intend to stare, but I must have.

A bearded man in a green linen sports jacket noticed me. His face lit up. "Annita!" he said, extending his arms to give me a warm hug I returned with relief: I was in the right place. "So good to see you," he said. Others near him smiled and greeted me. The welcoming stranger turned to the group. "Shall we eat?" He led us a few steps into a small, spare but tidy dining room. A narrow table set with perhaps twenty places filled the space.

He motioned to a seat beside him, and, grateful, I sat. By then, I'd surmised that this man was Allen, the lunch organizer. I waited until I'd heard him addressed by name at least twice before I delivered Meg's message. A broad grin lit up his face.

"Mind if I sit here?" a friendly, sandy-haired woman settled beside me. "It's fantastic to see you, Annita. I'll never forget you in *The Crucible*," she said, sounding very pleased. I marveled that people seemed to know who I was. Her enthusiasm disarmed me. I hadn't expected to feel at home so quickly.

"I might have been too authentic," I said, with a half laugh. "I was in the process of losing it around then."

At four-thirty, I found Sue in the lobby, as we'd planned. Now at least one person knew how tentative I felt, someone who would sit with me and talk if I asked, so I wouldn't be left entirely on my own. To my surprise, Sue felt the same way.

Upstairs in my hotel room two hours later, I confronted my reflection one last time: flat gray-brown hair that wouldn't fluff topped a small, slight frame. I was wearing black slacks, a turquoise linen blouse, and my favorite silk scarf—a mix of deep blue, bright red, and turquoise splashes. A black jacket, bought at Jacky's urging especially for the occasion, matched the slacks. I'd paid too much—I still worried about spending money—but it fit perfectly. Turquoise earrings and an opal pendant James and his wife had given me complemented my outfit. For good luck, I wore James' spiral silver ring; Jessica's basket of flowers brooch graced my lapel.

The murmur of conversations along with a jumble of tantalizing aromas enveloped me as I descended the stairs. Already a mass of people had gathered in the spacious carpeted lobby. A short, friendly man I didn't recognize directed me to a table where I could sign in.

Everywhere people greeted one another, calling out names, expressing surprise, hugging and laughing. I stared at the badge in my hands, at the girl with dark bangs and big eyes who smiled at me from the enlarged yearbook photo above my old name. I wanted to feel kindly toward her. If I looked at her from the perspective of a stranger, I could sense her appeal. But I fought contempt. I was used to thinking of her as a wimp, a compliant goody-goody who had acted out of fear. *She did her best to be the person she thought she was supposed to be: she smiled because it was expected.* Was that so terrible? She had also smiled because she had believed, as I did still, that life was lonely, and a smile, for a moment, could transcend any boundaries and connect two hearts. After all those years, why did I have so much trouble bringing us together? My last healing step was to embrace *her* as *me*.

I heard my name and turned. A small, dark-eyed woman dressed in black beckoned to me. She took my hand in hers.

"We were just talking about you," she said, nodding at a tall man beside her. "We were so glad to read your bio. You were with us in English senior year. Then you disappeared." She kept her grip on my hand, her eyes searching mine. Her friend reached for the other.

"No one told us where you had gone," he said. "We worried that you had died."

I stood, squeezing both hands, taking in their concerned, sad faces. I wanted to hold on and never let go.

Although some classmates who spoke as if they knew me remained a mystery, there were others whom I recognized easily, at least by the name on the badge. In a whirlwind, mostly listening, I moved from one group to another. I discovered that many of my classmates had kept in touch with each other. Good friends had stayed close. There were a number of couples now married who had been dating fifty years earlier. I pushed back grief, along with envy, at what I had missed. *Don't think it. Don't you dare....*

Along with dizzying accomplishments and genius offspring, I heard about hip surgeries, skiing accidents, elderly parents, and departed spouses. In companionable openness we shared tales of grandchildren and gardens, interesting hobbies, deferred dreams finally fulfilled. There were wry references to aching joints and failing memories, retracted retirements, unemployed adult children who'd returned to live at home. I wasn't the only one seeking perspective on a tumultuous and humbling life.

Perhaps this was more my wish than fact, but as a group we seemed to be no longer in thrall to pride. After fifty years, what bound us together was knowing firsthand that life was messy and unfair. Friends shared their teenage fantasies and laughed about behavior they would have died before admitting back then.

I did remember Bobby. While his wife, also a classmate, and I stood by sipping wine, he reminisced about his crush on me in junior high. "I'd make a detour from my paper route to ride past your house, hoping for a glimpse of you in your yard," he said. "I liked best when you'd see me and wave, giving your big smile."

I had never connected Bobby's bicycle trips with puppy love.

"Annita, I'm Roger. I'd like you to meet my better half." A soft-spoken man put his hand on my arm, reminding me who he was as he introduced his wife. Roger and I had also been in junior high together. I learned that he and his wife lived in the same college town as John, another classmate, now a retired classics professor. They'd all come to the reunion together.

"John's too embarrassed to say this himself," Roger began with a smirk, referring to his friend and our classmate, "but he said I could tell you that he saw you in a play in fifth grade and was smitten. You were his earliest love." Roger paused to scratch his head. "Of course, I'm not innocent here," he said, laughing. "We were talking about first crushes and both of us named you. Mine began in homeroom in junior high. I joined the stage crew so I could watch you rehearse. You smiled at me a lot."

"Talk about flattered!" I laughed. I wanted so badly to remember at least something. They were boys I knew I'd admired. John had been considered the smartest person in our school. I wished I could have enjoyed their attention. I'd had no clue.

I moved closer to the wall, sipping from a glass of white wine, slipping back to thoughts of my friends' adolescent crushes. As a youngster I'd captivated them. I must not have been the cringing, shameful creature I'd long imagined. Despite my introverted preoccupations, they had seen me as kind and intelligent. My persona as a filthy outcast didn't fit.

Attractive youngsters in black and white uniforms balancing trays of miniature cheese tarts, shiny mushroom caps, bite-sized pepperoni pizza, and assorted other greasy delicacies snaked through the growing crowd outside the dining room. I helped myself to a few tidbits as they passed by. Fragrances of warm cheese and wine mingled with Obsession and Old Spice. Savory roasting and baking smells permeated all. I began to feel hungry.

A little while later Roger approached me where I'd been standing alone. He looked serious.

"I read your bio," he said, his eyes on my face. "I wanted to tell you that for several years I had a summer job at New York Hospital—we called it Bloomingdale's—the psychiatric hospital here," he continued in a confidential tone. "I began in the bakery the summer after my sophomore year, and I returned for three summers, including during college."

"I was at that hospital then," I blurted out, almost interrupting. "What did you do there?"

Roger chose his words with care. "I never saw you; I didn't know you were a patient. The last two years I worked as an aide on the male floors. As part of that I escorted patients to all sorts of appointments. I assisted when they had shock treatment."

My brain had caught fire. I ran a hand through my hair, then fiddled with my scarf. "At some point, could we talk in detail about the shock treatment?" I asked after a pause, aiming for a detached, professional air. "I have my own picture of what happened, but there's no telling if I'm right."

We agreed to meet for breakfast the next morning.

The prospect of learning the truth about my shock treatment momentarily preempted all my attention. I smiled as classmates and said hello, but my mind was back fifty years earlier in New York Hospital, searching gray buildings and pale blue halls, struggling to remember. Gradually the cheerful chatter, welcome smiles, and dinner smells bombarding me came through with good effect. I rejoined the reunion.

In the dining room, I found Sue and her husband sitting at a table among others I didn't know. It turned out that they were former members of the football team. After peering at badges, we didn't advance much beyond friendly nods and grins. Words were useless in the clamor.

After dinner, I half-listened to speeches about events I didn't recall and watched a slide show created from old photographs. The band began to play. Several people approached and warmly shook my hand. I recognized some names, but talk was difficult. Much as I might have wished otherwise, I remembered far fewer people than seemed to know me. At around eleven, I left.

Upstairs, I wandered about the hotel room, exhausted, but too restless to consider sleep. A million bits of information bounced around my head. I wanted to gather them and hold them close—sort them, organize them—to piece together a sense of who I was. "In order to forget you were abused, it was necessary to forget the self you were," Jacky had explained to me. Blanking out trauma meant blanking out everything; one didn't get to pick and choose. With Jacky's help, I'd recovered a consistent sense of what I'd experienced as a child. I was aware of the shame and self-loathing that I'd directed at myself for much of my life, especially in childhood and during adolescence. Now I longed for a more balanced understanding of who that young person had been, of how others had seen me.

Here were people who remembered the girl I had come to call Anni. They had liked her. Some had loved her. I'd seen it in their faces. They'd respected her; they missed her—in contrast with my own hands-off way of keeping me and Anni separate.

Mulling over my observations, summoning the generous spirit that energized the gathering below, I sought to conjure up the person my classmates knew without turning on her, to approach my young self with compassion. As I borrowed their eyes to assess the present woman they called brave, I felt a window open. While it lasted, I understood: yes, it took courage to be honest, because everyone knew that a psychiatric history and diagnosis carried stigma. The threat of diminished respect and loss of standing was real. *But they welcomed you anyway. They are glad to see you now.* I struggled to fit the disparate pieces into one emotional box.

The next day at breakfast, Roger and I talked briefly about shock treatment, but when others joined us, we had to stop. Common sense had predicted this, of course. I tried not to show my disappointment.

Roger expanded on his reflections and sent them as an email message after he returned home:

...Another form of restraint was the cold wet pack or "CWP" used primarily for patients going for electric shock treatment (EST). I became quite proficient in the technique of wrapping patients mummy-style in warm wet sheets in preparation for treatment. Most patients were anxious anticipating scheduled EST but after the treatment would have no memory of the experience...

Once wrapped, and covered with a dry sheet, the litters with patients would be lined up in the unit in preparation for treatment. Indeed once wrapped, patients relaxed and frequently dozed until they were transported to the treatment room.

In EST the patient would be attended by a physician, nurse, and one or two attendants. The physician would examine the patient and the nurse would start an IV, administer a dose of Scopolamine as a muscle relaxant, and attach electrodes to the temples of the patient.

The mummy wrap would be removed, and a mouth guard would be held in place as the nurse and attendant would hold the legs and shoulders of the patient. A shock would be administered and the patient would go into convulsions lasting no more than thirty seconds.

*Following, we would cover the patient with dry sheets and a warm
blanket and transport them back to the unit.*

I garbled sentences and stumbled over words as I tried to take in everything at once. At first, bursts of anger surprised me. *What do you mean 'relaxed?'* Yet I knew people who relied on modern ECT to interrupt periods
of profound depression. Not everyone shared my terrifying experience.

I read Roger's note again. It fit! His recollections matched mine
down to details of mummy wrap and waiting in line. Now I could
counter doubting voices that had dogged me forever. I wasn't a liar. My
memories were reliable and my impressions had integrity. I would need
time to absorb the full magnitude of what this meant.

By late Sunday morning, rain was descending in sheets. Our picnic bar-
becue lunch had been moved into the high school cafeteria. After chatting for a few minutes in an interminable food line, I decided to explore
the rest of the building. I wanted to see if being in that physical space,
especially the hallways, might jog my memory. Maybe I could verify my
impression of lockers stretching toward infinity.

Student art and brightly-colored posters dotted the industrial walls,
but that hadn't lessened the cold factory feeling I carried from decades
before. As I walked the long, empty corridors, I listened to the echo of
my footsteps and tried to imagine myself as an adolescent there. My
mental picture of the lockers hadn't been too far off. Although I failed
to conjure up an explicit historical event, I did sense my reality as an
overwhelmed teenager, struggling to perform, sinking, even as I tried
so hard to swim against the tide. Tears welled in my eyes, but they disappeared as soon as I noticed them.

Back in the cafeteria, I found others reencountering their own
high school days who spoke with me while we ate. The juxtaposition

of perspectives dazzled me. One beautiful, popular girl, whom I remembered envying but knowing only from a distance, told me that she'd always admired my intelligence. She paused, a catch in her voice, as she thanked me for my present honesty. In that instant, I felt a deep bond. Audrey, another classmate whose name I recognized, described the fragile Annita she had witnessed in 1960, when her own mother had been dying.

Audrey, too, had struggled, working to hold her family together while she continued to shine in class. During our high school years, her traumatic situation had remained secret, as had mine. In those days vulnerability equaled moral weakness. Cancer, mental illness, divorce—all were treated as shameful. We hid them. Aware of her own painful circumstances, Audrey was one of the few friends who had perceived my distress. I grieved for young Audrey. Yet, even in retrospect, my friend's story lessened my loneliness. I felt relief knowing that someone had understood my precarious grip.

The wholehearted, appreciative reception I received from former classmates caught me off-guard. No one avoided or disdained me. They acknowledged the reality of stigma, but they respected me: I had to face down my own shame to be honest.

The truth stung. I took pride in my decision to be open, but that I'd been forced to make it wasn't fair. Anger, grief, regret, and gratitude interspersed with occasional bursts of joy swirled within me. Again I searched my heart for generosity to accept the girl I'd been and to feel warmly toward the woman who stood in the cafeteria smiling and accepting compliments.

The adolescent fear of my classmates' hostile reactions had been a projection of my own contempt for my condition. Some of my classmates had been puzzled by my withdrawal. A few had worried. At least one friend, and perhaps others, had interpreted my dissociated state as aloofness or snobbery—as my rejecting her. But most had respected and even loved me. While I focused on hiding my vulnerability, they were busy doing the same: many of us had taken in evidence to support our worst ideas about ourselves. We were adolescents!

Windshield wipers swished and rain pounded on the roof as I drove home. I dodged puddles along a parkway I'd traveled most of my life— to Sunday dinners with aunts and grandparents as a child, to see my parents in White Plains and to events in New York City as an adult. Snug inside my noisy car I traveled up and down the steep hills, over and under old bridges, past drenched blossoms raining off trees in the center divide. I was thinking about my life, especially high school and now the reunion. I felt disappointed that I'd wasted so much energy feeling alienated and ashamed, when most likely I'd never been shunned or feared. I wondered how many years I'd lost to living dissociated, not fully in this world, and how often I'd deprived those I loved of my genuine presence. I also felt closer to forgiving myself.

So many parts, not all in place.

So much behind me. So much ahead.

Imagining a teenaged Anni in the passenger seat beside me, I stretched out my arm and set my hand on her shoulder.

Acknowledgments

Although I can't come close to naming each of the many individuals who helped make this book possible, I'll attempt a start. The list begins with my family: I love you! Thank you to my brothers; to my cousins; to Will, my unfailing supporter; and to Garrett, my chief technical advisor. Thank you to my kind friends Chris, Ray, Judith, Barb, Linda, Ann, Sue, Bess, Bob, and Joyce. Thank you to my remarkable readers Laura Apol, Christina Askounis, Paul Austin, Miriam Camitta, Ann Sheybani, Dhana-Marie Branton, Susan Milmoe, Judith Ward, Betsy Wesman, and Kathleen Devereaux. Thank you to my high school friends, who shared stories and added perspective to that difficult time.

I have been in workshops with some of the finest, most generous teachers in the country; they inspired and encouraged me. I am profoundly grateful to Phillip Lopate, Ted Conover, Patricia Hampl, Scott Russell Sanders, and Jane Brox. I owe so much to Michael Collier, Norine Cargill, and the Bread Loaf Writers Conference community for the opportunity to live among writers, and, in time, to become one myself. The magical combination of solitude and creative fellowship I discovered in superb artists' residencies allowed me to grow and my writing to flourish. Thank you to Vermont Studio Center, Ragdale, VCCA, Hambidge, the MacDowell Colony, and the Millay Colony. In the New Haven Writers Group I learned how to write and then how to revise: thank you to Greg, Barry, Charlie, Ken, Beth, Erin, Sarah, Scott, Sam, Kate, Susan, Alex, and Cathy. I hope you feel proud.

I am indebted more than I can say to Kit Ward, who will always live in my heart, and to John Thornton—literary agents who gave me and my manuscript their valuable time and respect. I am grateful to Lee Gutkind and Andrew Gifford, who have helped to make my impossible dream come true. Thank you, Erica Harney, a very special Muse (of the amazing Lemoille Muses from VSC) who captured the whole story in one exquisite image.

And, of course, thanks beyond measure to Stan, Sandy, and Jane, who helped me grow wings, then told me to fly.

About the Author

An SFWP Literary Awards Program grand prize-winner, Annita Perez Sawyer has been a clinical psychologist in full-time practice for over thirty years. She received the 2012 Bellevue Literary Review Burns Archive nonfiction prize for her essay "The Crazy One" (also included as a Notable in *Best American Essays* 2013) and the 2012 Literal Latte Essay Contest first prize for "The Other Chair." Annita has been a Wesleyan Writers Conference Fellow and Bread Loaf Writers' Conference Scholar. She has also been a Fellow at the MacDowell Colony, the Millay Colony, Vermont Studio Center, Ragdale, VCCA, and Hambidge.

Annita speaks to mental health clinicians and groups around the country, using her own story of psychiatric misdiagnosis and consequent mistreatment to reinforce her message: pay attention; don't give up. She lives in Connecticut.

www.smokingcigaretteseatingglass.com/

A NOTE FROM THE PUBLISHER

Thank you for purchasing this title from the Santa Fe Writers Project (**www.sfwp.com**).

I started publishing because I love books. I publish titles that I would buy, and that I want to see on the shelves, regardless of genre. SFWP's mission is not about creating a catalog that the accountants can get behind. The mission is one of recognition and preservation of our literary culture.

I encourage you to visit us at www.sfwp.com and learn more about our books and our mission.

Happy reading!

Andrew Nash Gifford
Director
@sfwp

Santa Fe Writers Project